LAW'S DESIRE

Law's Desire provides a critical examination of the relationship of law and sexual orientation in the United States, the United Kingdom and Canada. Law is one of the primary means through which lesbian and gay male sexualities are constructed, monitored and controlled (albeit not necessarily successfully). Carl Stychin exposes this connection through an exploration of key questions of current interest and controversy. He examines the motivations behind legal restrictions and their impact both upon sexual subcultures and dominant society.

The book tackles the major areas of controversy that have erupted in the 1980s and 1990s: public funding restrictions on 'homoerotic art'; sodomy laws; the regulation of safe sex educational materials; gay pornography and feminist theory; lesbians and gay men in the American military; sadomasochism and the law; and legal restrictions on the 'promotion' of homosexuality. The author concludes with an examination of the challenges posed by the newly emerging queer identities and the likely direction of future struggles.

Carl F. Stychin is Lecturer in Law at Keele University. He has written extensively in the areas of law and sexuality and legal theory. Educated in Canada and the United States, he served as a law clerk to the Chief Justice of Canada. He is co-editor (with Didi Herman) of *Legal Inversions: Lesbians, Gay Men, and the Politics of Law*.

LAW'S DESIRE

Sexuality and the limits of justice

Carl F. Stychin

London and New York

First published 1995
by Routledge
11 New Fetter Lane, London EC4P 4EE

Simultaneously published in the USA and Canada
by Routledge
29 West 35th Street, New York, NY 10001

© 1995 Carl F. Stychin

Typeset in Times by LaserScript, Mitcham, Surrey
Printed and bound in Great Britain by
Mackays of Chatham PLC, Chatham, Kent

British Library Cataloguing in Publication Data
A catalogue record for this book is available from the British Library

Library of Congress Cataloguing in Publication Data
A catalogue record for this book has been requested

ISBN 0–415–11126–9 (hbk)
ISBN 0–415–11127–7 (pbk)

For my mother

CONTENTS

ACKNOWLEDGEMENTS

This book has been written in various forms over the past four years. The ideas upon which it is based began life when I was a graduate student at Columbia Law School in the City of New York. I owe a debt of gratitude to all of those with whom I came in contact at Columbia for providing me with a stimulating environment in which to write. In particular, I thank Professor Kendall Thomas for all of his assistance and support. The book was finished in my first two and a half years as a full-time lecturer in the Department of Law at Keele University. I am fortunate to work in an institution that has generously provided the material resources and support which allowed me to complete the book. I also wish to thank all those who read and commented upon various chapters of the book in different forms over the years. They are now too numerous to mention individually. However, a few people stand out for their intellectual and emotional support above and beyond the call of duty: Shauna Van Praagh, Didi Herman, Audrey Macklin, Gillian More, Davina Cooper and René Provost. I also thank Mari Shullaw and Anne Gee at Routledge for their encouragement and advice.

I acknowledge permission given to reprint material which has previously been published in the following articles: 'Identities, Sexualities, and the Postmodern Subject: An Analysis of Artistic Funding by the National Endowment for the Arts', *Cardozo Arts and Entertainment Law Journal*, 1994, vol. 12, pp. 79–132 (Chapter 1); 'Of Prohibitions and Promotions: A Comparative Analysis of Legal Interventions', *Australasian Gay and Lesbian Law Journal*, 1994, vol. 5 (Chapter 2); 'Exploring the Limits: Feminism and the Legal Regulation of Gay Male Pornography', *Vermont Law Review*, 1992, vol. 16, pp. 859–900 (Chapter 3); 'Inside and Out of the Military', *Law and Sexuality: A Review of Lesbian and Gay Legal Issues*, 1993, vol. 3, pp. 27–43 (Chapter 5); 'A Postmodern Constitutionalism: Equality Rights, Identity Politics, and the Canadian National Imagination', *Dalhousie Law Journal*, 1994, vol. 17, pp. 61–82 (Chapter 6); 'Unmanly Diversions: The Construction of the Homosexual Body (Politic) in English Law', *Osgoode Hall Law Journal*, 1994, vol. 32, pp. 503–36 (Chapter 7).

INTRODUCTION

This book is about the relationship between law and desire. More specifically, it is about how sexual desires are constituted and regulated by the law, with particular reference to gay male and, to a lesser extent, lesbian and bisexual sexualities. I attempt to uncover what the law desires – which, I will argue, is the 'homosexual', against whom a coherent heterosexuality can be promoted through law. Throughout the book, I seek to demonstrate that the relationship of law and sexuality is complex and dynamic. While law may be (and has been) a repressive force, it also is a regulatory one which plays a role in constituting and maintaining coherent sexualities. At the same time, regulation is never entirely successful, for gaps and inconsistencies are left within legal discourse. This creates spaces for resistance against, and opposition to, the legal and sexual hegemony. I hope that this book provides one such intervention.

I should make clear at this juncture that I do not (and cannot) provide a singular 'truth' in my examination of the sexual acts, sexual identities, and legal discourse upon which this book touches. My methodological approach is heavily indebted to a poststructural analysis that questions and interrogates such claims to universal truth. Moreover, I have not dealt in any sort of comprehensive way with many important issues, specifically those dealing with lesbian sexuality, the intersection of race and lesbian and gay sexualities, bisexuality, (dis)ability and sexuality, and, no doubt, numerous other identity-related issues. My belief, though, is that works such as this can be facilitative of an ongoing dialogue involving participants that historically have been denied the opportunity to express themselves fully within both dominant culture and the lesbian and gay communities.

To some extent, such a dialogue would have been unthinkable only ten years ago. The area of 'law and sexuality' (which, I concede, often remains a handy euphemism for the relationship of law and lesbian, gay and bisexual sexualities) is a definite growth industry, as is lesbian and gay studies more generally in the academy. For those of us who spend a good deal of our time thinking and writing about these questions in law faculties, our greatest debt is owed to the emergence and institutionalisation of both feminist legal theory and critical race theory in

1

recent years. Increasingly, voices from the margins have come to inhabit the centre of the university, and law schools have not been immune from this process. At the same time, we should never underestimate the extent to which the centre is resistant; and the legal centre often has a particular intransigence with respect to giving up its privileges.

This book is highly personal in the way that it reflects my own tenuous relationship to a national identity. Although I was raised in Canada and educated there, I began writing what later became chapters of this book while engaged in graduate studies at Columbia Law School in New York City. Many of the case studies that I use thus are drawn from both the American and Canadian contexts. After completing graduate work, I accepted a teaching position in the United Kingdom and the focus of my attention shifted to the British scene, which was replete with examples ripe for interrogation. Consequently, my focus is exclusively upon Western, late-industrial legal cultures. There are, however, differences between them, which the reader may find of interest. It is to these similarities and differences that I now turn.

THE COMPARATIVE LEGAL CONTEXT

Before delving into the case studies which form the basis of this book, some background may be useful in providing a context with which to compare legal cultures. America, Britain, and Canada have a good many similarities in terms of culture generally, and legal culture specifically. Indeed, they share a legal system (although Quebec is an exception in some cases), as well as many legal and political traditions. These similarities will become apparent in the case studies. Political and legal initiatives with respect to lesbian and gay sexualities sometimes display remarkable similarities, particularly as between America and Britain, including the language used by legislators, judges, and activists.

There are differences, however, in terms of legal culture that also deserve mention. For the purposes of my analysis, one of the fundamental divergences turns on the role of 'rights discourse' within the three societies. America is the paradigm 'culture of rights' and the role of the Bill of Rights in the American Constitution will be ever present within my legal analysis. For lesbians and gay men, an appeal to the vindication of rights is central to the claims made within the legal arena in the United States. Rights of speech (the 'First Amendment' of the Constitution), the Equal Protection of the laws (the 'Fourteenth Amendment'), and privacy (located in the so-called penumbra of rights emanating from the 'Due Process' clause of the 'Fifth Amendment'), will be central to these claims. The existence of a written rights document also gives rise to the review of legislation by the judiciary to ensure that it passes constitutional scrutiny. The pivotal role of the judiciary thus also is fundamental to the American legal experience.

At the same time, rights discourse is politically indeterminate. While lesbians and gay men in America employ the language of rights and the strategy of judicial review in an attempt to vindicate rights claims, other groups with very different

2

political aims also make claims to rights. Indeed, one of the fascinating aspects of American constitutional law is the way in which rights are employed by the 'right wing' both in the name of the 'majority of Americans', as well as religious minorities and other groups such as 'parents' as a response to lesbian and gay legal struggles. Such claims have achieved a fair degree of success, not only within the courts, but also through 'democratic' means such as the referendum, which has recently been utilised as a way to prevent the legislatures from enacting laws to protect the rights of lesbians and gay men. The constitutionality of this strategy, though, remains in doubt. Rights discourse thus emanates not only from those favouring 'progressive' legal reform, but also from those opposed to it.

At the other extreme is the United Kingdom, a country in which there is no written Bill of Rights pursuant to which individuals and groups are 'protected' from the will of the legislature. Rights discourse still plays an important role within British legal and political culture; 'I have my rights' is a familiar refrain. However, the absence of a constitutionally protected bill of individual rights inevitably means that the language of rights is less powerful both as discourse and as a pragmatic political strategy within the United Kingdom. There is no 'appeal' to the judiciary from decisions of the 'democratic' branch of government. The constitutional structure thereby constrains the range of options available for the deployment of law, although membership in the European Union may open up a new vista for rights discourse through appeals to the European Court of Human Rights. However, this is a cumbersome, time-consuming and expensive procedure which has yet to achieve anything approaching the effectiveness and centrality of judicial review within the American system.

Canada is something of a hybrid legal culture. Historically, it did not possess an entrenched rights document and in this regard resembled the United Kingdom, from which its system of Parliamentary supremacy derived. However, in 1982, Canada constitutionally entrenched a bill of rights – the *Charter of Rights and Freedoms* – which guarantees a series of individual and group rights from encroachment by governments, subject to certain limitations. The Charter clearly has transformed the Canadian legal system and culture and the extent of that change continues to be felt. Rights discourse has assumed an increasingly prominent place. For the purposes of the rights of lesbians and gay men, two provisions are of particular importance: s.2(b) which ensures freedom of expression, and s.15(1), which ensures rights of equality before and under the law on a number of different bases. Although s.15(1) does not specify 'sexual orientation' among its prohibited categories of discrimination by government, this has come to be 'read in' by judges as included within the Charter equality guarantees. The interesting question therefore becomes, if sexual orientation is a prohibited basis of discrimination, what are the implications for government? As well, the guarantee of freedom of expression, especially when read in light of the entrenched rights of equality, also has come to play an important role in the realm of lesbian and gay rights struggles, in particular around the issue of obscenity.

CHRONOLOGY OF EVENTS

This book deals with events which have occurred from the 1980s to the present. It is not an encyclopedia of legal engagements with lesbians and gay men. It is, rather, a collection of essays dealing with a number of major legal developments over this period. In my view, we are witness to an important historical moment for the engagement between law and sexuality. It is a time in which a number of Western nations have experienced increasingly vocal lesbian and gay rights movements (and shifting dynamics and agendas within them); the rising tide of conservatism in politics; the increasing politicisation of evangelical Christians around issues of sexuality; and the appearance of Aids, the realisation of its pandemic proportions, and calls by various constituencies for greater action from government to combat the scourge. Thus, a clash of fundamentally opposed interests and groups is occurring, and the legal arena has been the site of confrontation on a number of different issues.

In America, the election of Ronald Reagan in 1980 symbolised the beginning of this period. His promise to appoint politically conservative judges (a crucially important matter in a country with a bill of rights and judicial review) continues to have a dramatic impact not only on the rights of women (particularly concerning access to abortion), but also has had a deleterious effect upon the lesbian and gay rights movements. That struggle for rights suffered a monumental setback in 1986, when the United States Supreme Court in *Bowers v. Hardwick* upheld the constitutionality of laws, which continue in force in some states, prohibiting the sexual practice of sodomy.[1] The Court, by majority, held that these laws, historically enacted by state legislatures pursuant to their jurisdiction over the criminal law, do not contravene a right of privacy previously judicially recognised as implicit within the Bill of Rights. In effect, the Court held that there is no right to engage in same-sex relations in private free from laws which regulate sexual conduct. The symbolism, as well as the material and doctrinal impact of that decision, is enormous. Numerous courts have subsequently concluded that lesbians and gay men are not entitled to the 'strict' judicial scrutiny of laws pursuant to which government discriminates on the basis of sexual orientation. That is, government will rarely (if ever) be prevented from enacting legislation which discriminates against lesbians and gay men, provided a 'rational basis' can be demonstrated for the distinction drawn. This constitutional question is a continuing one, which has yet to be decided by the Supreme Court.

The latter half of the 1980s also saw an increasingly vocal anti-gay agenda enunciated within Congress. In particular, Senator Jesse Helms, a conservative Southern Republican, introduced a number of different legislative initiatives to counter what he (and others) perceived to be the legal and political gains made by lesbians and gay men. Many of these interventions have involved governmental funding of various different programmes. The argument is that government (and, by extension, the taxpayer) has the right not to fund the advancement of a 'homosexual lifestyle'. This position was manifested in several different laws. In

1987, Congress passed the first 'Helms Amendment', which prohibited the expenditure of public funds on safe sex educational materials that 'promoted' homosexuality. This law was enacted after a period of what many consider to be inexcusable inaction by Congress to deal with the Aids pandemic.

Furthermore, in what has now become an infamous episode, in 1989 Congress began a continuing confrontation with the National Endowment for the Arts. The Endowment funds a range of artistic projects with federal funds. Partly in response to the funding of a retrospective of the work of photographer Robert Mapplethorpe, Congress prohibited the provision of funds for 'homoerotic' art. Thus began an ongoing saga of controversy over arts funding that has continued largely unabated to the present. Both the safe sex material and NEA funding amendments were challenged successfully in the Courts on the basis that they infringed the right of free speech. These examples thereby demonstrate the particular effectiveness of speech rights in combating an anti-gay agenda in America.

The election of Bill Clinton in 1992 signalled a shift in the contours of the debates. Clinton entered office with commitments to the lesbian and gay communities (although those promises remained rather muted during the election campaign), and he began his term by attempting to lift the prohibition on homosexuals in the armed services. The ban has given rise to considerable constitutional litigation by dismissed members of the services. The hostile reaction and political damage caused by the attempt to change the policy demonstrated the continuing antipathy of substantial segments of the American public towards lesbians and gay men. It also forced a compromise solution, namely the so-called 'don't ask, don't tell' policy. Finally, 1994 saw the twenty-fifth anniversary of the Stonewall Rebellion – the event which marked the beginning of the modern lesbian and gay rights movement. The articulation of a wide-ranging agenda for social and legal reform that emanated from the marking of the anniversary can be juxtaposed against the other defining moment of 1994: the election of a Republican Congress. The latter event indicates that the tide of conservatism has not yet been stemmed in America. The impact of the new Congress on lesbian and gay rights struggles in law remains to be seen, but may well be significant.

The British political map in this same period bears considerable resemblance to that of America. The Thatcher years, beginning in 1979, were characterised by a conservatism that extended not only to the economic realm, but also to that of the social and 'moral'. Sexual relations between men in private were largely (but not totally) decriminalised in 1967 as a response to recommendations from the Wolfenden Committee (an independent body appointed by Parliament) ten years earlier. Subsequently, gay culture began to flourish in most areas of the country. However, the legalisation of same-sex sexual relations between men (lesbian sex had not been subject to criminal penalty) was never intended to sanction the expression of sexuality in the 'public' sphere, which has always been subject to a strict regime of police regulation. The corollary of decriminalisation thus was intended to be 'discretion'. That pattern began to change in a limited way in the

1980s, when some local government bodies began to make tentative steps to-wards inclusion of programmes designed for lesbian and gay constituents, and through the creation of 'positive images' of lesbians and gays within education and other sites. The reaction to these moves was hostile in some quarters, including substantial segments of the Conservative Party. The dramatic result was the enactment in 1988 of the now infamous section 28 of the *Local Government Act, 1988*, which sought to prohibit the expenditure of local government funds on the promotion of homosexuality, or the teaching of the acceptability of homosexuality as a 'pretended family relationship' in schools. The clause is important not only for its symbolic and material impact upon lesbian and gay life in Britain, but also because of the role of the debate in mobilising the lesbian and gay movements to articulate an oppositional position. Section 28 is an apt example of the use of law to regulate and contain sexuality as a response to what was perceived in some conservative quarters to be attempts at radical social change. It also signified a heightened anti-gay rhetoric within Britain and, at the same time, it fostered a measure of solidarity between the various constituencies that comprise the lesbian and gay movements.

The liberal consensus that led to decriminalisation, and the rigid separation between public and private spheres in terms of the role of law in regulating same-sex sexual conduct, came under attack in the early 1990s in what has become known as the 'Operation Spanner' case, *R. v. Brown*.[2] A group of gay male sadomasochists were arrested, charged and convicted of assault and wounding after police learned that they had engaged in private, consensual sadomasochistic sex (with each other) over an extended period. Their appeals to the House of Lords, the highest court in the United Kingdom, were dismissed. *Brown* is significant for the way in which freedom of sexual expression in the private sphere came under attack and, at the same time, for bringing the issue of sadomasochism into public view.

Finally, 1994 saw the lowering of the 'age of consent' for gay male sex to eighteen years (from the previous twenty-one). The original proposal made by a private Member of Parliament to lower the age to sixteen years (the age of consent for heterosexual sex) was defeated. The debate and mobilisation of constituencies to influence the voting was interesting in that it exemplified how the language of equality and 'equality rights' assumed a central place in debates over law reform. In terms of lesbian and gay politics, the issue also highlighted the division between what might be termed liberal assimilationist and more radical ('queer') positions over the relative importance of the issue and the acceptability of a compromise position. This tension is also present in the American movements, as demonstrated by the different reactions to the practice of 'outing' closeted lesbians and gay men.

By contrast, the 1980s and 1990s saw the emergence of a significantly different agenda in Canada. The phenomenon of constitutional litigation around equality rights for lesbians and gay men became increasingly commonplace. The implications of the acceptance of 'sexual orientation' as prohibited as a ground for discrimination by government began to be discussed, with the institution of marriage and the definition of 'spouse' in legislation appearing high on the agenda. One response from the political process, largely as a result of the impact of constitutional challenges, was the lifting of the ban on homosexuals in the armed services.

In a sense, Canada can be seen as a legal culture beginning to engage at a different level of analysis – with the substantive implications of formal legal equality for lesbians and gay men, no longer chiefly debating the question of formal recognition as a rights-bearing group. For example, in the context of the legal regulation of pornography, vociferous argument has ensued in the 1990s over the enforcement of Canada's obscenity laws in the particular context of lesbian and gay male erotica. The Supreme Court of Canada has upheld obscenity laws as imposing a reasonable limitation on the scope of the right of free expression, and in so doing it has relied extensively on a feminist analysis of pornography for its justification. The implications of that reasoning in the context of lesbian and gay rights remain to be seen. The issue highlights how rights claims can come into conflict. The ways in which legal liberalism will respond to this particular clash will be interesting. Finally, a conservative backlash to lesbian and gay rights also may be gaining strength in Canada, especially in some regions, and the impact of this emerging movement in legal developments also is beginning to materialise.

THEMES

Each chapter of *Law's Desire* deals with different legal events and controversies from the period under study. However, a number of themes continually emerge and link the case studies together. First, I argue throughout the book that legal discourse is an important site for the constitution, consolidation and regulation of sexuality and, in particular, the hetero–homo sexual division. Sexuality is socially constructed and law participates in this process. That is, sexual subjectivity comes to be naturalised through a matrix of different discourses. But if sexuality is established through practices of discourse, the consolidation of a 'normal' sexuality demands an excluded 'other' against which heterosexuality can be consolidated. Homosexuality provides that 'other', which means that it never in any sense exists outside of the discursive realm. Thus, the operation of power through law is not simply prohibitive regarding sexuality (or anything else). Law, like other discourses, also constitutes sexual identities and practices as deviant or normal and then seeks to regulate what is defined as beyond normality. This thesis has implications for theories and strategies of resistance to a sexual hegemony sustained in part through law. Legal 'prohibitions' can inadvertently create discursive spaces for the articulation of the identity of the excluded 'other' in a field of legal and political contest.

A related theme of *Law's Desire* concerns the politics of sexual identity. To reiterate, identities come to be formed in part through the exercise of power (including law) in oppressive ways. But, in addition, identities can be articulated and consolidated through acts of hegemonic resistance and political process. The articulation of coherent, oppositional identities is an important aspect of that struggle. Yet, at the same time, identities are subject to contestation – and to deconstruction – which reveals their own partiality, contingency, and exclusions. This tension between the assertion and deconstruction of identities has become particularly acute in lesbian and gay politics and theory. In my view, it is an irresolvable tension and a condition of late modern (or 'postmodern') culture, in which a singular *essential* truth of any identity category is rendered problematic. Instead, identities are revealed to be 'performative' – they come to appear natural through repetition within different discourses. As a consequence, strategies of reform and transformation have, of necessity, become more complex in order to respond to this increasing problematisation of identity. The concept of performativity facilitates a constructionist view of identities by suggesting that there is nothing essential or immutable in the way that we conceive of sexual (and other) identities.

By contrast, from the perspective of a conservative sexual politics, sexual identities do divide neatly into the normal and the 'perverse'. Moreover, homosexuality as the quintessential perversion of normal sexuality is particularly dangerous because it can be 'promoted' so easily. That is, the unwary can be seduced into homosexuality simply through its representation – its appearance within discourse in any sort of 'positive' or neutral light. Thus, for conservatives, sexual identity actually is contingent, mutable, and promotable. In fact, heterosexuality must be continually promoted in order to ensure its viability and supremacy. For lesbians and gay men, one interesting issue is how to respond to such arguments, without making claims grounded in the 'immutability' of sexuality.

Within conservative sexual discourse, the promotion of heterosexuality and the condemnation of 'perverse' sexualities has become particularly pressing in the age of Aids. For conservatives, Aids signifies the logical outcome of homosexuality and serves as a convenient justification for steps to consolidate and promote a heterosexual lifestyle. Aids has been deployed as a means to construct the gay man as disease carrier, as dangerous to the body politic, and as in need of legal regulation. A gay sexuality thus comes to be defined exclusively in terms of lethal sexual practices which, within this discourse, remain strangely seductive despite the consequences.

Another central theme of this book is the construction of boundaries through discourses of law and sexuality. Throughout *Law's Desire* I interrogate the binary divisions that have come to be naturalised in the law, such as homo/hetero; public/private; and inside/outside. This process of deconstruction is a feature of much theoretical writing on sexuality and is aimed at problematising what has been made to appear 'normal', in order to facilitate the project of envisioning a different set of societal possibilities. For lesbian and gay subjects, the problematising or 'queering' of the boundaries of socially constructed categories, in both the theory and practice of sexuality, is an important means of underscoring the social contingency of those apparently bounded categories. The transgression of boundaries is itself closely associated with 'queer politics' in the 1990s. Its effectiveness as a strategy of social transformation in itself is contestable, a point upon which I also touch.

Of course, identities never operate in isolation, and in several chapters the relationship between different legal identities will be explored. National, racial and gender identities are all examined, and the social contingency and performativity of each is emphasised. The role of law in inscribing, constituting, and regulating them proves important. At the same time, it also must be recognised that law is not an 'all-powerful' discourse. Too often legal scholars place law in isolation at the centre of struggles for (or against) social change. On the other hand, scholars in other disciplines are sometimes dismissive of the role of legal discourse. Neither position is viable. While my analytical focus is upon law and its 'desires', I do not mean to suggest that law alone can 'change the world'. Nor, for that matter, can it necessarily resist social change on its own. In interrogating legal discourse I recognise that those of us committed to social/sexual change must realise that the struggle extends to other sites and discourses and that there are connections that must be made between them. I am convinced, however, that legal discourse also deserves and demands interrogation in its own right. That is the project I have undertaken.

CHAPTER OUTLINES

The first four chapters of the book illustrate the role of representation in lesbian and gay legal struggles. Chapter 1 focuses upon the legal restraints placed on artistic funding of the 'homoerotic' which were enacted by the American Congress. In this chapter I also develop many of the theoretical strands which will be employed throughout the book, involving a postmodern conception of the subject and its application to sexual and gendered subjectivity. American rights discourse is central to the legal dispute in issue and judicial review ultimately proves highly successful in combating Congressional actions. The role and limitations of American constitutional discourse thus are analysed in detail. Chapter 2 continues the focus on representation and here I develop a comparative analysis of two issues that bear striking similarities: the section 28 controversy in Britain and the 'Helms Amendment' on safe sex materials in America. Both initiatives are attempts to constrain representations of homosexuality and are grounded in a fervent belief in the power of representation to seduce and convert 'heterosexuals' to a homosexual 'lifestyle'. The two examples also highlight the differing role of rights discourse in the two legal cultures. In Chapter 3, the focus shifts to pornography. In this chapter, I develop a theoretical model in which I answer claims by anti-pornography feminists concerning gay male erotica. I employ the poststructural analysis of the sexual subject which I developed in Chapter 1 in order to develop a rights-based defence of gay male pornography. The analysis of pornography has become increasingly relevant in the face of recurring debates around the homophobic enforcement of obscenity laws. In Chapter 4, I apply the analysis developed in Chapter 3 to a specific example – the application of Canadian obscenity laws and the role of equality and expression rights in Canadian constitutional discourse.

Chapters 5 and 6 deal with the intersection of national and sexual identities. In Chapter 5 I interrogate one of the many 'gays in the military' cases that have been argued before the American courts. These controversies all turn on the constitutionality – in terms of the guarantees of the equal protection of the laws – of the ban on homosexuals in the armed services. However, my interest in the case is not so much doctrinal, but rather I examine what the reasoning reveals about the legal constitution of both the homosexual and the nation-state. In Chapter 6, I continue to focus on national identity and the military. However, the analysis shifts to the recognition of 'sexual orientation' as a prohibited ground of discrimination in the specific context of lesbians and gay men in the Canadian Armed Forces. The different outcomes to this issue in Canada and the United States to date suggests radically different conceptions of national identity and the relationship of nationalism and sexuality.

Finally, in Chapters 7 and 8, I endeavour to look forward to the future and, in a sense, backwards to the past. In Chapter 7 I focus upon the recent criminal convictions of gay male sadomasochists in Britain. This issue drives the analysis back to the original agenda of the gay rights movement – rights of sexual privacy free from criminal sanction. At the same time, the reaction to the case suggests the emergence and articulation of new sexual identities around specific sexual practices that may intersect in various ways with the sexual identities of lesbian, gay, bisexual, and straight. This is also the theme of the last chapter, in which I interrogate the concept of 'queerness' as a sexual identity in the 1990s which, it is claimed, challenges and deconstructs sexual categorisation in general. I endeavour to apply queer theory and practice to legal analysis. The tension implicit in the emergence of a coherent lesbian or gay rights-bearing legal subject that I traced in Chapter 1 is thus itself scrutinised in this closing chapter.

1

IDENTITIES, SEXUALITIES, AND THE POSTMODERN SUBJECT

An analysis of funding by the National Endowment for the Arts

In this first chapter I examine the ongoing issue of arts funding by the National Endowment for the Arts (NEA) in America. Perhaps more than any single area of legal regulation in the United States (other than sodomy laws themselves), the NEA has featured as an arena of controversy in the past several years. This is due to the focus of attention on how funded (and 'defunded') cultural works touch issues of lesbian and gay sexuality. The conflict over arts funding heats up with a certain regularity and often with a fierce intensity, such as in the campaign by Patrick Buchanan to unseat George Bush for the Republican presidential nomination in 1992. Claims that the President was 'soft' on arts funding for gay-themed works were framed as an example of weakness in the face of subversive forces at work within the nation.

The NEA funding controversy highlights several themes which will prove central to the studies in this book. First, the implicit justification for the legal initiatives is that cultural representations have a tremendous power to promote sexual practices and identities and to erode the 'core' values of America itself. Second, the issue demonstrates the centrality of rights in American constitutional discourse and the power of free speech rights to 'trump' competing rights claims. The question of whether it is permissible for the legislature to provide funding for some artistic endeavours and not for others based on sexual content becomes transformed into an appeal to the language of rights by lesbians and gay men, as well as by religious minorities and 'mainstream' America. Third, the debates in Congress over NEA funding suggest that proponents of legal restriction on funding explicitly accept the social constructedness of sexual identity, since the rationale behind legal intervention in large measure is the cultural seductiveness of representation and its power to seduce the unwary into a homosexual 'lifestyle'.

In response to this perceived threat, the late 1980s and 1990s have seen numerous attempts to make grants to artists conditional upon assurances that their works do not depict the obscene. Some of these political interventions have been successful, and the contestation over the issue continues. Without question, the debate has largely focused upon the funding of artistic works which present lesbian and gay images. Grants have been denied to artists whose works depict a

11

lesbian or gay identity, and even when grants have been approved, the storm of controversy has not dissipated. Not surprisingly, this environment of content-based control of artistic funding gave rise to questioning of the constitutionality of explicit Congressional restrictions and their application by the NEA.

In this chapter, I first review the chronology of events in the NEA saga and the constitutional implications raised. I then argue that the constitutional analysis of this issue was less than robust given the constraints of American rights discourse. I develop an alternative approach which draws upon a number of theoretical strands – postmodernism, poststructuralism, and critical film and literary theory – and I argue that the restrictions on arts funding amounted to a fundamental violation of American constitutional values because, when successful, they have denied some citizens the right to articulate a political identity. This theoretical framework informs my analysis throughout the book. In order to substantiate this thesis, I analyse postmodern theories of the subject and their role in the cultural conditions of postmodernity; in this way I hope to provide a theoretical foundation for understanding how identities are formed and expressed in the cultural environment of the late twentieth century. Next, I focus on the importance of constructing new forms of political subjectivity through cultural production and consumption. This analysis of discourse theory will be explored using a vision of equality that emphasises the dialogic – the fundamental right to participate in a conversation in an ongoing attempt to define and contest identity. After establishing this theoretical groundwork, I turn to an example of particular relevance to the NEA – the formation and articulation of a gay identity within our cultural environment. Particular cultural practices will be explored in order to establish that restrictions on arts funding that limit the articulation of a gay identity are a denial both of the right to political expression and of a dialogically based right to the equal protection of the law. Moreover, such restrictions are unenforceable in a sense because they misconceive the role of culture and the diverse meanings of a representation. The uncontrollability of representations, in terms of their meaning to cultural consumers, ensures that any representation may become the basis for the forging of a new and potentially subversive political identity. Restrictions, then, are objectionable both because they are contrary to American constitutional values and, moreover, because they are impossible to enforce effectively due to the unpredictability of the ways in which a cultural artefact will be deployed.

THE NEA AND THE LIMITS TO REPRESENTATION

Recent political intervention in the National Endowment for the Arts has become well known and continues to raise controversy. Some background on the disbursement of grant money may provide a useful starting point for analysis. The NEA was created in 1965 as a means for public financial support of the arts through an agency with independent grant-making powers. The Endowment's mandate is to sponsor works of artistic or cultural significance through grants to individuals of exceptional talent. The Endowment was intended to be free from political influence in its grant-making decisions, which were to be based upon the recommendations of peer review panels of professional artists expert in particular fields. The final funding decisions have always rested with the Chairperson of the Endowment, an appointment made by the President of the United States, with the advice and consent of the Senate.[1]

It is not surprising that funding decisions in the past have occasionally given rise to controversy. Since the creation of the NEA, there has been criticism of individual funding decisions and general policy, often centring upon competing claims of cultural elitism and populism. In addition, dramatic budget-cutting in the name of national debt reduction produced an angry response from the arts communities in the early 1980s. However, the vehemence of the reaction to two funding decisions that came to light in 1989 was unprecedented and underscored how a new cultural agenda was being set in place. The first was the posthumous NEA-sponsored travelling exhibition entitled *Robert Mapplethorpe: The Perfect Moment*. This was scheduled to appear at the Corcoran Gallery in Washington D.C., but was cancelled by the Gallery in response to political pressure. The Mapplethorpe retrospective included his controversial *X Portfolio*, largely consisting of sadomasochistic gay male imagery. It also included the *Y Portfolio*, which comprised Mapplethorpe's frequently criticised photographs of African American men. The second work was by artist Andres Serrano, who had received NEA funding for his *Piss Christ*, a plastic crucifix submerged in a glass tank of urine.

In response to these funding decisions, Senator Jesse Helms intervened as a critic of the NEA. His attack alternated between the 'blasphemy' of Serrano's *Piss Christ* and the 'perversity' of Mapplethorpe's *X Portfolio*. In calling for an end to government subsidy of projects akin to these, Helms considered at some length the implications of Mapplethorpe's photographs. For the Senator, this work 'ha[d] a political and social dimension':

> the art critics acknowledge that Mapplethorpe's obscene photographs were an effort to gain wider exposure of, and acceptance for, homosexuality – which happens to be the stated political goal of all homosexual pressure groups. For instance, the catalog for the Mapplethorpe exhibit at the Whitney Museum of Modern Art concedes that Mapplethorpe felt sadomasochism . . . was an almost obligatory subject for him to treat and that "he reported it not as a voyeur, but as an advocate."[2]

Thus, it was the power of representations not only to expose a lifestyle to public view, but to further the acceptance and promotion of that lifestyle that was particularly troubling for Helms. This is the political dimension of the work which provided a rationale for a political response to its subsidy by a governmental agency.

Senator Helms proposed a statutory restriction as a condition for the appropriation of funding for the NEA, which he introduced on 26 July 1989. It provided that:

None of the funds authorized to be appropriated pursuant to this Act may be used to promote, disseminate, or produce –

(1) obscene or indecent materials, including but not limited to depictions of sadomasochism, homo-eroticism, the exploitation of children, or individuals engaged in sex acts; or

(2) material which denigrates the objects or beliefs of the adherents of a particular religion or non-religion; or

(3) material which denigrates, debases, or reviles a person, group, or class of citizens on the basis of race, creed, sex, handicap, age, or national origin.[3]

Clearly, Helms sought to respond directly both to the Mapplethorpe exhibit and the Serrano piece. With respect to Serrano, clause (2) attempted to foreclose such a funding decision in the future. With respect to Mapplethorpe, the prohibition on the obscene and indecent, and the explicit references to sadomasochism, homo-eroticism, and children cut a sufficiently wide swathe to include all of the photographs that Helms found offensive.

The original wording of the 'Helms Amendment' also was significant for the way in which it focused attention on group rights as a justification for restrictions on arts funding. Those groups that warranted protection from the 'harm' included religious minorities as well as racial, sexual and other groups. Clauses (2) and (3) explicitly deployed the language of group harm inflicted through another's self-expression. Previously, this argument had been used primarily by minority groups in the context of racial and sexual hate speech. Helms' appropriation of the idea of harm caused by representation also had a superficial resemblance to arguments developed by anti-pornography feminists.[4] In this context, though, the language of minority protection from hateful representations is reworked in order to protect the sensibilities of mainstream America and the American Christian community. The supporters of the amendment sought to analogise the treatment of Christians at the hands of Serrano to intolerance directed against religious and racial minorities. As one Congressman pondered:

one wonders how many of those who are aggressively opposing the setting of these standards would be doing so, if it had been a photo of Martin Luther King or a symbol of the Jewish faith that had been submerged in a bottle of urine at taxpayers' expense.[5]

Furthermore, it was alleged that the constitutionally imposed separation of church and state in America was infringed by government-funded 'anti-Christian' art. Opponents of the amendment also argued within a framework of religious faith, emphasising not only their own deeply felt Christian beliefs, but also the dangers of religious fanaticism implicit in 'an amendment which would give an Ayatollah Khomeini or the like the right to veto the grants of the National Endowment for the Arts'.[6]

After Congressional debate, the amendment was modified through the withdrawal of clauses (2) and (3) and the removal of the reference to indecency in clause (1). The focus thus shifted away from Serrano and religious offensiveness, and towards work that might be considered obscene. The justification for the amendment thus became more obvious and was clearly targeted at the Mapplethorpe exhibit. Simply put, it was argued that the taxpayer should not be expected to fund cultural work that is obscene, pornographic, or as Senator Helms argued, vulgar, sick, and unspeakable. However, there also was included a new provision which stated that work with serious artistic value was not precluded from receiving funding. But for those members of Congress supporting the bill (and indeed for most of those opposing it) there seemed no issue as to the merit of *Portfolio X* itself – one member claimed that '99.9% of Americans would categorically define [it] as obscene garbage'.[7] Some politicians went further, and attributed an overwhelming symbolic value to any representation of gay sexuality, finding that NEA funding decisions exemplified an ongoing battle against the 'eroding [of] the moral structure of our country' by something 'inherently evil'.[8] For one member of Congress, the battle lines were all too clear, and this controversy was:

> the symptom of a moral decay in a society that has lost the ability to say that there are standards in this world that govern mankind down through time and that are valid, traditional family values, where we have the courage as leaders of the country to stand up and say what is junk and what is good literature, what is pornographic, and what we are going to tolerate.[9]

In fact, the determination of what is unacceptable was explicit in the 'Helms Amendment'. The intent was to ensure that funds would not be made available to artists who would then produce a work that *might* be considered obscene and, given the definition, that meant anything that depicted the undefined 'homoerotic'. Moreover, because the amendment included in its list of prohibited representations 'individuals engaged in sex acts', the further inclusion of the term 'homoeroticism' logically implied something other than the depiction of same-sex acts. It suggested rather that funding of any representation of lesbian or gay sexuality was foreclosed. Carole Vance has argued that the amendment had a particular 'linguistic elasticity' because it left unanswered the question of whether peer review panels should reject *all* proposals that might offend any group, and whether any representation that the proponents of the amendment would object to is then necessarily deemed obscene.[10] Finally, the phrase 'may be considered obscene' suggested that the discretion left to the Endowment was sufficiently wide as to be beyond review in court.

There were other feats of linguistic gymnastics in the amendment. The exempting clause that permitted funding of works of serious value was difficult to square with the rest of the amendment. If a peer review panel determines that a project is worthy of funding, does it, by definition, possess serious artistic value which overrides the other statutory clauses? If that is the case, however, then the entire amendment becomes devoid of meaning, since it merely reiterates what already was obvious; namely, that funding is to be awarded on the basis of artistic excellence. The amendment also implied that representations of sadomasochism, homoeroticism, and the other examples necessarily are obscene by reason of content alone. However, in American constitutional law the definition of obscenity, which can be legally proscribed, is narrow, and convictions under obscenity law are extremely difficult to obtain.[11] The narrowness of this legal test appears to be replaced by a much broader definition that turns on offensiveness to groups in general. Finally, as a symbolic matter, the grouping together of homoeroticism, sadomasochism, sexual acts, and the exploitation of children further reinforces the construction of lesbians and especially of gay men as perverse and degenerate.

Despite its apparent incoherence, the 'Helms Amendment' was far from ineffective both symbolically and practically. It easily passed into law and, in response, recipients of funding were required to certify that no federal funds would be used to promote material that could be deemed obscene, including, but not limited to, the various categories of representation prohibited by the amendment. Not long thereafter, Congress also enacted a number of structural changes to the National Endowment for the Arts. The composition of peer review panels was to explicitly reflect 'diverse artistic and cultural points of view' and to include non-artists.[12] This was designed to allow for more representation of the views of middle America, in what was perceived to be the exclusive preserve of the East-Coast artistic elites. Written records were to be kept of panel meetings and the Chairperson of the Endowment explicitly was given final authority over funding decisions. Artists were required to file interim reports on their progress, and payments could be made by instalments, with a provision for reimbursement of funds that had been used to create a project determined by a court to be obscene. Clearly, these structural changes were aimed both at the funding decision stage (by ensuring peer review panels which would be less receptive to homoerotic work) and at the later stage of artistic production (by creating mechanisms to ensure closer monitoring of the content of the cultural production).

It also became increasingly clear that the focus of attention was specifically on the cultural production of the 'homoerotic'. This was apparent in May 1990 when then Chairperson of the NEA, John Frohnmayer, overturned the recommendations of the NEA's theatre review panel and denied funding to four performance artists – Karen Finley, John Fleck, Holly Hughes, and Tim Miller (the 'NEA Four'). Holly Hughes is openly lesbian and John Fleck and Tim Miller are out gay men, and the sexuality of all three forms an integral part of their performance art. Moreover, Karen Finley, although she does not identify herself as lesbian, creates work that tackles issues of sexuality, and it has been argued that her performances frequently are read within dominant culture as 'lesbian' because of her focus on 'policing displays of the body'.[13] As Finley explicitly employs her body (including orifices) in her performances, her art frequently is seen as 'unnatural' and, consequently, she is read as homosexual.

Although the NEA Four's 'defunding' decision marked the height of the controversy and was followed by resignations from a number of expert panelists

16

in different fields, subsequent events have suggested that these cultural contestations are far from over. In 1990 the 'Helms Amendment' was dropped by Congress, but in its place was inserted a provision which required the Chairperson of the Endowment to ensure that 'general standards of decency and respect for the diverse beliefs and values of the American public' was a consideration in funding decisions; and that 'obscenity' (as judicially determined) was not funded.[14] In fact, the Chairperson of the Endowment found himself increasingly unable to please critics on either side. In November, 1991, Frohnmayer approved grants to Tim Miller and Holly Hughes. And, in early 1992, Endowment support for a New York literary journal, *The Portable Lower East Side*, publications of which included *Queer City* and *Live Sex Acts*, spurred conservative organisations to send excerpts to members of Congress. In the midst of Frohnmayer's conversion to support for the independence of funding decisions by the NEA panels, and in the climate of a presidential election campaign, he was forced to resign with effect from 1 May 1992.

The Republican Administration elevated Deputy Chairperson Anne-Imelda Radice to the position of acting Chair of the NEA. A few days after assuming office, Radice vetoed two grants recommended by its advisory panel for sexually explicit works: an art exhibit at the List Visual Arts Center at the Massachusetts Institute of Technology entitled *Corporal Politics*, which featured violence, castration, and sexual fetishism; and a video and photography exhibit at the Anderson Gallery of the Virginia Commonwealth University called *Anonymity and Identity*, which included one work by photographer Annette Messager entitled *My Wishes*, which consisted of 'more than 100 tiny photographs of faces, lips, hair and, in one case, a penis'.[15] In protest, the Endowment sculpture panel announced the suspension of its grant meeting and the solo theatre arts panel resigned in protest. Two other panels criticised Radice's actions. In November, 1992, during the final weeks of the Bush Administration, the Endowment refused to award grants to three lesbian and gay film festivals on the basis of artistic merit.

Of course, the political climate changed dramatically with the election of the Clinton Administration and especially with the appointment of actress Jane Alexander as Chairperson of the Endowment. However, controversy still swirls around the cultural scene in America. Grant applications create heated debates in the NEA's advisory council meetings and, in a dramatic move, in August, 1993 the county commission of Cobb County, Georgia, voted to end all of its arts funding because of the possibility of inadvertently supporting gay-related cultural works. The vote occurred after complaints about a production of the off-Broadway play *Lips Together, Teeth Apart*, which includes peripheral references to gay male sexuality. Most recently, right-wing politicians have described as depraved and pornographic a performance by HIV-positive artist Ron Athey at the NEA-funded Walker Art Center in Minneapolis in April 1994. Athey carved symbols on the backs of audience members and made prints in blood of the patterns on paper towels. The performance has been cynically deployed as a rationale for threatened cuts to the NEA's budget.[16]

Clearly, then, the political process has been a tenuous arena in which to advance claims in response to the anti-funding critics. Arguments that taxpayers have the *right* not to have their money spent *promoting* lesbian and gay male sexuality through cultural funding generally get a receptive hearing at the legislative level. This is reinforced by arguments that lesbian and gay cultural representation *promotes* the destruction of the moral fibre and values of American society. Implicit in this position is the point that there is no right to governmental funding for any particular cultural endeavour, especially when the majority perceives it as obscene, indecent, pornographic, and incompatible with the national interest. Finally, the funding of representations of lesbian and gay life, it is argued, would violate the rights of practising Christians not to have their tax dollars spent on promoting (simply through representation) a set of sexual practices they view as inherently evil. The rights of both mainstream America and a religious minority group are thus invoked simultaneously (despite contradictions) to marshal arguments in favour of restrictions on financial support for the arts.

This set of arguments, as formulated by the right wing, has forced proponents of lesbian and gay cultural representation to rethink their response. While claims can be made in terms of the rights of lesbians and gay men as a group to participate fully and equally in American cultural production, group rights arguments cut both ways. The rights of religious minorities and 'the American public' have partially neutralised arguments framed in terms of equal cultural participation. Moreover, this argument frequently has been met with the response that no artist has a right to funding and that the marketplace of ideas will ensure that work of value finds an outlet. Thus, the argument is made that artistic freedom is not limited by funding restrictions. Rather, only state subsidy is curtailed

Interestingly, while the political process has been fairly hostile to claims of funding for lesbian and gay cultural representation, constitutional litigation has proven an effective means of eliminating funding restrictions. These 'victories' demonstrate the power of the doctrine of free speech in American constitutional discourse (the 'First Amendment') to trump other arguments also based in the language of rights. As Nan Hunter, a litigator in a series of cases dealing with restrictions on public funding of sexual expression has suggested, the argument has been made that cultural representations of lesbians and gay men are worthy of constitutional protection as speech of political and social value:

> Our claims set forth the first serious demand that speech about sexuality be treated as core political speech. This development marks a radical shift in First Amendment doctrine, provoking a category crisis of whether to treat sexual speech as part of a shared social dialogue or as second-tier quasi-obscenity. The change in legal doctrine has altered political thought as well. It signals the conceptualization of sexuality – and specifically homosexuality – as a political idea.[17]

Thus, while the legislative interventions have sought to define the 'homoerotic' as indecent, obscene, and pornographic, the constitutional arena provides the opportunity to challenge that characterisation and to assert a value in the expression of sexual minorities to which can be attached a constitutional *right*.

The issue of whether such restrictions on funding are a violation of the right of free speech raises one of the most vexing questions of constitutional law. On the one hand, it is well established that governments must make decisions all the time about what is deserving of funding (and what is not), and it is within the power of the legislature to determine that it will provide funding for some types of expression and not for others. To hold otherwise would mean that any attempt at public support of expression in America was unconstitutional. However, it also has been firmly established that the government 'may not deny a benefit to a person on a basis that infringes his constitutionally protected interests – especially his interest in freedom of speech'.[18] The difficult issue, therefore, is how to reconcile these propositions.

Two legal challenges in the context of NEA funding illustrate this difficulty and they both underscore the power of speech rights claims. First, in *Bella Lewitzky Dance Foundation v. Frohnmayer*, a District Court judge held that requiring grant recipients to certify that funds would not be used to produce obscenity was unconstitutional.[19] Judge Davies found that the certification requirement was vague and created a 'chilling effect' on the speech rights of grant recipients.[20] He reasoned that there was no question of the government's right to place conditions on the award of federal funding, but that such provisions could not be unduly vague. As a consequence of this decision, the NEA dropped the certification requirement.

Second, in *Finley v. NEA*, the NEA Four challenged the decency clause as part of their constitutional appeal against the decision to deny them funding in May 1990.[21] Judge Tashima found in their favour, holding that the requirement that artistic merit and excellence be determined in light of 'general standards of decency' was vague and too broad in its sweep to satisfy constitutional scrutiny. He found the words 'decency' and 'respect' to be 'inherently subjective' and 'contentless'.[22] With respect to free speech doctrine, Judge Tashima reasoned that artistic expression 'is at the core of a democratic society's cultural and political vitality',[23] and that governmental funding criteria are limited to 'professional evaluations of . . . merit'.[24] That determination of excellence did not encompass considerations of decency. Consequently, the decency clause was declared unconstitutional. The case currently is under appeal. In both cases, then, one can see rights claims based upon freedom of artistic expression overcome competing arguments.

The claims of indecency also highlight a deep ambivalence within dominant culture with respect to the representation of lesbian and gay male sexuality. The critics of arts funding for lesbian and gay culture assume without question that representations have a tremendous transformative potential which is sufficiently powerful to erode the dominance of heterosexuality in American society. Moreover, culture is seen as having the power to erode 'America' itself through the destruction of its traditional values. Proponents of these arguments implicitly accept both the social construction of sexuality and the nation-state, in that each is capable of a radical reconstitution through cultural means. Nor is there any attempt made by the critics to question the relationship between the messages intended by the artist and the meaning received by the audience or to acknowledge the possibility of multiple, contradictory, or ironic readings of any representation. There is, of course, an irony in the argument because, for Senator Helms and his supporters who have been an unanticipated audience for lesbian and gay culture, the works in question reinforce (rather than transform) their views about lesbian and gay sexuality. The solution offered by this audience is a truly conservative one, for they seek to stop any attempt at reforming public opinion through a denial of the material resources that are perceived as necessary for that project.

THE LEGAL SUBJECT AS BEARER OF RIGHTS

In the remainder of this chapter, I will analyse how the attempt to erase lesbian and gay artistic representation through a denial of funding violates constitutional norms which have not been easily articulated within American legal discourse. I will seek to expand on how both expression and equality rights are conceived by formulating a theoretical framework in an attempt to rethink both the immediate legal questions as well as more expansive issues of American constitutional theory and interpretation.

In order to engage in the reconception of the rights of equality and expression, it is necessary not only to understand the content of the rights but to examine how rights are held by their subject and, more fundamentally, to analyse how the subject itself is constructed. The universality and, indeed, the coherence of the subject increasingly has come under scrutiny in the glare of postmodern and poststructural analysis. The postmodern focus on the demise of the universal narrative has meant that one of the targets for decentring has been the narrative of the rational and coherent social subject.[25] The individual subject is rendered inextricable from discourse, 'a post through which various kinds of messages pass', which leaves her a point for the ever-shifting play of dissonant language games.[26] With the postmodern rejection of all projects claiming to be universal, the unity of the subject is deconstructed and revealed as plural, fragmentary, and contingent.

Moreover, the searching deconstruction of the subject has revealed that the universal rational subject of Enlightenment thought demanded exclusions from its category as the means for its own constitution as a universal: '[T]he philosophical and historical creation of a devalued "Other" was the necessary precondition for the creation of the transcendental rational subject outside of time and space, the subject who is the speaker in Enlightenment philosophy.'[27] Indeed, feminists have long argued that the definition of the subject as universal has been inextricably tied to its identification as exclusively male, leaving woman necessarily defined by her absence – by her otherness. The discursively constructed 'I' is male as a direct result of the exclusion of the female from its borders.

20

The recognition of the constructed status of subjecthood, and how its constitution as a universal has been achieved by the relegation of some to the status of other, has forced poststructuralist thinkers to determine the status of a deconstructed subject. If the unity and singularity of the subject is revealed as illusory, the question then becomes how we conceive of a post-Enlightenment notion of identity, or whether identity itself is a universal that must be deconstructed. This appears increasingly to be the postmodern project – a reconstitution of identity and subjecthood apart from a modernist, universal conception. In other words, a decentring of the subject does not mean that the subject ceases to have any coherent meaning. The ontological status of the body itself grounds subjectivity in a way that it is difficult to imagine transcending.[28] Thus, the rejection of the universal need not mean the rejection of all coherence for the subject. Not only does the body itself suggest some limits to the dissolution of subjecthood (if only through a firmly entrenched metaphor), but the ability to conceive of a decentring of one's self demands that there remain a grounded subject making use of the discursive space of multiplicity and identity fragmentation.[29]

Moreover, as a political matter, it is not surprising that feminist theory has generated an examination of limits to the dissolution of the subject. For women, who historically have been denied the position of speaking subject, the rejection of the universal appears to leave little opportunity for overdue claims grounded in the singularity of the subject position.[30] If the nodal point of subjecthood is unpacked and revealed as multifaceted, contradictory, and both subjected to and complicit in relationships of power, the question arises whether the singularity required to pursue legal claims will be undermined.[31]

This scepticism as to whether the dissolution of the subject will hinder claims that we have associated traditionally with the universal subject of rights demands a response. In fact, postmodernists increasingly have focused their attention on how a postmodern understanding of identity, agency, and a localised, situated subject provides the basis as a political and theoretical matter for the securing of rights. In other words, an understanding of subjecthood can be relocated rather than rejected. To begin with, the postmodern deconstruction of subjecthood has revealed the subject not only as socially constructed but also as a product of discourse. This discovery, however, need not mean that the status of the subject is reduced to nothing more than the intersection of various language games (to use Lyotard's formulation). Subjects are constructed by discourse, and as subjects we actively and creatively participate in our self-definition through discourse. Such a realisation demands that our understanding of subjecthood must transcend the binary opposition between liberal, universal conceptions and the poststructuralist dissolution of all notions of a grounded subjectivity. Rather, we must recognise individual activity in self-definition and interpretation.

It is the potential for interpretive activity that provides the grounding for a conception of agency apart from traditional notions of the subject. As a starting point, this understanding depends upon an appreciation of the necessarily incomplete delineation of the boundaries of any discourse – including law – through which an identity is inscribed upon the subject.[32] This partial suturing of discourses of the universal subject allows for intervention, resistance, and subversion of the terms of the system. The active role of the agent, through her creative intervention and resistance, ultimately contributes to the social construction of identity.

From this theoretical standpoint, the possibility exists for active intervention by the marginal subject, historically defined as the other against which the universal subject is constituted, in the very structure that creates the appearance of the universal. The power of the 'universal' metanarrative operates through a matrix of constraints by which 'the subjection of localized, fragmented knowledges . . . is a necessary condition for appearance of the "totalizing" discourses of authority'.[33] However, if discourse is never actually totalised, for the subject constituted as an absence discursive resistance remains possible. Thus, an identity can be forged within the very discourse through which one's subjectivity has been denied articulation. This potential for resistance also suggests that a measure of commonality may be found between a feminist and a postmodern conception of subjecthood.

The capacity for resistance can be linked to a political agenda that focuses on the formation of identities denied by the universal discourse of subjecthood. The destabilisation of the universal subject position through practices of resistance opens up a realm of cultural space for the establishment of identities that have been silenced. Thus, attempts to problematise the norm become a precondition for articulating difference. Moreover, by operating within the dominant discourse, subjects that have been historically denied participation can appropriate and redeploy the terms of the dominant discourse. It is this cultural phenomenon of discursive appropriation – a parasitic redeployment of the excess of discursive meaning – that amounts to the cultural practice of postmodern theory.[34] By operating within and utilising the terms of the dominant discourse in subversive fashion, new identities are shaped – subjectivities that emerge in an oppositional relationship to the universal.

The cultural conditions of postmodernity do not give rise only to isolated acts of resistance by individual agents. Resistance also occurs within 'a shared material and discursive history', which results in shared identities articulated in liberationist terms.[35] Attempts at articulation also can provide the means for rethinking the liberal tension between individual and community. On the one hand, to the extent that cultural interventions in a discourse are understood as emerging from a shared history, and therefore a shared identity, the narrative of identity itself may come to be shared and authored collectively. The logic of postmodernism also demands a recognition of specificity; 'that each of us is located at, indeed is, the intersection of various specific discourses and structures, and that we each possess knowledges produced in that location'.[36] The focus, then, cannot be on abstract notions of *collective* difference alone. Rather, a refutation of the universal subject equally requires an understanding of the specificity of agency – that an agent is unique (individual) because of a particular

22

location within a structure of hierarchies. A decentring of the universal subject opens up cultural space not only for the recognition of difference, which, by definition, still prioritises the universal. It also leads to articulation of an individuality that can be defined in terms that respect membership in collective subjectivities and also recognise the uniqueness of any location. The individual subject thus is defined in terms of membership in communities, but also provides a unique intersectional vantage point.

SUBJECTHOOD AND THE CULTURAL CONDITIONS OF POSTMODERNITY

I have argued to this point that alternative subjectivities can be articulated and identities forged through acts of resistance to the dominant discourse of the universal subject. It is necessary, though, to ground this argument in an understanding of how such an articulation of subjecthood can occur. In other words, what are the cultural conditions that give rise to the formation of a political identity in contradistinction to the universal subject position? To reiterate, the narrative of the universal rational subject was the product of discourse. The effect of the discourse was the emergence of 'centralising principles', and the task of postmodern analysis is to uncover what the centre has rendered marginal.[37] The postmodern redemption of the peripheral is possible because, as Foucault described, power also gives rise to:

> mobile and transitory points of resistance, producing cleavages in a society that shift about, fracturing unities and effecting regroupings. . . . [J]ust as the network of power relations ends by forming a dense web that passes through apparatuses and institutions, without being exactly localized in them, so too the swarm of points of resistance traverses social stratifications and individual unities.[38]

Increasingly, the postmodern analysis has turned to how a subversive fragmentation of the unities of discourse is to be realised in late twentieth-century Western society. That analysis has focused on the cultural conditions of postmodernity and the specific cultural practices through which alternative subjectivities may be constructed. Culture becomes the focus of attention as its potential as a site for a politics of resistance emerges from the role of the subject as cultural consumer.[39]

Not surprisingly, the inundation of the individual with cultural signs opens up a new terrain for the formation of an identity forged from resistance to, and through the subversion of, those signs. Such an understanding of culture demands the rejection of a singular meaning, located in the producer's intention, of any cultural representation. It requires a depriveleging of universal cultural meanings and a recognition of local, particularised, and contradictory cultural configurations. Thus, in the cultural environment of postmodernity, a modernist cultural tradition, which has allowed only articulation from the universal standpoint,

23

comes under scrutiny. Cultural practices reveal how points of resistance to a dominant discourse come to be articulated. The task, however, is not simply one of 'articulating the margins, or what has been projected as marginal' and appropriating those 'regimes of images that seem designed to silence those whom they embody in representation'.[40] The postmodern project also fundamentally must overcome the binary relation of universal and marginal subject – a relation in which the very recognition of one's historic silencing 'is implicitly to accept and to internalize the condition of marginality'.[41] Within the cultural circumstances that we face, the goal becomes the elucidation of how the cultural universal never fully expels the marginal. Rather, the margins continue to reside within the centre despite the constant attempts to silence, erase, and reduce them to the other.

One method by which dominant cultural productions are utilised as a means for cultural resistance is decoding. Through cultural consumption by historically marginalised subjects, the marginal, which resides within the 'universal' meaning of a cultural production, can be uncovered or decoded. Through decoding, the meaning of a message, as it is received by a consumer, becomes uncontainable from the standpoint of production, a phenomenon described by Jean Baudrillard in a now famous passage:

> [T]he mass does not at all constitute a passive receiving structure for media messages, whether they be political, cultural or advertising. Microgroups and individuals, far from taking their cue from a uniform and imposed decoding, decode messages in their own way. They intercept them (through leaders) and transpose them (second level), contrasting the dominant code with their own particular sub-codes, finally recycling everything passing into their own cycle. . . . [I]t is a way of redirecting, of absorbing, of victoriously salvaging the material diffused by the dominant culture. . . . [I]n the case of the media, traditional resistance consists of reinterpreting messages according to the group's own code and for its own ends.[42]

The practice of decoding ensures that a particular, local, resistant subject can come to be defined through her cultural consumption. Consumption thus is not a passive process, but in itself is a form of cultural production.[43]

The implications of this postmodern understanding of cultural consumption are considerable. The constitution of the resistant subject depends upon the ability to formulate cultural meanings from the materials that are available and can be appropriated from the dominant culture. Through this cultural appropriation the subject receives 'an education about the "self" and its relation to the world and to others in it.'[44] Moreover, appropriation opens up cultural space for the formation of collective identities. How images are consumed, appropriated, and redeployed depends upon the unique vantage point of the subject located at the conjunction of the matrices of power relationships.[45] The decoding and appropriation of cultural images, then, can become an act of discursive resistance to the positioning of the universal speaking subject, creating the possibilities of 'oppositional, independent or alternative symbolizations of the self'.[46]

The implications of a postmodern approach to cultural consumption for a theory of identity are significant. The postmodern approach suggests an ongoing struggle, both through the encoding and decoding of texts, to utilise culture for the purposes of individual and collective self-definition. It also implies that culture is political in its role as a forum for the deployment of images that can be reworked for a variety of political ends. The interplay of culture and identity – how culture forms the self and how culture may be subversively utilised for the definition of one's self – becomes a thoroughly political matter with no pre-determined outcome. Instead, the process is an ongoing contest over identity, which itself is a product of culture or, more accurately, the provisional outcome of a struggle over the meanings of cultural artefacts.

FROM CULTURE TO POLITICS: THE ARTICULATION OF A POLITICAL SUBJECTIVITY

I have argued to this point that cultural consumption is a means by which a subject resistant to a dominant discourse can be constructed. I also have suggested that this process of identity formation is a politically charged one – a continuing contest over the meaning of any cultural representation. In this section, the focus shifts from an analysis of culture to a focus on politics, although, of course, the two are intertwined. I will examine the implications of a postmodern analysis of the subject, particularly as the analysis touches upon our understanding of the 'rights' that traditionally have been perceived as essential to our understanding of identity and the capacity to define one's 'self'. I will argue that this analysis of the political nature of subjecthood demands a rethinking of the rights of equality and free speech, such that the two become linked to form a right of 'dialogic equality'. The focus of attention thus shifts to the right to articulate a political identity unencumbered by legal restriction.

This reconstitution of the subject outside of the constraints of a modernist, totalising system of thought is a project that has been undertaken by Ernesto Laclau and Chantal Mouffe.[47] Their enquiry is closely related to postmodern theories of cultural consumption; in fact, it can provide a theoretical foundation for an analysis of cultural representation. Laclau and Mouffe argue in favour of a 'proliferation of political spaces'[48] (such as the terrain of culture) through which new subjectivities can be formed through appropriation: 'The struggles of the working-class, of women, gays, marginal populations, third-world masses, must result in the construction of their own reappropriations of tradition through their specific genealogical efforts.'[49] Their focus, however, is on the politics of the subject. To this end, they examine the discontinuities and fragmentary nature of political struggle.

The multiplicity of subject positions cannot be interpreted solely in traditional Marxist relations of production terms. The unitary working-class subject is replaced by a pluralist conception in which categories of subjecthood are contingent and constructed. If the subject occupies a plurality of positions:

there is also a possibility that contradictory and mutually neutralizing subject positions will arise. In that case, more than ever, democratic advance will necessitate a proliferation of political initiatives in different social areas . . . [and] the meaning of each initiative comes to depend upon its relation with the others.[50]

This contingency has deeply political implications in terms of how the positions come to be articulated through discourse. Only through the conditions of political struggle can identities establish themselves in any particular power configuration. Moreover, Laclau and Mouffe argue that the political system never achieves a total closure that prevents the development of new and politically resistant identities that may come to be articulated in the social arena.

The partial and unfixed nature of subjecthood clearly has implications for a progressive political project. The search for the collective will of class politics must be abandoned in favour of a continual struggle aimed at the establishment of a precarious and constructed unity amongst the constantly emerging partial identities of social subjects.[51] This approach claims to be anti-essentialist in its articulation of 'the precarious character of every identity and the impossibility of fixing the sense of the "elements" in any ultimate literality'.[52] At the same time, articulation to some extent organises and constitutes social relations.

Identities never manage to be constituted fully, but always remain partial. This is due to 'overdetermination', which refers to 'the presence of some objects in the others [which] prevents any of their identities from being fixed. . . . [T]he presence of some in the others hinders the suturing of the identity of any of them.'[53] Subjecthood must be partially fixed and not completely dispersed, because otherwise any understanding of the differences and contradictions of identity would be impossible. These privileged points of partial meaning become the 'nodal points' of identity, and articulation is a means by which the nodal points are socially constituted.[54]

The logic of overdetermination and the contingency and political character of subject positions provides the basis for a theory of radical, pluralist politics that depends upon the articulation of previously unconstituted subjectivities. If the social subject is a 'meeting point for a multiplicity of articulatory practices, many of them antagonistic',[55] and if there is nothing inevitable about any particular social struggle or its emergence at an historical moment, then it is only through articulation of a subjecthood that a democratic discourse can develop. That discourse can facilitate the emergence of shared political subjectivities claiming *rights*. The concept of the subject and of rights thus becomes infused with new meaning. Rather than representing a universal conception that denies status to marginal social identities, subjecthood signifies multiple and diverse oppressed (as well as dominant) identities. That articulation can form the basis of an ambitious political programme.

This focus on the multiplicity of subjectivities fosters claims to rights which cannot be understood as emanating from the universal position. Such claims, of course, are linked to the postmodern emphasis on the particular, the local, and the contingent. The subjects of rights multiply in number and are limited only to the extent that the space of the political is discursively constrained. In not fixing the meaning of subjecthood as a unified and transcendental category, new identities appear, facilitating new egalitarian movements. This potentially enhances a pluralist democracy, for each struggle is given meaning only to the extent that it forms alliances outside of itself. The political indeterminacy of rights struggles, however, also means that collective identities can be formed around 'radically' conservative political agendas (as witnessed in the NEA funding case).

In the end, Laclau and Mouffe do provide a way out of the precarious relationship between postmodernism and subjecthood. A universal concept of subjecthood is abandoned, but in its place remains an identity – both individual and collective – which represents a continuing tension between coherence and fragmentation. A partial fixity must exist at any moment to give intelligible meaning to an identity, and through articulation that identity can be utilised in democratic struggles. The language of rights remains the discourse of those struggles but it is a local, situated use of language that is anchored in a history of domination. History thus becomes one of the means by which an oppositional identity comes to be constituted. It provides the subject with the language to make intelligible claims to rights. The focus, though, has shifted from the universal to the specific – a specific history of the denial of subjectivity for which reparation is sought through rights discourse.

To reiterate, the destabilisation of the universal subject position and the emergence of resistant political subjectivities is realised through the articulation of identities within dominant culture. The formation of an identity depends upon the ability to articulate a subjecthood and to forge connections through that articulation. This relationship – of identity, politics and culture – also provides insights into our understanding of free speech rights. It explains, moreover, how speech inextricably links itself to the constitutional value of equality in America. This link has been developed through the concept of a dialogic right. As some theorists of the postmodern have come to recognise, '[t]he de-centering of the subject does not spell its demise, but "renders subjectivity thoroughly communicative".'[56] Laclau and Mouffe argue that the emergence of new subject positions depends upon the ability to engage in a dialogue in which new social identities are articulated. Consequently, the optimal condition for the forging of identity is the opening of the political and cultural terrain to that dialogue.

Although speech rights traditionally have been founded in part upon individual and collective self-fulfillment, in our cultural climate it has become necessary to appreciate fully the far-reaching political implications of dialogue which surpasses our traditional justification for political speech.[57] If the formation of an identity is a product of discourse, then free access to the discursive space provides the means by which new political subjectivities can arise. This, in turn, facilitates a conception of ourselves, our communities, and furthers the relationship of a pluralistic self to a variety of communities. The benefits of dialogue flow to all of the participants in the conversation, as relations of equivalence between participants come to be constructed.

Indeed, dialogism speaks not only to our understanding of free expression, it also sheds light upon how equality rights are conceived. Dialogic equality demands a 'symmetric reciprocity between participants', in which a decentred subjectivity is communicative.[58] Communication in a dialogue, though, demands both a conception of the self as a speaking agent and conversation through which the self is continually reshaped and redefined. A reconception of the dichotomy between individual and community through dialogue also can be the means by which universality ceases to operate as an exclusionary device in constituting the subject.[59] This focus on equality of access to the dialogue informs the principle of dialogism – an equality (or sameness) in terms of access, but a right of access that arises from the uniqueness (specificity) of each agent which, in turn, makes her contribution to the dialogue valuable. Finally, the goal of the dialogic process can be expressed in terms of a 'commitment to universality' – the 'real possibility that generalizable interests will emerge in the course of that conversation. Understood in this way, universality is a commitment to a yet-to-be realized actuality rather than to an established reality.'[60] While the modernist focus on universality has not been totally abandoned, it comes to be infused with many of the elements of postmodern thought. A universal right of dialogic access arises from the differences and the particularity of agents. Thus, it is not the universality of the subject position from which a right emerges, but the specificity of subjecthood that demands a right to express one's agency.

However, given the history by which access to the dialogue has been denied to some – to those who have not been allowed to publicly articulate an identity – the traditional right of free expression has been far from universal. Dialogic equality demands more than an unencumbered liberty to speak. Rather, the conditions for dialogue must be conducive to the manipulation, reworking, and redeployment of the signs and symbols by which our culture permeates our lives. The expressive right, then, has a positive connotation in that it demands that subjects have access to the cultural tools by which a meaningful contribution to the dialogue can be made. The articulation of identity connotes the ability to reconfigure, in a unique manner, the signs of dominant culture. In so doing, the ways in which we conceive of culture, the subject, and the community all may be radically altered such that the dialogic contributions of all subjects come to have meaning for all others.

CULTURE, POLITICS, AND THE FORGING OF A GAY SUBJECT

Having examined the postmodern critique of the universal rational subject and the role of culture in the politics of oppositional subjectivities, I now move beyond abstract theoretical explanations and return to the issue of the funding of artistic representation through the National Endowment for the Arts. The current climate of legal restriction, both formal through law and informal through the determination of artistic merit, denies a right to articulate an identity, a right that now must be fundamental to American constitutionalism. Specifically, it silences the formation and articulation of non-heterosexual identities. In developing this thesis, I will draw directly upon the framework that I have developed to this point – the postmodern fragmentation of a universal subject, the discursive nature of all identity concepts, the role of culture in the creation of oppositional and resistant subject positions, the ongoing political struggle over control of the discourse of subjecthood, and the right to articulate radical alternative subjectivities.

Cultural theorists have examined how lesbian and gay identities are cultural, political, and are forged from a marginalised experience of subjecthood. That history of erasure and condemnation, and the tenuous development of an oppositional identity, have been analysed in terms of the binary of in and out.[61] Within the dominant discourse of subjecthood, the establishment of a universal sexual subject was dependent first upon the denial of sexual subjectivity to lesbians and gay men. The instability of a universal heterosexual subject also required that a negative subjecthood of the outsider be attached to the identity of the homosexual.

However, that discourse of inside and outside, like all discursive devices, has the built-in ambiguities through which it can be redeployed in an oppositional strategy. For gay men and lesbians, the language of out and in is not only the means by which subjecthood has been denied, it also provides the tools with which an oppositional identity can be constructed. Indeed, the term 'out' has a multiplicity of significations, demonstrating the ambiguities of the sign and the relationship of a dominant discourse of exclusion to a resistant counter-discourse that itself operates from inside.

The strategy, for those of us who seek to undermine the universality of the (hetero)sexual subject, must continue to be resistance to and subversion of its rhetorical privileging. One means of resistance is the appropriation of the binary of inside/outside. That challenge necessarily is ongoing, for resistance itself can reinforce the centrality of the universal.[62] Acts of resistance are made through the use of language, which also is the means by which cultural identities are forged and maintained. Thus, language not only acts as a point of resistance to dominant culture, it can provide a means for forging a collective and liberatory identity.

However, the articulation of a *subcultural* identity has been, in the case of a lesbian or gay subject, a practice always threatened by the intervention of a dominant heterosexist culture. The threats that emanate from the attempt at closure of discourse to the articulation of a gay identity have a material reality that impacts directly upon the subject. Indeed, the monitoring by dominant culture of the expression of sexual subcultures is pervasive. The inside/outside binary thus takes on an extraordinary importance in a consideration of the articulation of an identity. Language must be encoded within a community (available only to insiders) as a means of individual and collective self-protection. It becomes crucially important that the outsider is not privy to the meanings of the text.

However, the dichotomy of inside and out, while it may facilitate a communal identity through a discourse that might be read only by insiders, also can be rephrased as the metaphor of the closet. To the extent that the policing of discourse in dominant culture forces us to cling to private language, liberation at best will be partial and survivalist. Indeed, the consequences of a denial of public discourse – of a place in the dialogue – are potentially fatal, not only for the subculture, but for the subject, which has been so powerfully demonstrated by the simple equation of silence with death.

The erasure of a gay identity from the dominant discourse is understandable because of its threat to the naturalness of the universal heterosexual subject. If homosexuality is allowed to speak openly, then the universal and univocal heterosexual subject begins to lose a modicum of its priority. From the dominant cultural perspective, the result of the articulation of a gay identity is temptation and cultural seduction.

The threat from the articulation of a gay identity – an effect which may explain the recent history of NEA restrictions – is one that must be understood then in cultural terms. As Simon Watney has suggested, 'we are witnessing an increasing acknowledgment of the role that culture plays in the construction of sexual identities, and it is the field of cultural production that is ever more subject to frank political interventions'.[63] The cultural basis of identity, and specifically of a sexual identity, means that only an erasure (and a condemnation) within the dominant discourse will ensure that the universality of the heterosexual subject position is secure. Thus, dominant culture attempts to foreclose participation in the dialogue in order to prevent the threat to sexual and discursive stability of an alternative subjectivity.

The attempt to close off discursive access also can be explained by the threat posed by a gay cultural subjectivity to the coherence of the universal modernist subject. The gay subject underscores the culturally constructed status of subject-hood – that, rather than being prior to discourse, subjecthood, and particularly sexual subjecthood, is performative. As Richard Dyer has explained, the gay experience largely has been one in which subjecthood consists of a multitude of different roles – a fragmented (postmodern) experience.[64] For example, the gay male experience not only reveals the constructed status of subjecthood as a product of discourse, it also underscores the socially constructed status of masculinity as the universal subject position. The gay male subject is culturally situated in a specific location: in one sense he shares the privileged site of maleness which delineates the universal subject. However, as part of a marginal sexual subculture, his subjectivity is polyvalent and can operate in a resistant fashion.[65]

This fragmenting of the gay identity through performative multiplicitous roles mirrors the general postmodern fragmentation of all identity concepts and the appearance of multiple subjectivities through articulation (as described by Laclau and Mouffe). Thus, the gay subject is a misnomer, for the subject is in a continual state of oscillation between dispersion and coalescence. However, the ability of the gay subject to undermine the universality of the construct of sexuality is particular. As the gay subject reveals sexual orientation as having 'potential for rearrangement, ambiguity, and representational doubleness', the naturalness of sexuality begins to unravel.[66]

It is at this point that the danger posed by the gay subject as a social and cultural identity becomes clear. To the extent that identity is self-generated by lesbians and gay men through cultural representation, the unboundedness of sexuality becomes apparent, and an anti-essentialist account becomes possible. The NEA restrictions, for example, are an attempt to restore the appearance of a sexual essence through the reinforcement of a bounded category – the defined other of the homosexual. These regulations demonstrate the dominant culture's desire to prevent the disintegration of sexual identity concepts and to prevent alternative sexualities from emerging.

This rationale provides a convincing explanation of the recent history of NEA restrictions on homoerotic representation in state-funded artistic expression. It is not, in fact, the sexual expression that is particularly offensive to Senator Helms and others. Rather, 'the cultural acceptability of gay identity' threatens to undermine the universality of the heterosexual subject and to open up for public viewing a new terrain where the contingency of sexuality and its categories is revealed.[67]

GAY IDENTITY AND THE DECONSTRUCTION OF GENDER

Not only does an articulated gay identity undermine the universality of the sexual subject, it also potentially challenges the naturalness of gendered identity as it has been culturally constructed. In this section, I will explore how the cultural representation of a gay identity can draw into question a coherent and unified gender identity. This exploration provides a means of further understanding the motivations behind attempts at cultural erasure, as the coherence of gender comes to depend upon the removal of any intervention that exposes its contingency.

In exploring these issues, I utilise extensively the work of Judith Butler, who has brilliantly engaged in a postmodern analysis of gender, sexuality, and identity. Butler deconstructs all totalising identity concepts by which an 'I' is constituted. The subject necessarily is partial; 'its *specificity* can only be demarcated by exclusions that return to disrupt its claim to coherence'.[68] The subject thus must be continually constituted through repetition which, in turn, may expose its unstable discursive status. The instability of subjecthood ensures that a gay identity potentially can challenge received notions of gender. The strategy advocated by Butler draws upon the theoretical foundations formulated by Laclau and Mouffe and demands the opening up of all identity concepts, including gay and lesbian identities, so that sexual identity becomes a central site of political contestation.

By deconstructing sexual identities, the boundedness of the category of the other begins to disintegrate. The overdetermination of identity brings to the forefront what had previously been concealed, namely, that the other is itself a derivation or a copy of the constructed universal.[69] Once the boundaries of the otherness of homosexuality unravel, the naturalness of gender may be weakened. In fact, Butler argues that both gender and sex are culturally produced mechanisms for social control.[70] Thus, not only is sex a discursive function, but its appearance as prior to culture itself is constructed. Gender analysis, with its binary structure, provides the built-in limitations and constraints upon the discourse. Only by freeing these identity concepts to the play of signifiers can the sexual subject be fully understood.

For example, Butler argues that representations of sexuality may undermine the gendered subject to the extent that the coherence of sexual subjectivity is brought into issue. If subjectivity or personhood is tied to maleness, it also is tied to received notions of gender. A person is a subject because gendered. To the extent that, for example, lesbians and gays exhibit behaviour that does not conform to how gender has been understood in the dominant culture, the gendered subject may begin to unravel. This failure to abide by the rules of gender brings into the public arena a challenge to the binary of male and female. Gender thereby ceases to be recognisable as a cultural inscription on a prior essential set. In its place, the concept of gender becomes understandable only as performative.[71]

Once gender is deconstructed and rendered performative, then actions can be evaluated for their potential to interrupt and fragment the social construction. To the extent that a performative reveals the artifice of gender identity, it also may then undermine hierarchical gendered arrangements. This deconstructive power is particularly possible in a gay context because, although located at the margins of dominant sexual culture, gay culture is 'positioned in subversive or resignificatory relationships to heterosexual cultural configurations'.[72] That is, it may have the potential to resignify through a parody of gender categories. Thus, gay cultural representations reveal that homosexuality may be a copy of the dominant sexual and gender paradigm and that gender, far from being the original that is copied, is itself performatively constituted – a copy for which there is no original. The logical stopping point of the Butler critique is a model in which gendered subjectivity no longer is naturalised as it comes to be revealed as an effect rather than 'being', and the appearance of a coherent gender is shown to be a social construction.

Thus, the proliferation of gay representations has deeply subversive potential not only in destabilising a universal sexual subjecthood, but also in problematising the universality of a gendered subjecthood. The strategy, in part, for achieving a radical pluralist sex/gender system thus becomes the proliferation of images. This results in a loss of representational control and a destabilisation of both gender categories and the constraints on our conceptions of gender and sexuality that have been imposed within dominant discourses.

GAY IDENTITY, CAMP SENSIBILITY, AND STATE CENSORSHIP

Thus far I have attempted to develop a theoretical framework through which to understand the politics of cultural production and consumption and to examine the political implications of the representation of sexual identities. In this section, I will move beyond a discussion of postmodern theory in relation to culture and consider actual cultural practices, the conditions under which subcultural representations emerge and how an oppositional discourse develops despite attempts at erasure by the dominant culture through law. Specifically, I will explore the implications of one such representational strategy, 'gay camp', with reference to the current climate of artistic, cultural, and discursive contestation. The cultural conditions under which a camp sensibility developed provide insights into how a subculture can come to articulate an identity through a language spoken within the dominant discourse, but accessible only to those familiar with the 'decoding' necessary to comprehend the articulation. Moreover, the emergence of the gay identity through camp speaks to the difficulties in attempting to restrain the emergence of a subcultural language. Indeed, the prohibition itself proves to be the means by which the subcultural practices emerge in the gaps left within the dominant legal discourse.

Camp is both a mode of cultural production and of cultural consumption and, in the period prior to the Gay Liberation Movement beginning in the late 1960s, it was one means through which a gay male subcultural identity was forged. On the consumption side, gay men redeployed the images propagated by dominant popular culture in order to constitute an identity.[73] In particular, Hollywood female star images, usually of a bygone era, were appropriated by gay men as a means of identifying with the star. Thus, the cultural meaning intended on the production side within dominant culture was not necessarily that received by the reader. Rather, new unintended meaning was created through consumption as a way for gay men to establish a subjecthood through cultural symbols.

This identification across genders and sexualities has had important cultural implications for our conception of the universal subject. Through the choice of an apparently differently located subject with whom to identify, the camp subject articulated something about the specificity of his own cultural location and, in so doing, set in motion the development of a particular subcultural identity. Moreover, cross-gender identification through camp has implications for the destabilisation of gender boundaries and the naturalness and coherence of a gendered subject. Camp 'assist[s] in destabilizing what appears most permanent in the social order – distinctions between the sexes',[74] and it provides a 'comment upon the relation between nature and artifice in the presentation of the gendered self'.[75] Indeed, camp is the practice of Butler's theory of gender as performative, for the imitation of a star's qualities reveals that the star herself was engaged in a gender masquerade with no underlying original. Through camp, then, the universal gendered subject begins to fray at the edges, as masculinity and femininity

33

are redeployed in a subversive relationship to the dominant construction of gender. Furthermore, gay camp exemplifies how an identity can be formed through cultural consumption and the redeployment of images, despite the attempt at erasure of that identity in the dominant cultural discourse. For lesbians and gays, it was (and remains) precisely because of the 'lack of inherited cultural capital,'[76] the denial of 'the possibility of "masculine" and "feminine" positions of spectatorship, and exclu[sion] by conventional representations of male-as-hero or narrative agent and female-as-image or object,'[77] that subcultures have been forced to express identity in a parasitic relation to the production of images in dominant culture. Thus, attempts at foreclosure of the expression of an identity through cultural representation are rendered problematic because of the uncontrollability of cultural images and the manner in which they are employed.

Indeed, it is through the asymmetric relationship of encoding and decoding that prohibition can be utilised as a means to foster identity. This can occur not only at the consumption level, but also through production itself. An interesting example of this phenomenon is in the role of a gay camp sensibility in British theatre. The London, West End theatre was subject to strict censorship by the Lord Chamberlain prior to the late 1960s.[78] State censorship was vigorously deployed to foreclose the explicit emergence of any fragments of a gay identity, or, indeed, any mention of 'homosexuality'.[79] Alan Sinfield has documented, however, that the attempt at erasure of identity through representational prohibition was unsuccessful. Rather, it was the theatre that proved to be a central site for the formation of a gay sensibility and culture in the United Kingdom. As Sinfield points out, using a Foucauldian analysis, the very fact of prohibition served to produce a presence:

> By keeping homosexuality out of sight the lord chamberlain was acknowledging its likely presence; further, he helped to make theater a place where sexuality lurked in forbidden forms, the more insidiously because concealed. "Homosexuality is rife in the theatrical profession", accused the *Sunday Pictorial* in its 1952 series "Evil Men".[80]

First, the theatre became a subcultural meeting place for the gay male (white and middle/upper-class) cultural consumer. The theatre also was a profession to which gay men were drawn (which reinforced the performative aspects of a gay identity). Given the presence of gay men in the two central locations for cultural propagation – production and consumption of representations – it is hardly surprising that the prohibition fostered the formation of an identity. Sinfield uses the work of Nöel Coward as an example of the use of theatre as a site of cultural contestation and the emergence of a camp sensibility. The irony of the outright prohibition on the mention of homosexuality by the Lord Chamberlain, of course, was that Coward's texts make it obvious that '[t]he one unspeakable vice is so strikingly absent that it leaps into . . . prominence'.[81] Sinfield argues that this prominence was apparent to the subcultural insider within the theatrical community, for whom 'traces of homosexuality in the plays were heard and

34

appreciated distinctively'.[82] Thus, within a Coward play, cultural decoding was assisted by the playwright who included a subversive encoding within the script.

Instead of foreclosing a gay identity, the prohibition provided the conditions under which a gay identity (and, the redeployment of the term 'gay') could be developed. Rigorously enforced censorship was the cultural precondition for a subcultural appropriation of the dominant cultural texts and was an important historical moment in the development of a gay liberationist movement. While Coward and camp style would become passé in the era of liberation, Sinfield argues that the camp sensibility proved an important site as a precursor to the emergence of the cultural conditions under which a radical gay subjecthood could be forged. This exemplifies the theoretical difficulties in state attempts to foreclose articulation of new political subjectivities. Coward's plays and, more generally, a camp sensibility, demonstrate the contingency of the meaning of any representation and also show how the meaning of a statement can exceed its literality. Effective state control of such a discourse is soon undermined by the uncontrollability of a statement's meaning as it is received subculturally by the cultural consumer.

IDENTITY, CENSORSHIP, AND A PROLIFERATION OF SUBJECTIVITIES

I have attempted to demonstrate that cultural representation serves as a field of political contest over the definition of the sexual subject. I also have presented an example of an oppositional identity – a gay identity secured through the cultural phenomenon of camp – in order to demonstrate how an oppositional identity can be forged within dominant culture. Moreover, the explicit exercise of state power to control the contours of a discourse proved futile, as the prohibition served to create an encoded language in which a subcultural community conversed.

This theoretical model provides the basis for a legal critique of the diversion of NEA funding away from artistic endeavours that depict a lesbian or gay identity. The attempts by Senator Helms and his supporters to limit NEA funding are aimed, not at the sexually explicit, but instead are focused on controlling the cultural construction of sexuality. It is an attempt to manage a discourse through which an identity may be articulated:

> Helms not only extends those legal precedents that categorize homosexuality as obscenity, but, rather, authorizes and orchestrates through those legal statutes a restriction of the very terms by which homosexuality is culturally defined. . . . It is not merely that Helms characterizes homosexuality unfairly, but that he constructs homosexuality itself through a set of exclusions that call to be politically interrogated.[83]

Thus, it is over the terms through which an identity is created that control is sought. However, the attempt may lead to unexpected outcomes because of the uncontrollability of the subject. Moreover, this cultural control is further undermined by the important role of fantasy. The deployment of prohibitions on repre- sentation cannot control the constitution of an identity through fantasy. Rather, prohibition can eroticise a subjectivity, which renders far more complicated the relationship of a discursive prohibition to a representation. For example, in the case of Robert Mapplethorpe's photographs, the work's erotic appeal stems at least in part from the very fact of its subversiveness in relation to the cultural prohibitions. It is precisely because 'prohibitions of the erotic are always at the same time, and despite themselves, the eroticization of prohibition'[84] that prohibition serves to undermine any NEA content-based restriction on the disbursement of funds for cultural production. The means by which images are consumed and identities formed ensures that the relationship between prohibition and representation will be a complex and unstable one.

Attempts to restrict NEA funds for the creation of gay representational works are objectionable not only because of the unpredictability of their effect, but also because an attempt to restrict the terms under which a political identity is formed is deeply violative of a dialogic right of the subject. The forging of a politically charged subjectivity depends on the production and consumption of cultural representations. Restricting access to and deployment of our cultural resources is an attempt to inhibit the formation of an individual and collective identity and thus is violative of a positive right of self-definition. The discriminatory with-holding of funds based solely upon a sexual and political identity becomes an infringement not only of a right to free speech but also of a right to equality. In this context, rights can only be secured by a deregulation of representations, thereby ensuring a loss of control of how our culture is utilised by all subjects in the attempt to forge new and hitherto unimagined subjectivities. Through the proliferation of images, the possibilities for the redeployment of culture through its appropriation are enhanced, and this is the means by which discursive control will be challenged.

Although a prohibition may contribute to how an identity is subculturally forged, restriction remains objectionable in terms of how control is effected and how it forces the articulation of an identity in a private encoded fashion. Just as camp became a cultural phenomenon that existed under conditions of explicit state censorship, new sexual identities might well emerge under restrictions on NEA funding. A right to one's identity, however, also demands the ability to articulate a subjecthood in the *public* sphere. This, of course, is the difference between the survivalist use of camp and the discourse of gay liberation in the post-Stonewall era. As Sinfield recognised, Coward's plays were useful as a 'subordinate, negotiated discourse within a dominant discourse',[85] but the language of Gay Liberation is a 'radical, oppositional' discourse that can be publicly read as a text within dominant culture.[86]

In this chapter I have argued that a rejection of the universal subject can facilitate the deployment of the language of rights, but it becomes a localised use of the terminology which is anchored in an appeal to the specificity of a subject's location. As Andrew Ross has formulated this claim, it is a right of the 'liberatory imagination', a recognition of the political nature of claims which emerge from an oppositional standpoint.[87] A liberatory right thus demands access to the dialogue and the right to have claims to identity 'remain in the realm of public visibility'.[88] Through a situated application of the rights of speech and equality, the offensiveness of content-based restrictions on artistic funding become more apparent. The restrictions are understandable as a violation of a right to speech, but it is a right to political speech made by a legal subject defined by an oppositional location. The terrain of the sexual has been appropriated for an ongoing political struggle, and the state has attempted to silence the expression of a sexual and political subjectivity – a sexual politics. Ultimately, restrictions on representation are aimed at foreclosing the proliferation of subject positions and a postmodern fragmentation of identity.

CONCLUSION

The recent history of political and legal turmoil over arts funding is an attempt to seize control of the meaning of artistic representations through a legislative and administrative foreclosure of the scope of funded expression. In so doing, new identities are denied participation in a political and cultural discourse. From the perspective of rights, the project is to rethink our ideals of free expression and equality in order to recognise fully the offensiveness of the denial of a positive right to the unencumbered articulation of an identity. At the same time, an examination of the nature of representation and cultural consumption reveals that attempts to foreclose that articulation ultimately may be less than successful as identities come to be formed subculturally through the deployment of the available cultural tools. This, in turn, suggests that the restrictions on artistic representation in some sense are legally unenforceable given the uncontrollability of the meaning of a representation. However, the fact that new identities may come to be articulated in a private sphere, despite legal restriction, serves to highlight why representational control is violative of a right to participate in the public sphere. The current climate in America undoubtedly 'chills' public political speech. In relegating some to express their identities only in private, dialogue is limited, and equality of access to the dialogue is denied. The challenge is to reformulate legal discourse to capture the political and cultural implications of attempts at state control of representation and of identity. In the next chapter, I examine two cases of the attempt to effect that representational control directly through law.

2

OF PROHIBITIONS AND PROMOTIONS

In this chapter I continue to focus upon expression and the role of the state in constraining speech. As with the NEA controversy, though, censorship does not function directly through criminal prohibitions aimed at the content of speech. Rather, it is realised through a denial of public funding for expression that promotes homosexuality. Two examples from the late 1980s are useful for examining how homosexuality functions as a juridical construct in this public funding context. In both cases, the expressed fear is that a homosexual identity can be *promoted*. Sexuality is understood (at least implicitly) in these examples as highly fluid, changeable, and in need of restriction within public discourse in order to ensure that 'normal' sexuality is not dangerously undermined. The two cases of legislative intervention are similar in the way that sexuality is analysed, despite the fact that they arise in different countries: Britain and America. The central difference, however, lies in the different roles of 'rights discourse' in the two legal cultures, stemming from the absence of constitutionally entrenched rights in the United Kingdom. Thus, for that reason, the legal outcomes diverge. I will first provide some background on these legislative interventions and then consider their broader impact and the extent to which they have been successful means of discursive regulation.

SECTION 28 OF THE LOCAL GOVERNMENT ACT, 1988

The enactment of section 28 of the *Local Government Act, 1988* by the British Parliament was seen as an event of significance both by the promoters and detractors of 'the clause'. The wording of section 28 deserves careful attention. The provision which was finally enacted on 24 May 1988 reads as follows:

(1) A local authority shall not

(a) intentionally promote homosexuality or publish material with the intention of promoting homosexuality;

(b) promote the teaching in any maintained school of the acceptability of homosexuality as a pretended family relationship.

(2) Nothing in subsection (1) above shall be taken to prohibit the doing of anything for the purpose of treating or preventing the spread of disease.

In this section, I will examine the background to this enactment, its legal implications, and the broader impact of section 28 – what might be termed its role as a focal point of discursive and ideological conflict.

Despite the importance of section 28 in its own right, it should be viewed, not as an isolated event, but as part of a broader pattern of legislative intervention centring upon the regulation of sexuality by the state, especially with respect to the expression of sexual identities. For example, two years prior to Section 28, the Conservative Government enacted section 46 of the *Education (No. 2) Act*, which required that sex education only be provided within an overall discussion that had 'due regard to moral considerations and the value of family life'. The meaning of section 46 was elaborated upon in a government interpretive circular in 1987. This document highlighted the importance of teaching 'self-restraint' and the 'benefits of stable married and family life and the responsibilities of parenthood'.[1] Homosexuality was clearly a separate issue, cordoned off from the arena of stable family life. In an independent section, the government outlined its policy on this issue: 'there is no place in any school in any circumstances for teaching which advocates homosexual behaviour, which presents it as the "norm", or which encourages homosexual experimentation by pupils'.[2] Thus, the discourse of 'promotion' with regard to homosexuality was not unique to section 28 and had been developed previously by the government.

In fact, what subsequently became section 28 was introduced originally as a private member's bill in the House of Lords without government support. The government minister responsible, Lord Skelmersdale, held that the bill was unnecessary and open to 'harmful misinterpretation'.[3] Although the bill did pass the House of Lords, the general election of 1987 intervened and the bill fell. In 1987, however, the public discourse around sexuality was somewhat altered by the relationship of the central Tory Government to some Labour-controlled local authorities and, in particular, the government's reaction to efforts of those authorities to encourage the creation of 'positive images' of lesbians and gay men.[4] Ostensibly as a result of these local initiatives, the re-elected Conservative Government reversed its position when a Conservative MP proposed an amendment to the Local Government Bill similar to the earlier intervention from the House of Lords. The government supported the initiative and it became policy.

The change in position on the issue was explained as resulting from changed circumstances. The government maintained that there was growing unease about the use of public funds by local authorities to 'promote' homosexuality and parents had been complaining about their children being taught that homosexuality was 'on a par' with 'normal' heterosexual family life. Section 28, it was argued, was a much needed rectification of this imbalance designed to restore the primacy of heterosexual family life.

An analysis of the debates both in the House of Commons and in the House of Lords around these legislative interventions reveal much about how sexuality was understood by the Parliamentarians who led the debate. Interestingly, throughout the debate, most members who spoke in support of the bill made clear that they did not favour discrimination against individuals. Rather, their concern was with the promotion of homosexuality and the protection of the young, who were seen as particularly vulnerable to corruption.

However, the Earl of Halsbury, the promoter of the first private member's bill on the issue, was forthright with respect to the concerns which motivated his action. Male homosexuality, in his view, could be characterised in five ways:

Those who make the worst of their situation are the sick ones who suffer from a psychological syndrome whose symptoms are as follows: first of all, exhibitionism; they want the world to know all about them; secondly, promiscuity; thirdly, proselytising; they want to persuade other people that their way of life is the good one; fourthly, they boast of homosexual achievements as if they were due to and not in spite of sexual inversion; lastly, they act as reservoirs of venereal diseases of all kinds. Ask any venerealogist: syphilis, gonorrhoea, genital herpes and now Aids are characteristically infections of homosexuals.[5]

Not surprisingly, the Earl of Halsbury concluded that homosexuality is 'one of the worst mischiefs corrupting the fibre of our children and ultimately of society itself'.[6]

That corruption was realised in part through the 'Positive Images' campaign. Lord Campbell of Alloway explained the relationship between 'Positive Images' and the 'promotion' of homosexuality:

These positive images, as implemented as a matter of policy, involve a direct attack on the heterosexual family life – as the noble Earl put it, pushing us off the pavement. They do it in various ways, and two ways come to mind. One is that they attack the paternalistic disciplines of an ordinary family as being totally wrong because children should be totally free. Another is to teach the children that in some way the reproductive potential of the heterosexual relationship constitutes a positive social mischief in an over-populated world.[7]

In this construction of sexuality, homosexuality is not only promotable, but also is dangerously contagious for the general public, and especially for innocent children, who are particularly vulnerable to indoctrination. As Lady Saltoun of Abernethy vividly argued, 'the thing has to stop and not be allowed to go on as it is going on now, because it is spreading all the time'.[8]

Throughout the debate, supporters of section 28 adopted a view of sexuality that was far from biologically determinist in terms of how sexual identities were formed. 'Positive Images', in the view of Lord Kilbracken, would 'greatly increase the number becoming practising homosexuals though they were, genetically, perfectly capable of leading happy, fulfilled, heterosexual lives if their influence in childhood had been different.'[9] Lord Denning reiterated the point, arguing that 'the influence on youngsters under 16 may make them or mar them for the rest of their lives. Then we see them being made or marred by these booklets and publicity distributed at the hands of the local council in the schools.'[10]

The Peers also enunciated a view of adolescent sexuality that was particularly vulnerable to corruption into a homosexual lifestyle, which was likely irreversible:

> May I speak of adolescent boys and girls who, more often than not, go through a phase of experiencing deep feelings for older people of their own sex. It is a phase. If it is encouraged, if it is taught to be a way of life, there are some – and I say only some – who will not pass out of that stage, but will remain homosexuals and follow the homosexual way of life to their lasting unhappiness.[11]

In fact, the relationship between 'positive' education dealing with lesbians and particularly gay men, and sexual practices was taken one step further by Lord Fitt, who suggested that there was 'absolutely no doubt that a significant number of present Aids carriers within our society were given positive education in homosexuality when they were at school'.[12] Science also was used to buttress these conclusions. The Earl of Halsbury, for example, drew upon the findings of the Wolfenden Committee report, which in 1957, recommended the decriminalisation of consensual private sex between men:

> The Wolfenden report specified that people's sexual orientation was not fixed on leaving school. They needed a close period of several years so that those of them who may have had homosexual experiences at school had some free time to shake loose from it if they were not in fact permanently orientated that way. I have been told by psychologists that it is only at about the age of 24 that a person's sexual orientation is finally fixed. Therefore the idea of orientating them in the wrong direction for a very long period up to the age of 24 is very wrong indeed. It may lead to total unhappiness in later life.[13]

Heterosexuality thus becomes a fragile and tenuous identity that is easily displaced by any positive image of homosexuality received during adolescence. The government's spokesman for the Bill in the House of Commons, Dr Rhodes Boyson, highlighted the ultimate catastrophic consequences of positive representations:

> The Bill opposes the positive images of lesbianism and homosexuality, as though they were alternative ways of life that should be shown to all children in schools. Those images imply that one can live in a family with a mother and father, but there is an alternative way of life which is just as

reputable, in which one lives with a person of one's own sex, and the two are equal. *That could undermine the basis of our society . . .* One could say that the positive promotion of the images of lesbianism and male homosexuality as though they are equivalent to family life could bring death in one generation. I am not referring to Aids. I am talking about death in a generation, because there is no future in it – it is the end of creation. Any society that is concerned for its future in every way and for its continuation must have a clear view about what it is doing.[14]

Homosexuality thus is linked to death – not only the death of the individual gay male (for lesbianism largely is rendered invisible in this discourse) – but the death of the body politic through the failure to reproduce. The promotion of a positive image of gay sexuality is the causal link to these catastrophic consequences.

Interestingly, the arguments raised in Parliament in opposition to Section 28 focus on a view of sexuality that centres on its fixity, immutability, and the impossibility of promoting a sexual orientation. As Simon Hughes MP argued, 'homosexuals do not happen as a result of campaigns for their promotion, just as heterosexuals are not suddenly brought into active heterosexualism by having a campaign on their behalf.'[15] In a similar vein, Chris Smith (the only openly gay Member of Parliament), reiterated the impossibility of promoting any sexual orientation:

They say that they want only to prohibit the act, as they put it, of encouraging people to be homosexual. It is an absurd notion in any case. We are what we are. It is impossible to force or encourage someone into a different sexuality from that which pertains to them. What is needed is not to be involved in changing, persuading, forcing, encouraging people into different sexualities. *What is important is to enable people to understand the sexuality that they have, and that cannot be changed.*[16]

Thus, sexual orientation is described as an immutable characteristic, and consequently, any particular sexual orientation cannot be promoted. Peter Pike MP made the point summarily: 'it is quite clear that homosexuality cannot be promoted. People do not choose to be homosexual: either they are or they are not'.[17]

This debate is extremely revealing with respect to the relationship between sexual orientation and sexual practice and how orientation itself is understood. The significance of section 28 in part lies in the fact that it is grounded in the presumption that a particular sexual orientation can be promoted, such that it will be assumed by those who would not otherwise adopt it. Indeed, the clause was precipitated by the perception that a gay (male) sexual orientation could be successfully promoted simply through the presentation of any image that could be described as positive. While 'promoters' of the clause clearly recognised the difference between sexual *practices* and sexual *orientation*, it is the positive image of homosexuality that bridges the gap between isolated same-sex sexual practices (particularly in adolescence) and the crystallisation of an irreversible gay identity. In the face of this construction of sexuality, opponents of section 28 fell back on notions of immutability and the fixity of sexual orientation as the only viable response.

The debate thus provides an interesting case study of differing conceptions of sexuality. In contrast to much of the current theory and practice of sexuality that focuses on the ambiguities and fluidity of sexuality (its 'queerness'), opponents of section 28 resuscitated 'biological determinist arguments, by asserting that it is precisely because homosexuality is a "state of being" that there can be no threat to that other, by implication, discrete population of heterosexuals.'[18] A binary division of sexual orientation thus is reinforced which, as Evans suggests, is a view that increasingly 'is intellectually and politically untenable'.[19] As other writers have noted, there was little articulation during the debate of an oppositional viewpoint that recognised that a lesbian or gay identity indeed could be promoted and, moreover, *should* be promoted as an alternative sexual identity.[20]

The discursive interventions by proponents of section 28 centre upon the proposition that a gay sexual identity is both extremely dangerous and yet, at the same time, extremely seductive. Consequently, anything other than a complete condemnation of that identity will lead to its proliferation.[21] Moreover, it is not simply seduction into a sexual practice that is at issue. It appears that a 'one off' homosexual experience is not an irreparable situation within the terms of this debate. Rather, the risk that must be prevented is the seduction into an identity made attractive by its promotion:

> The unconscious logic thus runs that homosexuality can only exist as a result of the seduction of minors by predatory older perverts. This seduction may, however, be indirect, and effected via *cultural* means. In other words, there is a clear recognition that sexual identities are culturally grounded, and an acknowledgment that gay identity does not follow automatically from homosexual desire or practice.[22]

Sexuality thus becomes an historically contingent phenomenon in which heterosexuality is under constant threat from its 'other', which has the power 'to corrode the "natural" order of social and sexual relations'.[23] Section 28 seeks to shore up that natural order through a denial of the cultural acceptability of a gay identity and a condemnation of homosexual acts.

Thus, this legislative intervention highlights the extent to which a sexual identity is read as contingently dependent upon cultural conditions:

> for the first time in a British legal statute, it has been recognised that homosexuality can be 'promoted', precisely because it is not a condition but a status or role that can be learnt and adopted to extents dependent upon a range of social situational and interactional circumstances.[24]

Of course, the irony in these alternative constructions is that it is now commonplace amongst theorists of sexuality that sexual identities are highly dependent upon precisely the historical and social conditions in which we live. The notion of homosexuality as an historically specific social role, rather than a physical condition, was first pioneered by Mary McIntosh.[25] However, this argument gets turned 'on its head' in the debate over section 28, with opponents picking up the contrary proposition – that sexuality is fixed, immutable, and, in some cases, almost a condition.

At the end of the debate, and with the enactment of section 28, the question remained as to its meaning in law. The intention of the sponsors of the bill clearly was that it should have an impact in two separate spheres. First, the area of local authority spending and, specifically, local authority spending on programmes such as the 'Positive Images' campaign. Basically, section 28 makes it contrary to law for a local authority to use public funds to intentionally promote homosexuality or to provide funds to a voluntary organisation if the grant would be used for the promotion of homosexuality. The section can be invoked only against the local authority itself and, upon a successful application, the courts could restrain it from continuing to spend on the matter in issue.

This raises the obvious question of what constitutes the intentional promotion of homosexuality. The backers of section 28 no doubt had specific ideas of what the wording of the statute meant, namely, the prohibition of the advocacy or the toleration of a lesbian or gay identity within the sphere of public discourse and paid for by public funds. But, as a matter of law, the interesting questions are, first, what is necessary to establish an intention? And, second, what is the 'promotion' of homosexuality? As for intention, the law that has developed in other contexts is fairly revealing. Obviously, a deliberate motive to promote homosexuality (whatever that may mean) would satisfy the test of intention. However, in law, intention is a broader concept than that, because 'even in the absence of an explicit motive, a result may still be intended if the action is taken knowing that it is *highly likely* that such a result will happen'.[26] Consequently, a duty is now placed upon local authorities to examine the likely consequences of funding decisions:

> Section 28 means that local authorities are now bound to consider whether or not their decisions or actions intentionally "promote homosexuality" . . . In doing so, they must look fully at the *likely implications* of any decision or action. *Not wishing* to promote homosexuality does not necessarily fulful their obligations.[27]

Thus, the collective state of mind of the local authority is not determinative of the issue. Rather, that authority is under a duty to examine whether any funding decision has the likely result of promoting homosexuality.

This analysis raises the related question of *how* one can promote homosexuality. The Conservative Cabinet Minister Michael Howard, MP provided some indication of what he thought promotion entailed in the debate on section 28:

> Let me make it plain that it is no part of our intention in supporting this clause to affect the civil rights of any person. We are talking about the use

of public money to give preferential treatment to certain people, activities and tendencies.[28]

The Earl of Caithness made a similar point, finding that an attempt had been made in some quarters 'to sell homosexuality, to ensure that people see it in a favourable light . . . everything then is done to glamorise homosexuality to make all aspects of homosexuality seem attractive'.[29]

In a legal opinion commissioned to consider the meaning of section 28, Lord Gifford drew upon other legal contexts and concluded that the promotion of homosexuality required 'active persuasion'; it 'involves active advocacy directed by local authorities towards individuals in order to persuade them to become homosexual, or to experiment with homosexual relationships'.[30] The focus thus is on the active encouragement of homosexuality as a social/sexual option; in other words, 'persuading people to become homosexual who otherwise would not'.[31] In the end, then, for a local authority to run afoul of section 28, 'it must provide the grants or issue the licences with the express intention of promoting or facilitating or bringing about an increase in homosexuality, rather than the intention of making life easier for lesbians and gays'.[32] Interestingly, if this is the meaning of the intentional promotion of homosexuality, then there appear to be no documented cases where promotion actually has occurred, either before or after the enactment of section 28.

However, that fact does not negate the impact of the clause. Rather, in several different ways, the ban on the intentional promotion of homosexuality by local authorities has had an effect. First, there have been cases where funding has been denied, or restrictions imposed on groups on the basis of the existence of section 28. This impact might be termed the 'chilling effect' of the legislation on public funding decisions. These actions have included the cancellation of films and other cultural events; the insistence on changing the name of a 'lesbian literature' course offered by a Workers' Education Association; changes to the constitutions of the London Lesbian and Gay Centre and the Outcast Theatre Company by the London Borough Grants Scheme; and the refusal to give a lesbian organisation a grant for printing material.[33]

The 'chilling effect' on sexual expression also can be understood more broadly in terms of the constraints that operate on local authority policy-making: 'this effect has been aided by council legal staff, who now routinely express cautious opinions on the legality of proposed policies around sexuality.'[34] Moreover, in order to prevent possible legal challenges and unfavourable press attention, activities may become more covert – removed from the sphere of public discourse – in order to prevent controversy (which, of course, undermines the effectiveness of those policies). In addition, the presence of section 28 provides 'an easy excuse for continued inactivity' on issues of sexuality by local authorities.[35]

Finally, section 28 carries within its text a strong ideological grounding in the way that programmes launched by local authorities, and bodies funded by them, are characterised. This again turns on the question of how sexuality is understood in terms of immutability and fixity, or fluidity and contingency. As has been suggested, 'local governments working to tackle discrimination against lesbians and gay men must do so within a liberal approach that articulates sexual orientation as fixed and immutable – hence, it cannot be "promoted" and the section thus not contravened.'[36] Ultimately, such an approach has a constraining impact on the way that discursive interventions are framed and the way in which a theory of sexuality is enunciated when public funds are being allocated.

The second legal prohibition also contains a number of points of legal interest within its text. This provision forecloses a local authority from promoting the teaching in a maintained school of 'the acceptability of homosexuality as a pretended family relationship'. The background to this provision centred upon a perception by some Parliamentarians, fuelled by some elements of the popular press, that young children were being taught the acceptability of lesbian and gay family structures in state schools. This controversy largely was focused upon one children's book, *Jenny Lives With Eric and Martin*, which described the daily life of a young girl who lived with her father and his male partner. In fact, this book was stocked in an Inner London Education Authority Teachers' Centre to which only teachers had access. It was intended as a resource for teachers, but its existence was converted into the basis of a furore over education in primary schools. The book was frequently characterised as integral to a strategy of converting children to homosexuality as a 'pretended family relationship'.

Curiously, within the debate around section 28 as it concerned educational issues, there are frequent, albeit indirect, references to the English public school system, often noted within popular culture for its perceived inculcation of homosexuality. For example, the statement of Lord Kilbracken, from his speech in support of the clause, is particularly oblique in its reference: 'my belief is strongly supported by my own personal experiences when I was at Eton in the 1930s, and into which I have no intention of going.'[37] More startling is the statement made by the sponsor of the original clause, The Earl of Halsbury, who displayed a fascination with issues of sexual orientation and sexual practice, stemming from his own public school days:

> Schoolboy homosexuality starts as post-pubertal curiosity. I discussed it with my parents before I ever went to public school. I discussed it with my outgoing headmaster of my prep school. I discussed it again with my tutor at Eton. As an older boy, a captain of the house, I was expected to collaborate with my headmaster and housemaster in discouraging it wherever I could.[38]

Along with many of his colleagues, the Earl of Halsbury seemed to make this pursuit a lifelong task.

The actual legal impact of this provision, once again, is extremely limited on the face of it. Ironically, under successive Conservative administrations, jurisdiction over schools has shifted away from local authorities and towards school governing bodies. However, its symbolic effect may well be significant in constraining local authorities in curriculum development.[39] Moreover, the provision also may have a 'chilling effect' on speech in the classroom dealing with issues of sexuality and, finally, its existence 'seems to be related to a few cases of teachers being dismissed or suspended or resigning'.[40] Although proponents of the section argued that it did not prevent the discussion of sexuality as a factual matter, its role may lie in eradicating such discussions from the classroom.

The symbolism of section 28 focuses on the family and, in particular, the description of a lesbian or gay family structure as a 'pretended' or inauthentic form of family. As the clause makes apparent, at issue is not simply a same-sex sexual act. Nor, indeed, is identity alone the only danger. Rather, 'much more threatening, apparently, was the affirmation of alternative patterns of relationships'.[41] As the Earl of Caithness suggested in the debate on section 28, the underlying issue was that:

> the local authorities should not be using their powers under section 17 of the Education (No. 2) Act 1986 to encourage the teaching that relationships between two people of the same sex can and do play the same role in society as the traditional family.[42]

Paradoxically, in its focus on pretended families (and presumably long-term relationships that replicate at least in a formal sense the heterosexual norm) the legislature appeared more concerned with the legitimacy of the lesbian or gay *family*, rather than with the promiscuous sexual encounter which many Parliamentarians argued was endemic to (male) homosexuality. In fact, at several points in the debate, gay men are condemned for their inability to restrain their sexual impulses and confine themselves to mutually exclusive long-term relationships of commitment. Yet, if they do succeed in so doing, they have formed a 'pretended' family which is not to be promoted. Thus, on the one hand, homosexuality is constructed as unnatural and an inauthentic form of sexuality. On the other hand, it has an awesome seductive power and the capacity to recruit converts simply through its enunciation in a positive fashion within public discourse.

Finally, section 28 deals explicitly with information concerning the treatment or prevention of the 'spread of disease', which is exempted from the first two subsections. A government circular which interpreted this provision explained that:

> activities in the counselling, health care and health education fields undertaken for the purpose of treating or preventing the spread of disease, including Aids, will not be prohibited. This includes activities concerned exclusively with the needs of homosexuals.[43]

This apparent toleration of funded safe sex materials, though, must be juxtaposed against earlier government refusals to endorse official educational information of a sexually explicit nature.[44]

Despite the explicit provision in section 28 for the funding of activities designed to prevent the 'spread of disease', the debate surrounding the clause also contained a sustained discourse that sought to justify section 28 in Aids rhetoric. This was most obvious in the House of Commons debate on the clause and it was expansively employed in the speech of one of the key supporters of the Bill, Dame Jill Knight. One passage from her speech is revealing for its association of homosexuality with Aids, and speech promoting (or even concerning) a gay identity with the spread of Aids:

> millions outside Parliament object to little children being perverted, diverted or converted from normal family life to a lifestyle which is desperately dangerous for society and extremely dangerous for them . . . Very few hon. members fail to appreciate the seriousness of the danger that AIDS presents to the whole of our society, yet some of that which is being taught to children in our schools would undoubtedly lead to a great spread of AIDS: Even the knowledge of the danger of AIDS has not stopped the promoting of homosexuality among little children.[45]

Within this intervention, homosexuality leads inexorably to death from Aids, and positive (or neutral) images of lesbians and gay men will lead to the 'conversion' of children to a perverse *lifestyle* that, in turn, will lead inevitably to their early demise. The solution, according to this line of reasoning, is condemnation of that lifestyle and its erasure from public discourse. It should be replaced with a focus on abstinence from gay sex and the encouragement of 'normal' reproductive, monogamous family life. This provides the only true defence against the epidemic. The 'promotion' of homosexuality, then, is highly dangerous because of the contagiousness, not only of the disease of Aids, but also of the disease of homosexuality. In fact, the two become virtually synonymous (which, incidentally, further facilitates the erasure of lesbians from the discourse).

I have already discussed the impact of section 28 in terms of its 'chilling effect' on expression. However, the enactment of the clause, like many legal interventions in the arena of sexuality, has had an impact which is far from one dimensional. The reaction to the introduction, the debate and the enactment of the clause included mass demonstrations, lobbying tactics, and media attention on lesbian and gay issues. In this sense, rather than chilling speech, the debate over section 28 created the political and cultural conditions for the promotion of homosexuality. Section 28 'opened up a discursive struggle around sexuality',[46] was 'a watershed in the struggle for gay equality',[47] and provided a point of unity and solidarity across constituencies which previously had often been in conflict. Thus, while section 28 was designed to remove gay politics from the discursive realm, in the short term at least, it heightened its presence.

Consequently, it can be argued that section 28 'greatly contributed to an enhanced sense of identity and community' for lesbians and gay men in Britain in the late 1980s.[48] Of course, contrary to what opponents of the clause suggested in Parliamentary debate, a lesbian or gay identity (like all identities) is capable of promotion as legitimate, desirable, and fulfilling. However, it is not simply as a *sexual* desire that 'homosexuality' can be promoted. Rather, as a *cultural* matter, positive images and a presence within public discourse (other than as a condemnation) provides the basis for an 'integrated sense of self and community'.[49] The proponents of section 28 therefore are quite right in arguing that sexual identities can be promoted – heterosexuality being the prime example within dominant culture. The conservative treatment of homosexuality as culture rather than condition thus has a ring of truth. The critique of the conservative position, as embodied in section 28, should be formed, then, not through resort to the language of immutability, but instead through the assertion of a place – of a right – within public discourse for the articulation of a plurality of sexual identities.

THE 'HELMS AMENDMENT': PROMOTING HOMOSEXUAL SEXUAL ACTIVITIES

I turn now to another legislative intervention, this time in the United States, from the same period. Although it emerges within a different political culture and ostensibly deals with a different issue, the intervention in many ways bears a similarity to the section 28 controversy. Here again, the idea that a sexuality can be promoted, and may be contagious and fatal, underpins arguments for the erasure of representations of gay sexuality from the publicly funded sphere.

By way of background, in 1985 the American Centers for Disease Control commenced the funding of programmes aimed at changing sexual behaviour, including work undertaken by the Gay Men's Health Crisis in New York City. This organisation provides educational and other services to the community it serves. Some of these educational materials, aimed at sections of the gay community, included graphic and explicit descriptions of safe sex practices. As a matter of course, GMHC used private funds to develop their most 'provocative materials'.[50] As early as 1986, the Centers for Disease Control, concerned about possible negative reaction to such strategies, introduced restrictions on the content of programmes that received federal funding by requiring that any materials produced 'would be judged by a reasonable person to be inoffensive to most educated adults'.[51]

However, just as an isolated publication proved to be the lynchpin in the section 28 controversy, so too did a single series of publications focus the debate in the United States. In 1986, GMHC produced a number of 'Safe Sex Comix', which used cartoons combined with narrative to portray safe sex information aimed at a gay male audience. In keeping with the policy of GMHC, these publications were not produced directly with the assistance of federal funds. The comics were obtained by Senator Jesse Helms of North Carolina. Senator Helms is famous not only for his attacks on the National Endowment for the Arts, but as the proponent of a broad conservative agenda on issues of sexuality.[52]

In 1987, the Senator introduced an amendment to an appropriations bill in Congress to prohibit the provision of federal funds provided through the Centers for Disease Control to either private groups or state and local governments which would be used 'to provide Aids education, information, or prevention materials and activities that promote or encourage, directly or indirectly, homosexual sexual activities'.[53]

The debate on the 'Helms Amendment' bears a strong resemblance to the debate on section 28. Attention was turned to the promotion of both gay male sexual acts and identities and the unreasonableness of the use of federal funds to 'advance that lifestyle'.[54] The focus was not simply on the condemnation of sexual acts, but was more broadly based:

> I think it is appropriate for us to examine and find out a little bit more about how extensive the movement of homosexuality in America has become in terms of changing the cultural values of our society so that we will accept and equate homosexuality on a par with heterosexual life.[55]

This passage could as easily have been located in the British debate. Sexuality, in these terms, becomes culturally based, historically contingent, and therefore capable of promotion.

Moreover, as with the section 28 debate, gay male sexuality is not only dangerous because so easily promoted, but also because of its inherent contagiousness. This of course ties into a discourse of disease. Within the terms of the debate on the 'Helms Amendment', gay male sexuality became inextricably linked to the Aids pandemic, such that the gay male body is *the* vessel which contains and spreads HIV. According to Senator Helms, 'every Aids case can be traced back to a homosexual act',[56] and more graphically:

> Many of the experts, self-proclaimed, tell us that the source of the Aids epidemic is the Aids virus. That is like saying that the source of a fire set by an arsonist was the match that the arsonist used, rather than the arsonist who struck the match and set the fire.[57]

The promotion of homosexuality as lifestyle, then, leads to the spread of Aids. In this explanation, 'safe sex' cannot be gay male sex, for the gay man is constructed as a disease-carrying container.[58] Funding of safe sex materials, then, contributes to the spread of Aids because of the contagiousness of homosexuality. The only safe sex, for the incurably gay man, is no sex and that is what demands promotion.[59] Finally, and inconsistently, safe sex materials are derided for their ineffectiveness since, according to Senator Helms, 'it still is not doing any good because the people who are spreading this disease do not pay any attention to it anyhow'.[60] Yet, at the same time, safe sex representations are criticised for their power to promote the homosexual lifestyle and, moreover, are characterised as pornographic.[61] In the context of these interventions, the 'Helms Amendment' easily passed the US Congress and was enacted into law.

In response, the Centers for Disease Control propagated guidelines which utilised a standard of offensiveness to a general, mainstream audience. Funding recipients were asked to draw up a peer review panel and submit educational materials to it for prior approval. The panel would consist of a reasonable cross-section of the general public. Although the 'Helms Amendment' was rejected the following year in the debate on the appropriations bill, and was replaced by a more 'neutral' clause that focused on whether Aids educational materials were 'designed' to encourage sexual activity, the CDC offensiveness restriction remained until 1992.

The impact on Aids educators in one respect at least was analogous to the effect of section 28. In both cases, the legislative intervention in regulating the realm of public discourse had a 'chilling effect' on speech. In the case of the 'Helms Amendment', the standard of offensiveness had very clear implications in that it forced Aids educators to consider the directness and explicitness of information and, more generally, to ask whether 'realist portrayals of gay male sexuality are pornographic by definition to a mainstream culture that wants to hear nothing about it'.[62] The 'Helms Amendment' provided a graphic example of how 'the specificities of gay men's health education needs are obliterated by the mandate of the heterosexual majority'.[63] It also has been argued that the restriction discriminated against the less educated, less literate, and lower-income populations for whom graphic representations may be more effective educational tools than more circumscribed explanations.[64]

The CDC guidelines subsequently were challenged in the courts on constitutional grounds. The revised grant terms under consideration utilised a standard of 'offensiveness for a majority of persons outside the intended audience'. The United States District Court for the Southern District of New York found that standard to be outside the statutory authority of the CDC and the Court also held the grant terms to be 'unconstitutionally vague' with 'no core meaning'.[65] While the obscene legitimately could be proscribed, the Court recognised that obscenity and offensiveness were far from synonymous in the context of gay male safe sex representations:

> Because the obscenity standard is inherently narrower than the offensiveness criterion, there is a vast amount of material that could be developed that would be deemed offensive, but not obscene. As such, the Court finds that reference to the obscenity standard offers no real guidance or clarification to either Aids educators or PRP [peer review panel] members.[66]

The Court recognised the 'chilling effect' on speech of such restrictions, citing evidence of self-censorship by Aids educators.[67] The guidelines thus were struck down as unconstitutional, thereby ending another attempt at prohibiting the promotion of a sexual identity by foreclosing its expression in public discourse.

UNDERSTANDING PROHIBITIONS ON PROMOTION

The 'Helms Amendment' and the section 28 controversy are interesting, not only for their similarities, but also for their differences. The two cases are similar in the way that a discourse of promotion is employed to foreclose governmental funding of representations of sexuality. In both instances, additionally, gay sexuality is described in terms of contagion, conversion, and ultimately the destruction of the body of the individual and the body politic. However, in terms of outcome, the two cases differ. The 'Helms Amendment' was defeated the year after its enactment and the Centers for Disease Control guidelines subsequently were held to be unconstitutional. Section 28, on the other hand, continues to sit on the statute books. Although increasingly it appears to be a statutory provision largely devoid of meaning and unlikely to be invoked successfully, it still carries a symbolic resonance.

From a comparative perspective, the issues do highlight the importance of free speech doctrine in American constitutional law and the absence of any equivalent in British constitutional jurisprudence.[68] As I argued in Chapter 1, freedom of speech, far more than other strands of US constitutional doctrine, has provided the most consistent support for the protection of lesbian and gay rights. Although in many cases courts have decided these issues on fairly narrow doctrinal grounds such as 'vagueness', the underlying political implications, as I articulated in the context of the NEA in Chapter 1, can serve as the basis of a political theory of lesbian and gay expression.

At issue in both the section 28 and 'Helms Amendment' controversies is the expression of sexual identities in the public sphere and the right to articulate an identity publicly as part of a shared dialogue to which access is assured by means of membership in the greater community. The linkage between the articulation of an identity and its development and continued existence is all too apparent. As Mark Barnes has argued:

> explicit sexual images and the freedom to create and use them has been essential to the emergence of gay and lesbian cultures and identities over the past four decades. Explicit sexual images have allowed gay men and women to develop new eroticisms, to dismantle the view of homosexuality as pathological, to define a new culture apart from the dominant hetero-sexual ideal, and to establish new sets of norms and expectations. Censorship of sexual images – in the context of Aids as much as in other contexts – therefore threatens the vitality and even the survival of gay culture.[69]

Prohibitions on representation seek to reestablish gay identity as pathological and indeed, from a cultural perspective, to silence that identity by erasing it from the publicly funded sphere. In that sense, prohibition constitutes a 'direct disenfranchisement' and the denial of a right to participate in dialogue.[70]

However, in attempting to expurgate lesbian and gay identities from the social, identities also can be consolidated outside the boundaries of 'normal' sexuality. As Judith Butler has suggested, if sexuality is established through the practices of discourse, then 'this demarcation will produce a domain of excluded and delegitimated "sex"'.[71] The excluded 'sites' of sexuality operate ostensibly outside the social sphere that is continually shored up to prevent disruption by the sexually unthinkable. These domains though remain internal to the regulatory system, and are necessary for the consolidation of 'normal' sexuality, but they forever threaten to undermine it. Prohibitions on promotion of homosexuality present one example of a discursive attempt to fix and maintain this boundary between the normal and the abject.

The paradox, though, is that in seeking to silence an identity and to deny a right of sexual citizenship, the prohibition on expression creates a discursive space for the identity of the excluded. A prohibition must acknowledge the existence of the prohibited and this brings the prohibited practices into the public domain of discourse and 'thereby produces them as potential erotic enterprises and so invests erotically in those practices, even if in a negative mode'.[72] For the proponents both of section 28 and the 'Helms Amendment', these unintended effects can be glimpsed in the degree to which contributions to the debate seem almost erotically charged when the 'unspeakable' is described so graphically.

The effect of prohibitions on promotion, then, is not straightforward. While the laws enacted both in the United Kingdom and America have had a 'chilling effect' on expression (with, quite probably, fatal consequences for many individuals as a direct result of the 'Helms Amendment'), they also have facilitated the articulation of sexual identities as subject positions in a field of political contest.[73] These debates have been important in structuring that field and, in this sense, the discursive interventions have a performative function in the production of sexual/social identities. Categories of sexuality are invoked and consolidated through articulation and the relationship of those categories to the political terrain is made explicit.[74] The 'law' of desire that is performed through its repetition in discourse ultimately is unable to maintain the sexual order that it seeks to create because this performative also facilitates the articulation of oppositional identities. This is the production of 'the subject who is "queered" into public discourse through homophobic interpellations of various kinds'.[75] It is indeed a queer consequence of the prohibitions on promotion that they produce the subject that they seek to erase from the discursive realm.

CONCLUSION

In this chapter, I have examined two attempts to control the expression of sexual identities through law. Both interventions employ the language of 'promotion' to limit the expenditure of public funds. These laws are constitutive of an understanding of heterosexuality as unstable, contingent, and fragile. Yet, at the same time, male homosexuality is understood as overwhelmingly seductive, contagious, and dangerous both to the individual body and to the body politic. Lesbianism largely is erased from public view.

While both of the examples that I have analysed have been partially successful in controlling the discourses at which they are aimed, a consequence of these interventions also is that they facilitate the articulation of oppositional identities within the public sphere. Thus, the unintended result is the *promotion* of a collective, gay identity.

The offensiveness of such attempts at discursive control through law is that they deny to some a right of citizenship; that is, a right to articulate a sexual identity within a shared communal space. Finally, the material reality of these laws should not be ignored. Individuals have been lost unnecessarily, young people who are confused and miserable have been denied access to information that might instil a positive image, and prejudice and bigotry have been given an official outlet and *promoted. That* is the ultimate offensiveness of both section 28 and the 'Helms Amendment'. The inability of their advocates to fully control and suture the discourse merely creates spaces that can be utilised to develop strategies for ongoing political struggle and contestation.

3

THE PORN WARS

Feminism and the regulation of gay male pornography

In the next two chapters I examine the relationship of anti-pornography feminist legal theory and the regulation of gay male pornography. This chapter interrogates one theoretical model that has been developed to promote and justify legal regimes of regulation. In Chapter 4, I focus upon a particular example of the implementation of the model and the ramifications that have followed its adoption. The regulation of pornography through law in recent years has come to be appropriated as a central theoretical and political issue by elements of the feminist movement. The critique of pornography frequently is all-encompassing and it focuses on the perceived objectification of women which, it is argued, is central to pornographic representation. In order to guarantee the civil rights of women, pornography, as a site for the social construction of male domination, must be attacked directly. In this chapter, I argue that the breadth of the feminist argument proves to be its weakness. Specifically, I will suggest that the failure to differentiate between heterosexual and gay male pornography, in terms of a model of legal regulation, is problematic for a number of reasons. First, the anti-pornography position is insensitive to how the meaning of a representation, when relocated in a different sexual context, may change and cease to be primarily oppressive. Indeed, from this perspective, pornography may prove to be liberating rather than objectifying. Second, gay pornography may be situated uniquely to destabilise the coherence of the male subject, a construct which, many feminists argue, allows for the oppression of women through their definition as other to it. Pornography thus becomes a subversive practice in relation to phallocracy. Third, gay male pornography may be useful as a means of revaluing submission and objectification. The representation of gay male sexuality through pornography thereby proves to be a location for subversion of the meaning that has been imposed by dominant culture on sexuality. Finally, in light of these criticisms of the anti-pornography civil rights approach in the context of gay male pornography, I will attempt to formulate a new model of legal regulation. This approach focuses on the political dimension of pornography and specifically on the experience of the gay male subject. From a political history of sexual minorities, I will formulate a rights-based defence of gay pornography. Pornography becomes characterised as political speech, but in a liberatory rather than a liberal model in which the subject of rights emerges from a history of oppression. Thus, the analysis shifts from sexual to political subjecthood and pornographic representation provides the expression primarily of a political rather than a sexual experience. The emphasis, then, is placed on respect both for the *differences* of sexual minorities and on how the rights of minorities can be secured through pornography. In legal terms, gay pornography becomes protected speech, but based upon its role in securing the political rights of a subject forged from a marginalised political experience.

THE FEMINIST–CIVIL RIGHTS APPROACH

It is beyond dispute that the development of a uniquely feminist critique of pornography has been an important project in the feminist movement. Its success can be measured not only in terms of the intellectual sophistication of the approach, but also in terms of the usefulness of the issue in providing a point of unity. In placing the pornography issue near the top of the agenda, many of the cleavages within the feminist movement (racial, socio-economic, sexual preference) temporarily were buried beneath the guise of an issue that was interpreted in a particularly essentialist manner: *all* women are oppressed by *all* men through the representation of women in pornography.[1]

Much of the credit for this agenda-setting manoeuvre is given to Catharine MacKinnon and Andrea Dworkin. The ingenuity and novelty of their approach lies in the linking of sexual oppression, dominance by individual males, sexuality, and pornography. In their model, male dominance becomes the dominance of individual women by individual men, which is realised through their sexual relations:

> what is sexuality [*sic*] is the dynamic of control by which male dominance
> – in forms that range from intimate to institutional, from a look to a rape –
> eroticizes and thus defines man and woman, gender identity and sexual
> pleasure. It is also that which maintains and defines male supremacy as a
> political system. Male sexual desire is thereby simultaneously created and
> serviced, never satisfied once and for all, while male force is romanticized,
> even sacrilized, potentiated and naturalized, by being submerged into sex
> itself.[2]

Sexuality, as the tool of male domination in a patriarchal society, becomes equated with heterosexuality because, in the final analysis, sexuality is *defined* in terms of the dominance of men and the submission of women. The gender division becomes, therefore, the fundamental social construct that arises out of sexual relations. As this construct is eroticised, the assumption of male and female roles of dominance and submission becomes the paradigmatic sexual encounter.

The eroticisation of dominance and submission readily can be reformulated in terms of the subject and object positions. The hierarchy of sexuality is equally the model of the relations between men and women in the public domain. Men assume the position of subject – the autonomous, objective position – and women are relegated to the other, that which only can react to the actions of the subject.[3]

The transformation of woman into object provides man with the freedom to exercise control and to act upon her in order to achieve sexual pleasure. Indeed, it is the objectification of women that allows hierarchy to be exercised freely because it is only by transforming another autonomous being into an object that dominance ceases to be objectionable. Objectification, then, is always present in the sexual relations of men and women, since it is precisely the basis upon which sex is defined. However, objectification represents only one end of a spectrum of male sexuality which, by definition, is hierarchical. Violence against women is the other logical end point.[4] In fact, the spectrum of sexual relations becomes characterised in patriarchal society solely in terms of the freedom of the male subject. The greater the sexual freedom of the male to objectify and demean, the greater is the erotic experience. This is made to appear natural *because* it is hierarchy itself which has become eroticised.[5]

Pornography has a central role in the construction of this model. It is the means through which the sexuality of male supremacy is institutionalised 'which fuses the eroticization of dominance and submission with the social construction of males and females'.[6] Thus, pornography is a site for the maintenance of gender and of sexuality. Given how the erotic is defined, the degree to which pornography presents the dominance of males and the submission of females will be the measure of its success as a locus for the maintenance of sexuality.

Pornography is not simply a forum for the constitution of male sexuality, it is a primary site because of the hierarchical nature of sex. If sex is the objectification of women, then pornography, which necessarily objectifies, fractures, and dehumanises, creates the appearance of a sexuality which is repeated in the daily sexual encounters of men and women. In both 'life' and in pornography, the erotic is mediated by the objectification of a subject. Its success is apparent as sex ceases to be understandable except to the degree that this mediation occurs. Moreover, the positions of male and female – dominant and submissive – become completely impermeable. Thus, in the final analysis, the representation of sex in pornography is the reality of sex between men and women. The objectification in representation *is* the objectification of women. Pornography both reflects and constructs that reality.

Not only does pornography succeed as a forum for the defining of sex as the relationship of subject to object, it also functions as the means by which men learn how to evaluate objects in terms of their erotic potential. It creates the image of a woman, and in pornography as in life, men experience sexual pleasure by having intercourse with an image – an image of an object defined in terms of its 'usability'.

The definition of pornography thereby can be completely assimilated to the objective stance accorded men and to the resulting eroticisation of dominance over an object. Pornography is dehumanising because it *necessarily* denies to women the values accorded the subject. It is only in so doing that pornography can be sexy, and the extent of the dehumanisation defines the sexual freedom and liberation which the male experiences. Sadomasochistic imagery becomes a powerful pornographic experience for men because it involves the ultimate defiling of the other – the total denial of the values which are fundamental to the subject.[7]

This theory of pornography, indeed of sexuality itself, has served as the foundations of a model for the regulation of pornography which has come to be described as the civil rights approach.[8] The model has shifted attention away from the traditional focus of obscenity laws on 'community standards', to 'the sexually explicit subordination of women, through pictures or words'.[9] The approach is a logical response to the theory advanced by anti-pornography feminists. If pornography objectifies women, then, by definition, it denies to them those essential human attributes necessarily accorded to the individual subject. Consequently, it denies and encourages the denial to women of their civil rights as autonomous individuals. Unsuccessful attempts have been made at implementing the civil rights model at the municipal level in the United States. The ordinances which were drafted for the cities of Minneapolis and Indianapolis by MacKinnon and Dworkin utilised a civil rights remedial approach through the mechanism of a civil action for damages to victims of pornography.[10] Individuals could bring complaints directly into court based upon the discrimination against women which pornography propagates.

In this chapter I do not propose to engage in an extensive discussion of the civil rights model of regulation *per se*. However, it was in the development of the city ordinance approach to pornography that the potential breadth of regulation became apparent. In defining pornography, the Minneapolis ordinance specifically included an enumerated list of actionable representations.[11] Immediately following the enumeration was a subsection which stated that 'the use of men, children, or transsexuals in the place of women' was included within the definition of pornography.[12] Thus, gay male pornography was completely subsumed in the civil rights model under a constitutional guise of neutrality.

This expansive approach to regulation was not inadvertent, nor was it solely an attempt at ensuring sexual equality in a formal sense. In fact, in the MacKinnon–Dworkin approach to pornography, the theoretical underpinnings to the regulation of gay male representation have been elaborated at some length. Not surprisingly, the discussion of gay pornography is grounded in a consideration of gay male sexuality itself. MacKinnon, for example, has argued that a close nexus exists between the gendered social system and homosexuality, and she concludes that the latter can in no sense be understood as 'outside' patriarchy:

Nor is homosexuality without stake in this gendered sexual system. Putting to one side the obviously gendered content of expressly adopted roles, clothing and sexual mimicry, to the extent that gender of a sexual object is crucial to arousal, the structure of social power which stands behind and defines gender is hardly irrelevant, even if it is rearranged.[13]

Moreover, gay men not only exist within the system of male domination over women; by having sex with other men they *affirm* the social construct of sexuality:

> To the extent that gay men choose men because they are men, the meaning of masculinity is affirmed as well as undermined. It may also be that sexuality is so gender marked that it carries dominance and submission with it, whatever the gender of its participants.[14]

It is difficult to discern precisely how sexuality is so deeply 'gender marked' in this theory of sexual hierarchy. At one point, Dworkin suggests that gay male sex differs from heterosexual intercourse in that it *lacks* the conflation of objectification with eroticism. In gay male sex, she posits 'in no sense is the beloved annihilated. His virility continues to animate his own behavior, either in relation to others or in the sphere of social power'.[15] However, in the context of her theory of gay male sexuality, this statement surely must be interpreted to mean that while gay male sex may (perhaps necessarily) involve objectification, the object maintains the social power granted to him in the public sphere.

Given that pornography is a site for the construction of male sexuality generally, an understanding of gay male sexuality can be gleaned from an understanding of pornography. At a minimum, such an enquiry should reveal how homosexual relations differ (if at all) from heterosexual sex. MacKinnon and Dworkin describe objectification as central to gay male pornography, but it remains specifically the objectification of women. Dworkin is most explicit in her description of the role of women:

> Without the presence of the female, masculinity cannot be realized, even among men who exclusively want each other; so the female is conjured up, not just to haunt or threaten, but to confirm the real superiority of the male in the mind of the reader . . . The feminine or references to women in male homosexual pornography clarify for the male that the significance of the penis cannot be compromised, no matter what words are used to describe his (temporary) position or state of mind . . . superiority means power and in male terms power is sexually exciting. In pornography, the homosexual male, like the heterosexual male, is encouraged to experience and enjoy his sexual superiority over women.[16]

MacKinnon also accepts that gender is central to *all* pornography. Her understanding of gay pornography is grounded explicitly in gender terms – the representation of 'gender plus' homosexuality.[17] It is unclear, though, whether, in arguing for the centrality of gender, MacKinnon is referring to the representation of lesbianism for male audiences of pornography, to the exploitation of women in male pornography (Dworkin's view), or to the objectification of men (or women) through the assumption of positions of subordination. Indeed, it is conceivable that all of these possibilities represent MacKinnon's views.

The theoretical grounding of the critique of gay male pornography has been developed further by John Stoltenberg, a close associate (and partner) of Andrea Dworkin. Stoltenberg emphasises the representational quality of pornography. Because pornography mediates between the audience and the object, Stoltenberg concludes that the result is an alienation of the individual rather than a communitarian sexual experience:

> the sex acts in gay sex films have the illusion of forging a connection, in the sense of hooking up plumbing; but they seem to be experienced as acts of abstracting-apart, of getting off by going away someplace, of not being there with anybody.[18]

This criticism, though, surely must be directed more generally at all representation, which necessarily fragments and objectifies through the presence of a medium. Therefore, for Stoltenberg to claim that this is 'the difference between the reality and the representation' undoubtedly is correct, but also trite.[19] It does suggest, though, that gay male pornography may be qualitatively different from heterosexual pornography where the representation, according to MacKinnon, *is* the reality.

Second, Stoltenberg argues that gay male pornography objectifies in a more specific sense. In his view, it represents for the viewer the same hierarchy of subject over object as depicted by straight pornography.[20] The same values of dominance and submission are present, as is the denial of the subjecthood of the other in sex. The criticism, then, is focused on the alienation of the subject from the object of desire. Specifically, for Stoltenberg, the fact that a subject may dominate a submissive object, is a sufficient basis upon which to draw an analogy to heterosexual pornography. This strand of criticism might be described as objectification by male subject of male *qua* female object mediated by the additional objectification of pornographic representation.

Finally, Stoltenberg takes the argument one step further and asserts that gay male pornography objectifies not simply by representing dominance and submission, but in demeaning women and 'feminine' men. He elides the two to create a critique of pornography as specifically and explicitly anti-female.[21] Thus, gay male pornography is condemned not only because of its similarity to heterosexual pornography, but also for its specificity. The representation of dominance and submission, on the one hand, is criticised because it objectifies. On the other hand, extreme forms of dominance and submission do not, in gay male pornography, victimise the submissive party. Indeed, Stoltenberg explicitly argues that it is this combination of force and mutuality which demonstrates conclusively an anti-female bias. Gay male pornography, then, is subject to criticism in the civil rights approach not only for its objectification of other men but also because its treatment of men demeans women. The depiction of gay male sex differs from pornographic representation of heterosexual sex in order to reassure the viewer that he will not be objectified in a feminine way. At the same time, despite the interchangeability of positions, the focus on domination reveals that gay pornography engages the same values of hierarchy that infuse heterosexual relations.

The inadequacies of the feminist anti-pornography argument as applied to gay male pornography are multifaceted. In the remainder of this chapter, I will explore several of the arguments that rebut the reductionist approach of MacKinnon, Dworkin, and Stoltenberg. First, I will argue that the civil rights approach fails to examine the possibility that gay pornography amounts to a resignification through the misappropriation and subversive use of the signs and codes of dominant patriarchal culture. Tied to this argument is a general critique of the anti-pornography feminist understanding of sexuality. Second, an argument will be raised concerning the anti-pornography movement's conception of the coherent sexual subject. The work of Judith Butler and Andrew Ross again proves particularly instructive in this task. Finally, a deconstruction of the sexual subject leads to an examination of the relations of dominance and submission in psychoanalytic theory as developed by Jessica Benjamin. This reconception of subject and object relations will be related to the analysis offered by Leo Bersani, who has advocated a celebration of submission, which further underscores the inappropriateness of the anti-pornography model. After engaging in this deconstruction of the *sexual* subject, my focus shifts to the reconstruction of a rights-holding subject forged, not from a coherent sexual experience, but from a *political* experience of sexual oppression. The expression of that experience, which necessarily is defined as pornographic in the dominant culture, becomes, in American constitutional terms, 'political speech' worthy of legal protection. However, under this approach, gay pornography is defended not in a liberal rights model of free expression, but in a liberationist model which calls for an experiential enquiry into how pornography sometimes may prove to be both a means of resistance to the dominant sexual culture as well as a means of gay liberation.

RE-PRESENTING GAY MALE PORNOGRAPHY

At a minimum, it is beyond controversy that pornography can be defined as representation. The significance of pornography – its relationship to the 'real' – is of prime importance as is an understanding of the function of representation itself. If pornography is understood in these terms, then it is through the invocation of signifiers that the sexual act is created for the viewer.[22] At issue is the unity and coherence of the signifier in pornography when the context shifts from the heterosexual to the homosexual depiction of sex. The enquiry is important not only for what it suggests about gay male pornography, but also because it speaks to the relationship of gay male sexuality and patriarchy.

It is indisputable that representation objectifies. MacKinnon lays great stress on this fact because it is through pornography that an objectified sexual experience continues to be constructed. As a starting point, however, it is worth

61

recalling that representation shares with reality the fragmentation of images into something less than a complete unmediated subject. The filtering of images operates through the human senses and, in this way, mediates reality for our ultimate consumption. Obviously, this argument in itself does not answer the anti-pornography position. It does suggest, though, that the objectification of women in pornography must be particularly and uniquely offensive and that the enquiry is not centred merely on the objectification of bodies through representation. Thus, an attack on objectification *in itself* would not seem to be part of the social project of the anti-pornography movement. Alternatively, if the ultimate goal is to facilitate the consumption of images without their fragmentation into objects, then the project indeed is a mammoth one, for it demands a fundamental change in how observation is made. If that is the case, then pornography is an insignificant factor or, to rephrase the point, all images are consumed pornographically.

However, if it is assumed that there is something particularly harmful about pornography in terms of *how* it objectifies – its particular role in creating male hierarchy and the domination of women – then the enquiry turns to the context. For MacKinnon and Dworkin, pornography, despite presenting a range of increasingly objectifying images, is an essential unity because of the underlying hierarchy of all men over all women.[23] The emphasis on the homogeneity of male sexuality is a logical outcome of this position. In shifting the focus of attention from the patriarchal system to the oppression of individual women by individual men through the mechanism of sexuality, the categorical conclusion necessarily is that all men, because of their gender, are oppressive and complicit. Since dominance and submission are the defining characteristics of sexuality, the ultimate erotic experience logically is sadomasochistic. From this premise, the indictment of gay pornography becomes simply a matter of conflating the dominance of male heterosexual pornography with the assumption of dominant and submissive roles, particularly sadomasochistic roles, by gay men in pornography and in reality. The signifiers in pornography thus have a unity and coherence that cuts across differences in male sexuality. The male focus on dominance and objectification is the meaning of the signifier both in terms of the images produced and the images received at the level of fantasy by all male viewers.

This ellision of signifiers, though, is problematic in several respects and ultimately imposes a false unity. First, the anti-pornography model fails to recognise the importance of the fusing of sexuality with heterosexuality in dominant culture. Desire is defined not only in terms of male dominance and female submission, but also necessarily in terms of sexual relations between men and women:

> there is no unmediated desire. We experience sexual arousal only in the context of difference or mediation and in hegemonic sexual culture, that mediation has been defined almost solely through the discourse of sexual

difference and the corpus of visual codes, strategies, and injunctions that support the "naturalness" of that difference known as heterosexuality.[24]

This is significant because it suggests that the representation of gay male sexuality is potentially a site for the development of resistance to heterosexual male hegemony. Although MacKinnon and Dworkin are correct in arguing that gay male sexuality operates within the dominant discourses, they underestimate the subversive potential of a representation of the marginalised. Points of resistance, as Foucault suggested, can operate strategically in undermining apparent unities in relations of power.[25]

Gay male pornography may be particularly well situated as a point of resistance in an oppositional discourse to male dominance. This is because it makes visible what has been made invisible by male heterosexual culture. While gay male pornography may be a forum for the construction of male sexuality, it also represents a marginalised sexuality that is culturally outlawed. In fact, the term pornography takes on a different meaning depending on context. The dominant culture appropriates the term pornographic to describe gay imagery generally, not because it represents the paradigmatic sexual experience of domination, but because it r*epresents* what cannot be presented. In other words, 'if the linkage of male homosexuality has operated as an epistemological aid, it has also assured that homosexuality – even in becoming visible to itself – might never be produced out of sight of the pornographic'.[26]

This argument, while it might diminish the force of the anti-pornography critique, does not answer it completely. Although MacKinnon concedes that homosexuality undermines masculinity as a social construct, her contention is that it also affirms that construct simultaneously. The affirmation is played out through the mechanism of dominance and submission. Gay male pornography reinforces masculinity through the same anti-female and objectifying stance that is displayed in heterosexual pornography. While the representation may serve a useful function for gay men in representing their marginalised sexuality, more importantly it signifies the same underlying values as straight pornography. Stoltenberg's focus on domination, anti-femininity, and the appropriation of masculinity in gay male sex films is a further elaboration of this argument. Indeed, Stoltenberg is correct that the signifiers in both genres of pornography often literally do present a linear model of sex culminating in penetration. Dominance and submission are emphasised and, in the case of sadomasochistic imagery, extreme hierarchy is represented. On a literal reading, then, gay pornography may appear to appropriate the values of masculine dominance and feminine submissiveness characteristic of the dominant sexual culture.

The weakness in the argument, however, is the failure to recognise that the marginalisation of gay men may mean that the reception of the pornographic signifier by the viewer can change the very meaning of the sign *because* of its relocation. The statement thereby assumes a new meaning because of its reception at the fringes of dominant culture. In other words, if the meaning of an image cannot be discerned outside of the context of its spectatorship, then the dominance and submission of pornography may assume *different* significations because it is received outside of a straight male context. Thus, the 'meaning of any particular sex act, representation, or subjectivity cannot be reduced to a single valence'.[27] Underlying this argument is the proposition that there are no pure signifiers and, if so, then the categorical anti-pornography approach completely fails to capture the complexity of a representation. This further suggests that a highly personal, experiential enquiry is demanded to uncode meaning:

> If we want to study sexuality, we need more information about individual responses to symbol and image. We need to know what the viewer brings with her to make an interpretation: a cultural frame, resonances, connections, and personal experience. The question of context is important too, since viewers read symbols differently depending on the material they are embedded in and the relationship they have to other symbols, as well as individual interpretive frames which are somewhat idiosyncratic.[28]

Once the focus of interpretation shifts to the response of the viewer, then the signifiers of pornography cannot have a single categorical meaning. Rather, a definition of pornography necessarily becomes contingent. In the context of gay male pornography, the analysis suggests that the signification of the phallus is far from unified:

> the problem to be addressed in this case is the relation between the phallus of male homosexual desire and the phallus of male heterosexual desire, where "phallus" indicates both the power of the Symbolic order and the sexual organ associable with its articulation . . . Recent gay male culture has indeed appropriated masculinity as a representational strategy for its own self-empowerment, and that appropriation has been equivocal at best in its commitment to other political questions. But this masculinity, appropriated, no longer takes its meaning solely within the structure of heterosexual institutions and practices; it is wrenched into intertextuality with numerous homosexualities as well.[29]

As masculinity is reappropriated into a new, unauthorised context, the representation of that masculinity takes on new unauthorised meanings.

The sign to some degree also becomes uncontainable because of the fluidity of fantasy – a crucial element in an analysis of pornography. Interestingly, the anti-pornography feminist attack on objectification extends into the realm of fantasy.[30] It cannot account though for the unpredictability and individuality of fantasy. Through fantasy the appropriation of the values of male heterosexuality may operate as a counterhegemonic force. While pornography represents the sex act, its reception at the level of fantasy may infuse the sign with unexpected meaning:

> Pornography is like fantasies in this respect; no one would dream of

recounting the narrative form of either. Pornography, for the most part, provides a stimulus, base, or foundation for individual fantasies to be built upon and elaborated. It merely provides the conditions – stock, generic, eroticizable components such as poses, clothing and sounds – under which the pleasure of fantasizing, a pleasure unto itself, can be pursued. It cannot, of course, determine the precise nature or shape of the viewer's fantasies; it is aimed in the direction of his or her fantasmatic pleasure. As a result, it does not possess anything like the power of a realist Hollywood film to shape or control the effect of its representations.[31]

In fact, gay male pornography may be particularly situated to achieve this destabilisation. The ability of gay men to assume different roles, both dominant and submissive, leaves the element of fantasy open and unbounded:

> it is important to remember that sexual identification on the part of gay men is always mobile, able to assume different roles and positions, which are always also power relations. "Content" and "effects" based approaches to pornography can never begin to consider the deeper question of how different pornographic images stand for differing desiring subjects, or the terms on which fantasy identifications may be controlled or mobilised.[32]

Fundamentally, my critique of the feminist anti-pornography position is aimed at the categorical nature of the discourse. In adopting an overarching theory of male hierarchical rule, the argument assumes a completely literalist approach to representation which is unable to answer the complexity of the reception of images by a viewer. On a more general level, the anti-pornography interpretation exemplifies the tendency of some theorists to miss the nuances of sexuality in terms of the tenuous relationship of gay men to the values of the dominant culture and, in particular, to the value of masculinity. In arguing that sexuality is always gendered, MacKinnon loses sight of how gay sexuality is both a repressed and subversive force. As Gayle Rubin has persuasively argued, anti-pornography feminists forget that 'sex is a vector of oppression. The system of sexual oppression cuts across other modes of social inequality, sorting out individuals and groups according to its own intrinsic dynamics.'[33]

To this point, the argument that I have advanced would appear to lead to the conclusion that gay male pornography is politically 'good porn' and that gay male sex is politically 'good sex'. The dominance and submission, sadomasochism, anonymity, and apparent alienation indicted by Stoltenberg is a misreading both of gay male pornography and of reality itself. The weakness of the MacKinnon, Dworkin, Stoltenberg view thus would seem to be not beyond redemption since the critique is not based on their condemnation of the eroticisation of hierarchy. Instead, it is simply a revisionist approach which focuses on the specific cultural position of gay men. The criticism, then, is levelled at the failure to accurately read gay male sexuality, rather than at the failure to understand the constructs of dominance and submission or the relations of subject and object. Thus, to this point, the civil rights model of pornography itself as a general apparatus remains uninterrogated. Rather, the liberal values which underpin the model simply have been reinterpreted in a more sophisticated manner and applied in the context of gay male sexuality.

RETHINKING GENDER AS PERFORMATIVE

In the previous section, I criticised the anti-pornography model for its failure to acknowledge that the meanings of a representation can change and diversify as it is appropriated by a gay male subculture. That possibility for change meant that gay male pornography does not necessarily operate as an affirmation of the social construct of male dominance. Rather, gay pornography also enhances the subjectivity of gay men in a heterosexist culture. Thus, in terms of the values of the civil rights model, gay male pornography is not caught by the purpose of the model – to eliminate objectification.

Anti-pornography feminist theory can be analysed from another dimension, which focuses on the coherence of the subject position itself. My analysis here again benefits greatly from the work of Judith Butler. Although she has developed the argument in the broader context of gender relations, I have found it particularly useful in a discussion of gay male pornography. Clearly, the position of MacKinnon and Dworkin is embedded in a view of sex that is, in some sense, prior to discourse. Male patriarchal culture, through its mechanisms of domination such as pornography, inscribes a gendered meaning onto the sexes and this becomes *the* primary mechanism of differentiation for the purposes of a hierarchical arrangement of society. Gender is the means whereby male culture inscribes dominant (subject) and submissive (object) positions onto individuals, and sexuality is the daily forum for the maintenance of those relations.

The validity of this explanation obviously depends upon the coherence of gender as the chief inscription of cultural meaning on the individual. However, to reiterate the point I made in Chapter 1, Butler has argued that both gender and sex itself are culturally produced mechanisms for social control:

> Gender ought not to be conceived merely as the cultural inscription of meaning on a pregiven sex (a juridical conception); gender must also designate the very apparatus of production whereby the sexes themselves are established . . . This production of sex as the prediscursive ought to be understood as the effect of the apparatus of cultural construction designated by gender.[34]

Thus, not only is sex a discursive function, but its appearance as prior to culture itself is constructed. Gender analysis, with its binary structure, provides the built-in limitations and constraints upon the discourse. To the extent that anti-pornography feminism focuses on gender as a binary division of two prediscursive sexes and on the corresponding division of gender into subject and object positions, it reproduces the same discursive style of the dominant culture:

'the effort to identify the enemy as singular in form is a reverse-discourse that uncritically mimics the strategy of the oppressor instead of offering a different set of terms'.[35] Consequently, anti-pornography feminism becomes tied into the same set of concepts that have been attacked.

Butler argues that it is only through the opening up of these identity concepts that a theory of the subject can be fully developed. However, the construct of subjectivity itself is open to examination and deconstruction. The focus of feminism, then, should not be on the appropriation of the universal subject position for women, because the concept of subjecthood already is shot through with power relations. In this regard, the anti-pornography position leaves no room for the examination and deconstruction of the stabilising hegemonic subject. Instead, its sole aim is to appropriate the subject position for the advancement of women. The hierarchy of dominance and submission, according to anti-pornography feminists, is a cultural construct maintained through the institution of pornography. But if the appearance of sex as prior to cultural inscription is a cultural apparatus, then anti-pornography theory has not taken its deconstruction nearly far enough. First, fantasy contributes to the multiplication and shifting of identity concepts and, therefore, contributes to the disintegration of identity as a coherent construct. The 'I' becomes both the observer and the participant in fantasy, giving rise to at least a duality of identification.

Second, in the analysis of gay male pornography, anti-pornography theory becomes complicit in uncritically accepting gender, sexuality, and sex, which are the central tools of hegemonic rule. As I argued in Chapter 1, the representation of sexual minorities can undermine rather than reinforce male supremacy because it brings into question the coherence of sexual subjectivity – a concept which some feminists assert forms the foundations of hierarchy. The failure to abide by the means of cultural construction of gender brings into the public arena the concepts of male and female and raises the issue of whether they are understandable except as functions of discourse.[36]

Gay male pornography, then, might not best be understood as reinforcing objectification. Rather, it may prove to be a site where sexual subjectivity is redefined and opened up to new possibilities. This approach to gender and to sexuality suggests that Stoltenberg's assimilation of gay and straight male images of dominance and submission is deeply flawed. The repetition and representation of heterosexual male values in an unauthorised cultural setting demonstrates their purely constructed character. This, in turn, undermines heterosexual hierarchical gender construction.

Consequently, not only can gay representation resignify the meaning of the symbols of dominant culture, it also reveals, through a parody of gender, the contingency of the relationship between signifiers and signified. This is particularly realisable in a gay male context because, even though located at the margins of the dominant sexual culture, gay culture is 'positioned in subversive or resignificatory relationships to heterosexual cultural configurations'.[37] Pornography, like camp and drag, has the potential of parodic displacement because it exists within a realm where subversion and confusion can be created.[38] For example, the dominance and submission of some gay male pornography, including sadomasochism, may operate to parody the hierarchy of social arrangements and categories of dominant culture. The literalism of the anti-pornography analysis is unable even to consider this possibility.[39]

Rather than attempting to broaden the existing concepts of identity and subjectivity to encompass women as a gendered and sexed category, the more fundamental strategy thus may be the undermining of the coherence of gender. The destabilisation of gender boundaries through subversive parodic performative strategies may also undermine the subject–object dichotomy in heterosexual relations. This is because the idea of a coherent gendered subject would be made increasingly incredible. The concept of sexual subjectivity thereby is rendered problematic because identity, in gendered terms, is fragmented and multiplied.

The deconstruction of subjectivity is particularly problematic for the civil rights approach to pornography. If one of the principal motivations of the anti-pornography model is to control the 'harms to society through social conditioning'[40] resulting from pornography, then sensitivity to how gay male representation may undermine that hierarchical social conditioning is demanded. More fundamentally, the focus of the civil rights model on autonomy is a limiting one, since it depends ultimately on a coherent sexual subject. Thus, the model is valid only to the extent that gender difference, and the corresponding cleavage between subject and object positions, remains a coherent construct. The logical outcome of my argument then would be to develop a model in which gendered subjectivity no longer is the goal. This can occur only within a theory in which subjectivity has lost its foundational status.[41]

Moreover, the regulation of pornography itself may undermine the aims of the anti-pornography movement because the prohibition also serves to eroticise the representation. The regulatory approach, with its assumption of a single literal meaning to any representation, also becomes the means by which identity is defined and constrained:

> The claim that the text permits of a single interpretation is itself a construction of the pornographic text as a site of univocal meaning; if pornography is a textualized fantasy of dissimulated and unstable identifications, then *the claim* that pornography enforces a foreclosure of the text's possible readings is itself the forcible act by which that foreclosure is effected.[42]

This criticism goes to the core of the anti-pornography approach for it suggests that the focus on the sexual subject in contradistinction to the demeaned object of erotic arousal is an inadequate explanation of sexuality. It demands, as a strategy, the proliferation of images in order to destabilise and undermine both gender categories themselves and the constraints on our conceptions of gender and sexuality which have been imposed by anti-pornography activists.

EXPLODING THE BOUNDARIES OF SUBJECTIVITY

The deconstruction of the construct of sexual subjecthood is important because it draws into question the appropriateness of the focus of the civil rights model on individual sexual autonomy. The weaknesses of the anti-pornography position can be further elaborated upon by applying the work of Leo Bersani and Jessica Benjamin respectively. The civil rights model can be turned inside-out by shifting the analysis away from the denial of subjecthood to women in patriarchal culture and towards the denial of the *value* of the objectified. That, in turn, further weakens the anti-pornography position, with its focus on autonomy and the reclamation of the sexual subject.

First, Bersani has explored this argument specifically in terms of gay male sexuality and pornography.[43] His analysis both responds to the position of MacKinnon and Dworkin but also raises questions about much critical theory concerning gay male pornography. Bersani is particularly sceptical of the view that the resignification of masculinity through its appropriation by gay men can be valuable for its subversive potential in relation to the dominant heterosexual culture. In Bersani's view, the appropriation instead may leave the straight male secure in the knowledge that his values of dominance and hierarchy are pathetically imitated by those aspiring to his signifying practice:

> the macho male's rejection of his representation by the leather queen can also be accompanied by the secret satisfaction of knowing that the leather queen, for all his despicable blasphemy, at least *intends* to pay worshipful tribute to the style and behavior he defiles. The very real potential for subversive confusion in the joining of female sexuality . . . and the signifiers of machismo is dissipated once the heterosexual recognizes in the gay-macho style a *yearning* toward machismo, a yearning that, very conveniently for the heterosexual, makes of the leather queen's forbidding armor and warlike manners a *per*version rather than a *sub*version of real maleness.[44]

Thus, representations of masculinity in gay subculture result in an unending failure in appropriation. They are expressive of an inadequacy necessarily felt by the viewer who aspires, but inevitably fails, to realise the power of the phallus as signifier. Consequently, Bersani argues that:

> gay men run the risk of idealizing and feeling inferior to certain representations of masculinity on the basis of which they are in fact judged and condemned. The logic of homosexual desire includes the potential for a loving identification with the gay man's enemies.[45]

This critique, however, does not amount to an endorsement of the anti-pornography position. Even though the underlying values of hierarchy within representations of masculinity may not be subverted by gay male pornography, the dominant patriarchal culture ultimately is not reinforced. Instead, Bersani argues that the anti-pornography position is open to attack on a different level. First, he posits that the argument is disingenuous because the indictment of pornography cannot be limited to the representation alone. Rather, if the representation is the real, then pornography is nothing more than an accurate depiction of sexuality and the real itself should be subject to the same indictment.[46]

Bersani's critique, then, starts not from the position that the anti-pornography reading of the representation is too literal. Rather, his criticism of many of the detractors of MacKinnon and Dworkin is that they have failed to appreciate that gay male pornography may be an accurate depiction of homosexual relations. Thus, gay sex (and its representation through pornography) does not become politically correct sex – a non-hierarchical communion of equal, autonomous sexual subjects – through a resignifying of masculinity.[47] Consequently, Bersani agrees in large measure with the MacKinnon–Dworkin analysis of sexuality. He differs, though, in his rejection of the attempt at recreating sex outside of the framework of objectification and dominance. His position, therefore, might be considered essentialist in its acceptance of the fusing of sex with the exercise of power.

The sadomasochistic relationship thereby becomes the paradigm of erotic pleasure. Moreover, pornography, to the extent that it represents that human sexual essence, should be encouraged because it is shorn of the cultural baggage that surrounds the social construct of sexuality. The understanding of sexuality offered by Bersani is far more radical than that advanced by MacKinnon and Dworkin. It is a theory which questions the very concepts – autonomy, subjectivity, the self – which have been valued in the civil rights model and ostensibly in dominant culture. Rather than focusing on how sexuality objectifies, the emphasis shifts to how a male heterosexual discourse has valued only the position of subject and the individual's clearly demarcated boundaries of sexual autonomy. The civil rights model of pornography replicates that hegemonic practice because it attempts to construct a theory of pornography, indeed of sexuality, defined exclusively in terms of individual autonomy and respect for its boundaries.

The prescription then is a revaluation of the powerlessness essentially involved in sexuality. This redemption of the value of the loss of the coherent self in sex thus becomes a profoundly anti-phallocratic manoeuvre.[48] Gay male pornography and sexuality are subversive to the dominant order because they represent a decision to shatter the boundaries of the self in an act of eroticism. The alleged focus of gay male sex on sadomasochism underscores that a male sexual identity can centre upon the demeaning and debasing of the self, which may in turn undermine existing definitions of maleness:

> Gay men's "obsession" with sex, far from being denied, should be cele-
> brated – not because of its communal virtues, not because of its subversive
> potential for parodies of machismo, not because it offers a model of

genuine pluralism in a society that at once celebrates and punishes pluralism, but rather because it never stops re-presenting the internalized phallic
male as an infinitely loved object of sacrifice. Male homosexuality
advertises the risk of the sexual itself as the risk of self-dismissal, of losing
sight of the self, and in so doing it proposes and dangerously represents
jouissance as a mode of ascesis.[49]

The gay male identity underscores the oscillation between dominance and submission – power and powerlessness – and demonstrates the absurdity of equating
value as a human being with the arbitrariness of the sexual choice to be a 'top' or
a 'bottom'. In this respect, Stoltenberg's critique of gay male sex films is open to
attack even if its premises are correct. The flexibility of positions – of both
fucking and being fucked – does not reinforce male power. Instead, it demonstrates the ridiculousness of suggesting that real value is coterminous with sexual
position. The specific quality of gay male pornography, then, is that it exemplifies
that the explosion of the boundaries of sexual individuality – graphically demonstrated by penetration – cannot be taken seriously. Sadomasochism, moreover,
underscores the willingness of the individual to entrust his sexual subjecthood to
another and to allow the boundaries of his autonomy to be undermined, knowing
that he will reappear no less a subject. Ultimately, then, as Scott Tucker has
described, our ability to 'selectively entrust ourselves to annihilation'[50] reinforces
Butler's claim that there is no naturalness to subjectivity, for the boundaries of
the sexual subject can be penetrated and the resulting fluidity of subject and
object leaves neither position with greater value. Rather, it undermines the
attempt at valuation.

Bersani grounds his theory of sexuality within a psychoanalytic framework in
which submission becomes the means by which the ego continually overcomes
the crisis of separation and individuation. This theoretical ground also has been
developed extensively by Jessica Benjamin in her analysis of master and slave
sexual arrangements.[51] Benjamin approaches the issue of dominance and submission in terms of fantasy and her thesis is that 'the fantasy of erotic domination
embodies the desire for both independence and recognition . . . the impulses to
erotic violence and submission express deep meanings for selfhood and transcendence'.[52] For the submissive party, masochism is the means by which the
individual receives recognition from the other and thereby transcends the bounds
of individuation.[53] Similarly, through the use of force, the dominant master
overcomes alienation through the possession of that other.[54] Thus, the transcendence of the self only is realisable through the presence of another person and,
furthermore, only when one party temporarily becomes less than a coherent
sexual subject.

Benjamin suggests that this process of both asserting and transcending the self
has become increasingly urgent as the felt need to connect – to break down the
boundaries of the self and the alienation of the individual – has intensified in
Western culture:

the individualistic emphasis on strict boundaries between self and other promotes a sense of violation and unreality. Paradoxically, the individualism of our culture seems to make it more difficult to accept an other's independence and to experience the other person as real. In turn, it is difficult to connect with others as living erotic beings, to feel erotically alive oneself. Violence acquires its importance in erotic fantasy as an expression of the desire to break out of this numbing encasement.[55]

Gay male sexuality may well be situated to exhibit, both through the real and through its representation, the willingness to transcend the boundary division through a 'jouissance of exploded limits'.[56] At the same time, it avoids degenerating 'into a relationship that condemns sexuality to becoming a struggle for power'.[57] What Stoltenberg perceives as the abstraction and anonymity of gay male pornography, instead is the paradigm of connection and continuity.

In this regard, there is little indication in feminist anti-pornography theory as to what the erotic would resemble in a reconstructed sexuality outside the limits of objectification. The focus of the civil rights model is on respect for the boundaries of individual sexual subjecthood, rather than on how those boundaries might be transcended to give meaning and to give pleasure. It is appropriate that the MacKinnon–Dworkin approach to pornography has been poured into a civil rights mould, because the criticism both of the anti-pornography position and of a liberal rights model turn on the same failure to recognise the tension between individual identity and the other. Pornography graphically demonstrates that tension, which ultimately is reconciled through penetration. In fact, gay male pornography underscores the transcendence of boundaries in various ways. For example, in the forum of the gay pornography theatre, boundary analysis can be approached on at least three different levels: a disruption of the public–private distinction through the (private) sexual encounter which is common in the quasi-public theatre; the connection forged in the sex act itself; and the fusing of reality and fantasy in the subject viewing the representation. Thus, what Stoltenberg interpreted as alienation and separation, can be inverted to become the site for a deeply subversive boundary disruption.

TOWARDS A NEW REGULATORY MODEL: LIBERATION AND THE POLITICAL SUBJECT

Gay male pornography provides a useful example, not only of the inadequacy of the feminist civil rights approach in the context of a sexual minority group, but more fundamentally it demonstrates the difficulty of applying a liberal rights model to questions of sexuality. Once the sexual subject has been deconstructed, a liberal approach that is centred on sexual autonomy and subjecthood is rendered problematic. Gay pornography is an important analytical tool because of the way it acts as a point of resistance to universal heterosexual subjectivity. What all of the critical approaches to the feminist model share is a greater degree of sensitivity to the sexual difference in gay male sexuality and this underscores the weaknesses in adopting concepts of universal sexual rights. However, a rejection of sexual subjecthood does not mean that subjectivity ceases to be a useful and perhaps necessary means of grounding a legal model for the regulation of pornography. Subjecthood must take on a new content, though, as the focus shifts from the sexual to the political subject of rights. An appeal to the difference of sexual minorities calls for an analysis of specific political experience and history. That history allows for a fuller discussion of subjectivity and facilitates an examination of gay pornography as *political* as well as *sexual* speech. The appropriation of the American constitutional discourse of free speech does not mean that gay pornography should be understood in terms of a liberal rights approach to expression. Instead, it is through the concept of the gay subject, forged from a history of sexual oppression, that pornography comes to be interpreted not only as destabilising to heterosexual male values, but also as liberating for a marginal sexual group. This approach requires greater recognition of the interests of sexual minorities in any regulatory model. Andrew Ross, for example, suggests that this can be achieved only through a framework free of fixed concepts of gender and their universalising tendency:

> Gender-based reforms, such as those proposed by anti-porn groups, are likely to be antagonistic to the interests of sexual minorities, and have, in fact, already added to the suppression of minority rights only tentatively extended under the protection of the privacy of sexual conduct. A politics of sexuality that is relatively autonomous from categories of gender may be needed to achieve and guarantee the full sexual rights of sexual minorities.
>
> Such a politics is the domain of what I will call the *liberatory imagination*. Unlike the liberal imagination, which exercises and defends autonomous rights and privileges already achieved and possessed, the liberatory imagination is *pragmatically* linked to the doctrine of "positive liberty", which entails the fresh creation of legal duties to ensure that individuals will have the means that they require in order to pursue liberty and equality.[58]

A focus on the 'liberatory imagination' demands that the claims which arise from difference be not subsumed within the existing liberal rights framework. It is perhaps ironic that the context of this analysis has been a response to a feminist position – a theory which focuses on the unique position of women and which emphasises how a civil rights model must be sensitive to how women have been constructed universally as the other. A shift from a liberal to a liberatory model demands a rethinking of *all* universalising concepts in light of the different political experiences of the subjects of rights.

One of the interesting respects in which an examination of history and political experience reveals an unusual alliance is in the relationship of sexual minorities to consumer capitalism. Ross argues that the amorality of the marketplace has proven a useful tool for the liberatory imagination of gays. In the face of

73

widespread regulation and oppression in the name of morality, capitalism has provided the most consistent doctrine in support of sexual liberation. The alliance between sexual minorities and capitalism, from the perspective of gay liberation, is purely pragmatic. The example of gay male pornography demonstrates how the political expression of an oppressed sexual group historically has been realised despite the constant threat of censure from the dominant culture.[59]

I do not mean to suggest that the alternative to an oppressive model of regulation based on the morality of the dominant heterosexual culture is a deregulated, purely market-driven sex industry. Rather, in a liberatory model, the marketplace can be replaced with a regulatory approach that is sensitive to sexual difference and historical experience and which also ensures that failures of the market will be rectified. In the context of pornography, that means a focus on employment standards rather than moral sanction. The depiction of safe sex practices, for example, is important not only in representing the erotic in the age of Aids, but also in ensuring a safe environment for workers. The employment of children can be halted based on their political history of exploitation as workers generally, and particularly in the sex industries. Finally, under this regulatory approach, provision could be made for greater participation of sexual minorities in the production and control of the pornography industry. Thus, as a force for liberation, the market can be strategically useful, creating greater possibilities for the subversion of dominant culture which ultimately may help secure 'the culturally constructed body . . . an open future of cultural possibilities'.[60]

CONCLUSION

In this chapter, I have argued that the regulation of gay male pornography within a feminist anti-pornography model is of interest on different levels. First, it highlights how anti-pornography theory has failed to capture the subtlety and complexity of the relationship of sex, gender, and sexuality. Through an examination of gay male pornography, as the representation of a sexual subculture operating at the margins of the dominant heterosexist society, the relations of power are revealed as dense and multifaceted. More generally, in terms of a legal theory of rights, gay male pornography provides a useful reference point for an analysis of the failures of universal conceptions of the subject. It exemplifies how feminist theory at times has mimicked dominant culture in developing universal (and univocal) rights. It is ironic that this manoeuvre, which often has worked to the disadvantage of women, is itself utilised within a particular feminist model to isolate a sexual subculture. In response to this approach, I have argued that the coherent sexual subjecthood upon which universal sexual rights are grounded can be deconstructed. The final outcome, however, need not be the rejection of a discourse of rights and subjectivity. Instead, the project entails a reconstructive aspect which focuses on a liberationist conception of rights based on the particular (and political) experience and history of a subject position. Rights thus become a means to recognise a subject forged from an experience characterised

74

by the *denial* of subjecthood within the dominant culture. In other words, it is only through an appeal to experience that a *particular* subject position becomes understandable and coherent.

From a legal standpoint, gay male pornography becomes an important legal issue because the political nature of the speech is discernible from a history of oppression. Pornography may be a means of achieving both resistance to the dominant culture and, potentially, gay liberation. Legal protection is necessary because of the likelihood of censure by the dominant culture (an example of which I will analyse in the next chapter). This threat of censorship is not surprising given that gay male pornography is a practice with subversive possibilities in relation to phallocratic power. The implication of this analysis is that a model claiming to aspire to the goal of sexual equality must be sensitive to the liberationist aspirations of sexual minorities and must accept that sexuality at the margins of the dominant discourse is qualitatively different. Ultimately, this demands a general rethinking of universalising concepts of sexuality.

I have argued that the limits of sexuality, as explored by gay men, must be approached with great caution within any model of regulation. To do otherwise is to fall into a replication of the dominant phallocratic sexual discourse and to become a hegemonic practice. Any narrowing of sexuality at the margins runs the risk of foreclosing a point of resistance by curtailing the force of the liberatory imagination. On the other hand, by respecting the marginalised sexual practices of gay men, a feminist model itself can overcome the limits of gender analysis and help to facilitate the appearance of subversive sexual performative acts. As a strategic matter, then, anti-pornography feminists might benefit from recognising the usefulness of the subversive acts of gay men operating at the fringes of the dominant sexual discourse. An exploration of those acts, in turn, demonstrates the limitless potential of sexuality as a counterhegemonic force. That exploration can be both a point of resistance and a liberatory practice. How these debates have played themselves out in practice forms the basis of the next chapter.

4

OF REPRESENTATION AND REALITY

In this chapter, I continue to focus upon questions of representation in the context of gay male pornography. In Chapter 3 I developed a theoretical justification for a liberationist approach to the regulation of gay male pornography. Now, I seek to ground the discussion in a concrete example that is currently unfolding. In so doing, I also will respond directly to criticism of the position that I outlined in Chapter 3 and I will further elaborate upon the theoretical basis of my approach. My example is drawn from Canada, a nation in which constitutional discourse has assumed an increasingly central position and in which rights claims are explicitly 'balanced' against competing interests. How that balancing of interests is effected in the context of pornography proves to be of crucial importance to the legal analysis in this context.

BEYOND *BUTLER*

In 1992, the Supreme Court of Canada ruled on the constitutionality of the obscenity provisions of the Canadian *Criminal Code*. The Code is a federal statute and the relevant language is highly indeterminate:

> for the purposes of this Act, any publication a dominant characteristic of which is the undue exploitation of sex, or of sex and any one or more of the following subjects, namely, crime, horror, cruelty and violence, shall be deemed to be obscene.[1]

The question of law that arose was whether the obscenity provisions were unconstitutional as violating the guarantee of freedom of expression in the Canadian *Charter of Rights and Freedoms*. By way of background, Canada has had an entrenched bill of rights since 1982, which includes in s.2(b) a guarantee of 'freedom of thought, belief, opinion and expression'. It is also important that the structure of the Charter includes a saving provision which states that the guarantees of rights and freedoms are 'subject only to such reasonable limits prescribed by law as can be demonstrably justified in a free and democratic society'. The question, then, was whether the obscenity provisions were an unconstitutional infringement of freedom of expression and, if so, whether they could be justified as a reasonable limit on the scope of the right. Thus, the Court was forced to engage explicitly in a balancing of competing interests.

In February, 1992, in *R. v. Butler*, the Supreme Court of Canada unanimously upheld the obscenity provisions as a constitutionally valid limitation of the right of free expression.[2] Historically, the courts have interpreted obscenity law by focusing on whether the exploitation of sex in the work is 'undue'. The test for determining the undue exploitation of sex is the community standard of tolerance test – what Canadians would not tolerate other Canadians viewing. Furthermore, the community standard is national in scope and not, for example, that of a subcultural community or a particular municipal or provincial community.

Of particular interest is the fact that the Supreme Court accepted many of the arguments that were raised by counsel advocating a feminist anti-pornography approach. In a sense, the 'classic' MacKinnon–Dworkin framework was grafted onto the obscenity 'undue exploitation of sex' standard. The issue of undueness thus began to shift in the judgment of Justice Sopinka, writing for the majority, away from notions of morality and the preservation of the moral fibre of society, and towards human degradation as a justification for regulation (which, of course, also is a moral issue). He recognised that material which may be said to exploit sex in a 'degrading or dehumanizing' manner would necessarily fail the community standards test, 'not because it offends against morals but because it is *perceived* by public opinion to be harmful to society, particularly women'.[3] The justification for regulation thus is harm. The Court held that judges must determine as best they can what the community would tolerate others being exposed to on the basis of the degree of harm that may flow from the exposure. It also found that harm includes predisposing persons to act in an anti-social manner – a manner which society formally recognises as incompatible with its proper functioning.[4] The stronger the inference of a risk of harm, the less likelihood of tolerance.

Justice Sopinka also expanded upon the relationship of representation and harm through a threefold categorisation of pornography. He held that: (1) the portrayal of sex coupled with violence will almost always constitute the undue exploitation of sex; (2) explicit sex which is degrading or dehumanising may be undue if the risk of harm is substantial; (3) explicit sex that is not violent and neither degrading nor dehumanising is generally tolerated in our society and will not qualify as the undue exploitation of sex unless it employs children in its production.[5] The infringement on the constitutional right of freedom of expression thus is justifiable under the reasonable limits test because the focus is not on moral disapproval but the avoidance of harm to society, which is a pressing and substantial concern. Moreover, the obscenity provisions do not proscribe sexually explicit erotica without violence that is neither degrading nor dehumanising, but are designed only to catch material that creates a risk of harm to society. A nexus, therefore, implicitly is found between exploitation, degradation, a process of moral desensitisation, and social harm.

One of the intervenors in the case was the Women's Legal Education and Action Fund (LEAF), and the decision of the Supreme Court was hailed by them and others as a great victory. Some of the material at issue in the *Butler* case was gay male pornography, and the relevant passage from the brief written by LEAF underscores the application of the argument to gay male representations:

> Individual men are also harmed by pornography, although this is exceptional in that this harm does not define the social status and treatment of men as a group. Indeed, there is no systemic data to support the view that men as such are harmed by pornography. However, LEAF submits that some of the subject pornography of men for men, in addition to abusing some men in ways that it is more common to abuse women thorough sex [*sic*], arguably contributes to abuse and homophobia as it normalizes sexual aggression generally.[6]

Kathleen Mahoney, the lawyer who represented LEAF, explained the strategy behind the success, and one passage is very telling for its relevance to gay male pornography:

> We showed them [the judges] the porn and among the seized videos were some horrifically violent and degrading gay movies. We made the point that the abused men in these films were being treated like women – and the judges got it. Otherwise, men can't put themselves in our shoes. Porn makes women's subordination look sexy and appealing; it doesn't threaten men's jobs, safety, rights or credibility.[7]

I will return to the significance of this statement later, but I raise it here to show the deliberate deployment of gay male pornography as evidence in the *Butler* case.[8] Writing as a member of the LEAF 'team', Karen Busby has argued that the principle at issue, in the context both of lesbian and gay male pornography, is whether the material in question itself contributes to 'social and sexual inequality'.[9]

The aftermath of the decision has been all too predictable. In the wake of *Butler*, one of the prime targets of the police and customs authorities (and this is a continuation of previous practice) has been lesbian and gay erotic visual representations, but with a newly added constitutional justification. Furthermore, there has been no noticeable increase in criminal prosecutions and customs seizures of heterosexual pornography.[10] One case in the Ontario High Court of Justice demonstrates how the decision may impact upon lower courts. In *Glad Day Bookshop v. The Queen*, a judgment delivered in July, 1992, the Court considered the constitutionality of a detention of shipments of gay pornography by Canadian customs officials under the obscenity provisions.[11] These materials were destined for Glad Day Books, Toronto's primary gay bookstore and had been seized a few years prior to the *Butler* decision, as had numerous other materials in the past. Various constitutional questions were raised before the trial judge and of particular interest is the way in which the 'degradation' language of the Court in *Butler* is applied. The standard for the determination of obscenity is 'proof beyond a reasonable doubt', which is the highest legal standard of proof. In *Glad Day Books*, Mr Justice Hayes characterised the material as follows:

> The publications are in the form of what might be termed magazines and publications containing short stories. The pictures and short stories generally relate to explicit sexual activities between males. The text of the material describes in intimate detail the explicit sexual practices, reactions and feelings of the participants with excessive, lewd and disgusting detail.[12]

Interestingly, there was expert evidence led by counsel for Glad Day Books as to the specificity of gay male pornography and how the concerns raised by the Supreme Court in *Butler* were simply not relevant to the facts. For example, a professor of sociology gave evidence on how the 'abasement' of the individual in gay pornography was depicted from the perspective of the man seeking abasement and in that sense control was maintained by him in the scenario. Therefore, the reasoning in *Butler* was inapposite. This analysis was rejected out of hand by the trial judge who, after referring extensively to the *Butler* decision, reached the conclusion that everything seized satisfied the test of obscenity. The magazines in issue depicted explicit sexual scenes and gave descriptions of sexual scenarios between men, often with no representation of violence. Mr Justice Hayes' analysis is very revealing, as representations are found degrading and an undue exploitation of sex on the basis of explicitness alone. Indeed, in some cases, there is no actual visual representation of sex. For example, from comic strip formats and short stories describing bondage and sadomasochism, the Court is willing to draw an inference of harm. In one case, a publication (*Advocate Men*) was described as a:

> magazine of explicit pictures of nude males and stories of explicit casual sexual encounters relating to oral and anal sex. The description and activities are degrading and without any human dimension. The dominant characteristic is the undue exploitation of sex. I find it to be obscene.[13]

Explicit descriptions of gay male sex and magazines of nude men are constructed as degrading *per se* and an undue exploitation of sex. It is never entirely clear who is degraded nor why there is an undue exploitation of sex rather than just 'due' exploitation or no exploitation of sex at all. Of course, it simply may be that this judgment is a misreading of the direction given by the Supreme Court in *Butler* and should be reversed on the proper application of the test of obscenity.[14] Furthermore, it might be argued that community standards must be defined so as to explicitly include the sensibilities of sexual subcultures. To do otherwise itself may be an unconstitutional violation of the right to equality on the basis of sexual orientation, a right which I describe at length in Chapter 6.

In my estimation, though, there is nothing anomalous in the *Glad Day Books* decision, and the Court's willingness to construct representations of gay men as pornographic is not surprising. The language of exploitation and degradation is applied to justify the seizure, but the switch from moral disapproval to a feminist analysis of social harm (the *Butler* approach) appears to be a change at the level of discourse, rather than actual police practice. *Glad Day Books* demonstrates that while the Supreme Court of Canada may have focused upon the degradation of women through pornography, the enforcement of the law in practice may be undertaken in very different terms, so as to impact directly upon lesbian and gay male subcultures. In fact, the Conservative Member of Cabinet responsible for customs inspections at the time, Otto Jelinek, explicitly endorsed widespread seizures. He claimed that:

> the majority of Canadians – maybe they're the silent majority, they're the normal people who don't speak out as loudly – they don't want this stuff coming in . . . Most Canadians not only support us stopping this trash but want us to move further.[15]

As this comment suggests, anti-pornography feminists in Canada might be faulted for not engaging in a thoroughgoing analysis of the state in terms of its not so latent homophobia (and misogyny) in the context of the enforcement of obscenity law.[16]

The construction of gay sexuality as obscene also is evidenced by the long-standing bureaucratic rules for determinations by customs inspectors on whether a picture or story is to be barred from Canada. Until fairly recently, all depictions of anal sex were degrading *per se*, and currently only 'rational and unsensational' descriptions will pass customs inspection.[17] However, that standard is applied in a far from uniform manner. In January, 1993, Canada Customs informed the publisher of *Blueboy* magazine that if a list of dangerous activities was not omitted from an article giving safe sex advice, it would be subject to seizure.[18] Within the legal framework of customs inspections, then, there is a tension between the wording of the regulations which appear at least to condone the production of safe sex representations, and the construction of gay sex as unrepresentable in Canada. This conflict leaves little room for the appropriation of the genre of pornography for the production of safe sex techniques and fantasies.[19]

In fairness to LEAF, the discriminatory enforcement of obscenity laws has been condemned by some supporters of the *Butler* decision.[20] Moreover, it is entirely possible that the decision in *Glad Day Books* eventually may be reversed on appeal.[21] It also is conceivable that customs authorities, if given proper administrative guidelines, will interpret the law in a less homophobic fashion. Of course, it also is possible (and perhaps probable) that the enforcement of Canada's obscenity laws will continue largely unchanged in the future.

SADOMASOCHISTIC PORNOGRAPHY AND PRACTICE

Leaving aside the question of the administration of the law, a more fundamental issue remains. While some may criticise the seizure of lesbian and gay male erotic material that clearly does not fall within the parameters of the *Butler* decision, the more difficult issue is how one analyses, for example, gay male representations that *prima facie* fail the community standards test as it has been reinterpreted by the Supreme Court of Canada. In other words, are images that portray objectification, domination, and violence in a sexualised context necessarily a denial of the value of equality that underpins the *Butler* test? Are such images analogous to hate speech, which can be legally proscribed in Canada? Are these representations no different in substance from heterosexual imagery of the same ilk, because both promote misogyny and homophobia? These are the difficult questions that now confront Canadian courts.

In Chapter 3, I attempted to respond through a theoretical analysis of gay male pornography, highlighting the problems with the MacKinnnon–Dworkin model. To reiterate, there are long-standing difficulties thrown up by this anti-pornography framework that are only beginning to be addressed. In the anti-porn analysis, the indictment of gay male pornography becomes simply a matter of conflating the dominance and submission of heterosexual pornography with the assumption of dominant and submissive roles, particularly sadomasochistic roles, by gay men. The signifiers are given a unity and a coherence that cuts across sexual difference. The male focus on dominance and objectification, then, is the meaning of the signifier both in terms of images produced and images received by all male viewers. However, if gay male pornography reinforces male values that are shared across lines of sexuality, then the harshness of the response within dominant culture becomes difficult to comprehend. Consistently missing from the anti-porn analysis is a consideration of the ways in which desire is constructed, not only in terms of male dominance and female submission, but also necessarily in terms of heterosexual relations. One can then ask whether the readiness of the state to censor gay imagery speaks in part to the subversive potential of a representation of a marginalised sexual group within dominant culture. Furthermore, it is necessary to focus on how the reception of a sexual image may give the representation a distinctive meaning. Thus, if an image cannot be understood outside of the context of its spectatorship, then the dominance and submission of pornography assumes different significations because of its reception outside of a heterosexual frame.[22]

This analysis renders the earlier statement of Kathleen Mahoney on the Canadian jurisprudence fraught with difficulties. First, in pornographic representations, are men being treated like women? Arguably not, because the representation underscores the willingness of one who has been gendered male (and all that culturally implies) to entrust his sexual subjecthood to another – a *choice* to be objectified that is not open to women (but which appears to be in heterosexual pornography). Mahoney and others ignore the possibilities for reciprocity, changing positions and hierarchies, and shifting identifications, which render the meaning of a gay male sexual representation far more complex than they are prepared to recognise.[23]

The second problem raised by Mahoney's statement is that she proves too much. The representation, she argues, allows men to put themselves 'in women's shoes'. This suggests that there is a positive value in allowing straight men to recognise that a man can choose to be objectified and dominated sexually. Apparently, to see this debasement of a fellow male will horrify the heterosexual sufficiently to alter his attitudes and behaviour. The representation alone thus has a transformative potential on how straight men see the objectification of women. As an aside, her comment implies that LEAF was deploying the judiciary's homophobia as a conscious litigation strategy. I am more sceptical than Mahoney of the transformative potential of most straight men.[24] However, her argument suggests that we should strive for a *proliferation* of gay male sexual represent-ations in order to transform gender relations; to *expose* a transgressive relationship between maleness and domination in order to transform the relationship of straight men and women. Thus, gay male representation serves an educational function for homophobic and misogynist men.

A somewhat more sophisticated critique of the position I advanced in Chapter 3 has been developed by Christopher Kendall, who has described views such as mine as myopic, frightening, and dangerous.[25] In fact, he explicitly challenges me (and others) to answer his claim that 'if you defend gay male pornography you defend a gay male identity that promotes and encourages violence, cruelty, degradation, exploitation.'[26] According to Kendall, the hierarchies of dominance and submission – indeed of top and bottom – in some pornography reinforce rather than subvert traditional heterosexual male values and undermine any challenge to rigid gender norms. Moreover, in his analysis, representation and reality are ontologically merged such that the representation has the power to reinforce the social reality of oppression and inequality. Furthermore, the repre-sentation cannot be divorced from the reality of the *production* of pornography which also, it is claimed, is oppressive to those involved. Finally, gay male pornography, to the extent that it represents these 'male' values, contributes not only to sexual practices that reinforce them (such as sadomasochistic sex), but also leads to non-consensual violence and abuse. The decision of the Supreme Court of Canada in *Butler*, then, should be hailed as a victory for all women and for gay men. The language of *Butler* and its model of equality-based expression rights thus *should* be applied in the same manner to gay male pornography.

It is thus argued that the glorification of 'maleness' (the values of male power and masculinity as they have been constructed within a misogynist society) in visual representation reinforces those values within gay male culture and society at large. Moreover, as we know, those values are deployed so as to oppress women, people of colour, gay men of all races, and others. Thus, the represent-ation has a direct impact on the reality of people's lives, undermining the value of equality that is at the core of the Canadian Constitution. The representation is the reality of male sexuality and male power in our society, and the repre-sentation, in turn, reinforces (rather than undermines) that reality. At the same time, within this analysis, the power of law and especially of constitutional law, to achieve social change is idealised and fetishised.

I now will respond to each of these three aspects of the anti-pornography critique: the lack of employment standards in the production of pornography; the sexual practices that are represented and encouraged by pornography; and, finally, the argument that the representation of the underlying values of male hierarchy reinforces the social practices of misogyny, homophobia, and non-consensual acts of violence.

First, on the question of production, Kendall, for example, argues that gay male pornography is exploitative of sex workers employed within the industry. Citing an unpublished study by a law student, the research for which consisted of some interviews and the observation of the making of two films, as well as a twenty-five year old American government report, he draws scathing conclusions about how the industry treats its employees.[27] Kendall's most damning comment is that the production of 'degrading and objectifying scenarios, like those in heterosexual pornography, probably requires actual physical subordination'.[28] This statement, however, is not supported by evidence. Rather, it is presented as self-evident. After a moment's reflection, though, it is clear that it cannot be true as a general proposition. The implication is that any non-documentary representation of degradation on film necessarily can be created only through the degradation of the actor. Such an idea is incredulous. Although I have no doubt that the Hollywood film industry in general is highly exploitative of workers, it would be trite to suggest that the actors who portrayed Jews in the film *Schindler's List*, for example, were degraded in the way that the characters they portrayed were within the narrative structure of the movie. As Carole Vance points out, 'when we see war movies, for example, we do not leave the theatre believing that the carnage we saw was real or that the performers were injured making the films'.[29] Although an actor, in the course of the production of any film, may experience physical restraint (or emotional distress) if that is the character's experience, the actor's reality and the representation surely are different (unless the film in fact is the documentation of abuse). To make such an argument withstand scrutiny, therefore, one must claim that the structure of pornography *is* purely documentary, such that it represents reality *literally*. I have yet to see evidence which supports such a claim.

More generally, with regard to the exploitation of workers, a profit-making pornography industry undoubtedly exploits many employed within it, whether they be described as actors or sex workers. Although I suggested in Chapter 3 that the production of gay representations within a capitalist system has proven useful for gay men as a means for fostering an identity, that utility has been purely strategic. Capitalism, by definition, can be exploitative and, historically, sex-related industries have been no exception. In large part this is because they operate at the fringes of the legal system, outside the scope of routine employment regulation. The case of prostitution provides an apt example. Thus, while I agree that exploitation of the vulnerable is a significant problem (as it also, but perhaps to a lesser extent, is in the entertainment industry generally), criminalisation is an unlikely remedy for the situation. Here again, the criminalisation of soliciting for the purposes of prostitution and the drive by sex workers to both legalise and regulate sex industries is directly analogous. On this point, as I argued in Chapter 3, the importance of safe sex practices amongst sex workers is crucial and, in my view, should be strictly regulated through employment law. However, criminalisation of production is an unlikely means to achieve this end.

Furthermore, we may have reached a stage where the production of pornographic representation is slowly beginning to shift away from the private sector and towards community-based, non-profit production. This has become an urgent priority in the age of Aids, and it opens up possibilities for representing the erotic in creative ways in order to reinforce safe sex practices.[30] In addition, the pornography industry in general has responded to the Aids pandemic through the representation of safe sex.[31] Both the discovery of the HI virus and the social responses to it have operated to constrict the range of sexual practices open to gay men, and now many are working to creatively re-imagine and re-present sexuality and sexual practices in exciting and safe ways.[32] We may be entering a period of self-discovery, where our bodies, which have been constructed as disease-carrying containers, are tools with which we can explore new erotic possibilities. It also is a fact that, with respect to sadomasochism, 'some sexual practices which have been stigmatised as deviant are amongst the [sexually] safest'.[33] However, the social reality that gay men face is rendered invisible within much anti-pornography analysis. At one point, for example, Kendall cites statements of sex workers to the effect that pornography may have created an interest amongst gay men in the sexual practice of 'fisting'.[34] Whether or not this is true (and I cannot imagine why anyone would care), the implicit message is that some sexual practices are not sufficiently 'moral' for gay men to adopt (including penetration itself), even if they can be made safe sex practices. For those involved in safe sex education, such an analysis detracts from a focus on the politics of a safe sexuality, which is surely one of the primary moral issues surrounding our sexuality today.

Another issue that has been raised with some frequency is the representation of men of colour in gay male pornography. For example, it has been argued that gay male pornography reinforces a white supremacist ideology through the representation of racial minorities in conformity with racist stereotypes, including sexual stereotypes about people of colour.[35] In support of this proposition, the groundbreaking work of Richard Fung on pornography and Asian men is sometimes cited.[36] Fung analyses how Asian men are almost without exception portrayed as submissive 'bottoms' in gay male pornography, which may reinforce a racist stereotype about Asian men generally. However, in fairness, Fung's *analysis* of the meanings and contradictions of pornography also must be cited. As Fung argues, the failure of commercially produced gay male pornography lies in the constricted erotic possibilities provided to Asian gay men through representation: 'it is not that there is anything wrong with the image of servitude *per se*, but rather that it is one of the few fantasy scenarios in which we figure, and we are always in the role of servant'.[37] Consequently, the solution offered by Fung is not a censoring of images, but an opening up of space for the production and consumption of representations with specifically gay male Asian audiences in mind. While Fung acknowledges that such a project may appear 'utopian', it is a persuasive response given the importance that pornography carries for gay male racial minority groups. This is particularly true for those gay men who may be economically and politically disenfranchised, isolated, or young. Fung's analysis of the racial dynamics of gay male pornography thus suggests a radically different prescription from that of the anti-pornographers.[38]

In anti-pornography discourse, the visual representation of gay male sexual practices also frequently is linked to a condemnation of the reality of those same practices. In particular, this critique has been levelled at gay male (and lesbian) sadomasochism.[39] Sadomasochistic sexual *practices*, as well as their representation, are vehemently criticised because, it is claimed, they are imbued with heterosexual male values of power, objectification, domination, and subjugation. A sexual relationship involving sadomasochism thus becomes, by definition, a non-egalitarian (and perhaps non-consensual) relationship that undermines the goals of gender equality and sexual liberation. Thus, since the representation is the reality, both the representation and the reality of sadomasochism can be condemned together.

Of course, the obvious problem with this analysis is that there is no evidence that sadomasochistic pornography leads to sadomasochistic sexual practices.[40] However, this question is not my primary interest in this chapter. My concern, rather, is with the meaning and implications of the sexual *practice*, from the perspective of the goal of gender equality and also with the meanings of its representation. Like most people, I do not favour relationships that are non-consensual and inegalitarian. My starting point though is that *all* relationships of substance in which we engage, sexual and otherwise, are invested with power dynamics. In particular, all sexual relationships necessarily are a complex matrix of power turning on a variety of factors. The key ethical question, then, is how one negotiates and controls the manifestations of power (and lack of it) in one's everyday dealings with people. This, of course, includes how a teacher deals with students; how we interact with our friends; how we manage living with other people; and, indeed, how we conduct our sex lives. With regard to the last category, the most blatantly inegalitarian and non-consensual 'relationship' is between rapist and rape victim. Such a relationship of course is ethically indefensible. However, there are less stark examples of inegalitarian relationships, including cases of partner abuse, both physical and emotional. Less dramatic but still ethically indefensible are cases of emotional manipulation, deceit, and coercion. Moreover, I would readily agree that traditional heterosexual male values of hierarchy and dominance are closely bound up with all of these unethical practices in a variety of ways.

Where I part company with critics of gay male sadomasochism, however, is over the question of whether a consensual sexual practice necessarily can be analogised to a relationship of abuse arising from inegalitarian power dynamics.

85

More specifically, if people take sexual pleasure in a sadomasochistic relationship where one (or more) dominates and subjects the other(s) to acts that may be read by some as humiliating, I am not prepared to concede that such a practice (or its representation) is ethically indefensible.

Sadomasochistic relationships may involve highly inegalitarian power dynamics, as may any other type of relationship, such that the feelings and needs of the other have been ignored or disrespected. As Susan Keller argues, the 'reality' of a sadomasochistic sexual relationship 'is likely to be further complicated by the existence of power relationships that include but also extend beyond the sexual realm'.[41] However, in my view, these power dynamics – the possibilities of deceit, coercion, manipulation as well as physical and emotional abuse – are not readily connected to particular sexual practices *per se*.

Critics of sadomasochism sometimes argue that sadomasochistic relationships are founded upon and fetishise power imbalances. Rather than negotiating power in an ethical fashion taking into account the views of the other, power is wielded by the master in a brutal manner and accepted by the slave for reasons which are not easily understood. Such an approach is an oversimplified interpretation of the sadomasochistic relationship and wrongly conflates a relationship of sadomasochism with a relationship of abuse. The power dynamics in an abusive relationship are dramatically inegalitarian and may exist either (or both) within or outside the purely sexual realm. Sadomasochistic relationships may be abusive, but there is no evidence that they are abusive *because* sadomasochistic. Rather, I would suggest, the two are completely separate issues.

As I will argue in Chapter 7, the primary difference between a sadomasochistic sexual relationship (that is non-abusive in terms of my definition) and an abusive relationship is that in the former the infliction of pain (or, alternatively, the appearance of the infliction of pain) is part of a shared ritual designed to give both partners sexual pleasure.[42] It ideally exists within a framework involving rules and boundaries that should be mutually agreed upon and respected. This is fundamentally how one differentiates abuse from 'classic' sadomasochism. In fact, the negotiation of those boundaries demands an active awareness of the needs of the other and a concern to ensure that what one does is what the other wants. Pleasure thus is made explicitly a product of discourse, and to the extent that this is not actually the case, the relationship may well be founded on an inegalitarian basis. Unlike an abusive relationship, in a sadomasochistic one sexual power ideally is negotiated and, in fact, the power dynamics of the relationship may bear no direct relationship to the sexual practices involved. Because of the importance attached to the pleasure received by the sexually dominated partner, it has been argued that the 'bottom' is possessed of relatively more control in the sexual scene because it is incumbent upon the 'top' to ensure his sexual gratification.[43]

Returning now to the representation of sadomasochism, if representation and reality are conflated then presumably the same defence of the representation can be offered as for the sexual practice. However, it has been argued that the representation of sadomasochism may have a broader impact because it may give rise to abuse in (presumably) non-sadomasochistic relationships, due to the frustration felt by men who otherwise are unable to live up to the male values that are represented. Scenarios of sadomasochism thus lead to physical abuse. The abusers are driven to acts of violence in the attempt to imitate and realise the practices that have been represented.[44]

While I concede that representations in general can have an impact upon a social reality, and that there are connections between representations and social practices, the shift from representations of gay male sadomasochism to relationships of physical violence is problematic. Of course, we live in a world where we are bombarded with representations of 'male' values of hierarchy, dominance, and control. We also exist within a society where we are witness to representations of violence, degradation, and humiliation all the time. These representations are central to the mainstream media and, in fact, are central to our shared way of life. Undoubtedly they have an impact upon the way we think, feel, and act. However, the relationship is complex, multifaceted, and representations do not necessarily make us more violent or abusive or less sensitive to the experience of actual physical abuse. Moreover, it is not easy to see why gay male sadomasochistic representations in particular are singled out for criticism. The argument has been made that representations of violence in the media lead to violence in society, demanding greater censorship of such imagery. However, if that is the argument being advanced, then critics of gay male pornography are being rather disingenuous and should 'come out' as supporting the censorship of representations of violence generally. Given its much broader audience, representations of extreme violence and degradation on television and in Hollywood films must have a broader and more immediate impact than the vastly smaller circulation of representations of gay male pornography.

A similar point can be made with respect to the argument that gay male pornography reinforces male/female stereotypes and thus undermines gender equality. Masculinity, it is argued, is always presented as the defining and preferred construct for men.[45] In response, however, I find it incongruous that the argument is made that representations of two men engaged in sexual acts reinforces male/female stereotypes in some indirect way to such an extent as to require legal censure, particularly when we are constantly faced with representations that *directly* reinforce male/female stereotypes within the mainstream media.

The question of voice also demands further attention. Kendall, for example, asks 'why is the "option" of being an effeminate little queer grovelling at the feet of a muscular, straight acting dominant so subversive and empowering?'[46] First, why is the voluntariness of the option questioned? One of my fundamental disagreements with the MacKinnon–Dworkin model is that, like others, I am sceptical of claims of 'false consciousness'. Of course, all of our life options are socially constructed, but I fail to see why the option of a gay man to be objectified is somehow less of an option than any other. Assuming that the sadomasochistic relationship is non-abusive, then the choice of sexual practice is not directly related to the power dynamics of the relationship.

Moreover, anti-pornography analysis frequently reduces sadomasochistic sexual practices to nothing more than self-hate. Given that gay men are faced with hatred every day within dominant culture, such an easy dismissal of what a gay man may 'get out of' sadomasochism in itself becomes an objectification of the sexual practice. The participants are silenced, and denied a space to articulate both their sexual pleasures and how they have been marginalised within the gay community and mainstream culture. For example, when I see a man of colour in a subcultural space unclothed from the waist up except for a chain draped around his shoulders, I am forced to confront the history of enslavement, objectification, and sexual exploitation of people of colour within a white supremacist culture. I also must be reflective about my own positioning in a homophobic but racist society, and consider how I negotiate the power dynamics in which my social position places me. It is an oversimplification to assume that the image that he is creating is no different from the reality of slavery and merely reflects internalised self-hatred. The reasons why a person of colour may create such a representation (and may participate in either master or slave sexual roles), are, I suspect, multifaceted. The point, however, is that it is time to open a discursive space to allow the articulation of those reasons rather than silencing that voice and denying the sexual agency of the individuals involved. Throughout history, for too many people, sexuality has been 'at the hands of an oppressor'.[47] But for some gay men, engaging in sadomasochistic sexual practices *may* be a response to sexual and/or racial oppression. The choice of sexual practice is a means to intervene and to assert one's self in a discourse in which one may have been historically objectified and demeaned.

Furthermore, it has been claimed that the appropriation of a masculine style by gay men is a form of 'passing' as male – of imitating the heterosexual norm in order to be accepted as a 'real' man.[48] However, in no sense does one pass as the genuine article by culturally appropriating masculinity.[49] As I argued in Chapter 3, imitation never occurs without an excess of meaning, and it is that excess which is potentially destabilising for the norm. How else can one explain the homophobic verbal abuse and physical violence that the hypermasculine 'leather queen' is subjected to on the street? In no sense is he seen by homophobic men as an ally because he reinforces the values of male supremacy that they hold dear. Rather, masculinity is reduced to a form of 'drag' that one can slip into and out of, and the nexus between masculinity and social power is thereby loosened.[50] The appropriation of masculine style does not hold out the promise of privilege for the gay man. It potentially promises retribution instead, because it is an unauthorised use of heterosexual male privilege. Appropriation thus may become an anti-assimilationist stance.

To reiterate, I have argued that all social relations are invested with power, and the question then becomes how we negotiate our way through in an ethical fashion. In my opinion, attempting to discuss, manage, and even to replicate the production of power openly is an important step in a world where aggression, control, and dominance are part of our everyday lives. Appropriating those signs in order to give sexual pleasure to others (as well as one's self) reinforces the primary importance of the other in a sexual relationship. Sexual position and power dynamics become increasingly provisional, which runs completely contrary to male supremacist ideology.

Thus, I would disagree with the argument that the appropriation of masculinity is a means to avoid breaking ranks with heterosexual male privilege. Rather, there are numerous examples which underscore how dominant culture is deeply troubled by the appropriation of masculinity by gay men. For example, the reaction to the 'gays in the military' issue in America highlights how uncomfortable heterosexual culture is with the idea that gay men can successfully 'pass' as macho military types. This is an argument I will pursue further in Chapter 5. It also explains why Jesse Helms focused upon representations of gay male sadomasochism in his attacks on funding decisions by the National Endowment for the Arts. In addition, it provides a reason why sadomasochistic imagery was central to the hearings of the Meese Commission on Pornography in America.[51] Finally, it illustrates why the criminal law has been invoked against gay male sadomasochists in the United Kingdom, which I will discuss in detail in Chapter 7.

In the end, I do not disagree that gender inequality has sexual manifestations. However, as Carol Smart has argued, in the context of recent events in the United Kingdom, symbolically at least, 'when women say "No" to rape they mean "Yes" but when men say "Yes" to homosexual sex they mean "No"'.[52] When a gay man who actively chooses to submit to sadomasochistic sexual practices states that he experiences his relationships as consensual, pleasurable, and loving, it seems to me to require considerable justification to claim that he is misguided and wrong. So too, when an abused person says that a relationship is hierarchical, non-consensual, and founded upon violence and hate, such a verdict speaks for itself. However, my point is that to conflate the two or to see the former as 'causing' the latter is to trivialise abuse and may possibly deflect attention from an examination of the power dynamics and social responses to abusive relationships of all kinds demanded in our society. Furthermore, accusing gay male sadomasochists of fostering misogyny may divert our scrutiny away from the central role of compulsory heterosexuality in creating and maintaining a system of gender inequality.[53]

I do not want to suggest that gay men constitute a group that in some way is immune from the effects of the values of maleness, nor that there is a singular gay male 'reading' of pornography. Gay men often are in relatively powerful positions in our society and many do employ that power in a politically and ethically indefensible manner. Moreover, I agree that in so doing gay men have incorporated traditional 'male' values of hierarchy, dominance, and control; and their resulting stance properly can be described as assimilationist *vis-à-vis* the dominant heterosexual male culture.[54] Nor do I claim some 'moral' high ground in this regard. Whether in the workplace, the home, the 'clubs', or on the street, gay men *can* be as uncaring and, indeed, as abusive in their dealings with people as anyone else (and, frankly, sometimes it seems more so). But to link such behaviour primarily to pornography or sadomasochistic sexual practices is dangerous because it can too easily let gay men as a group 'off the hook' (so to speak). Rather than focusing on sexual practices and representations, as gay men we need to examine how we treat our employees, students, co-workers, friends, as well as our sexual partners in our everyday lives, and the extent to which our dealings undermine (or reinforce) systems of gender, racial, and sexual oppression. At a time when right-wing gay men are articulating an explicitly conservative and assimilationist political, social, and sexual agenda, this task has become more pressing.

CONCLUSION

Returning to the decision of the Supreme Court of Canada in *Butler*, it is significant that some commentators (and some judges) seem unable to engage in any kind of reading of gay male pornography other than through the lens of degradation. While issues of reciprocity and shifting identifications of the subject may be argued, such notions are beyond the limits of their recognition. The sexual submission of a male subject necessarily is interpreted as degrading, for no real man can freely abdicate sexual authority to another. It is the degradation, not of the individual, but of the phallus that is at stake. Images of dominance and submission between men are never read in terms of the codes, negotiated limits, or laws that may surround sexual performance. The difficulty in making such legal arguments rests in the failure of many to recognise the complex relationship of law and desire. Gay male pornography is condemned because it represents a transgression to the laws of male power. Yet those representations may operate within the context of a subcultural legal order. In this way, gay male pornography highlights both the lawlessness of sexuality that so often operates within a heterosexual framework and the everyday degradations and undue exploitations that pervade the dominant sexual culture.

5

INSIDE AND OUT OF THE MILITARY

What they're claiming is that us queers are unfit for their beautiful pure Army and Navy – when they ought to be glad to have us.[1]

The constitutionality of classifications based upon sexual orientation is a persistent issue in American constitutional discourse. That is, can the government draw distinctions in law between citizens upon the basis of their 'sexual orientation' without contravening the guarantee in the Bill of Rights of the Equal Protection of the laws? This question continues to prove contentious and vexing for judges. One recurring example in recent years has arisen in the military context – the permissibility of explicit regulations which attempt to exclude lesbians and gay men from serving in the armed forces. The question of the validity of this military policy is interesting, first, because it raises for examination the appropriate level of constitutional scrutiny and the persuasiveness of the state interests used to justify the classification. Second, it warrants analysis because the military context underscores how sexual identity is discursively constructed and controlled through the binary division of inside and out (of the military). In this chapter I attempt to explore how this binary division has been deployed by the judiciary to expel lesbians and gay men from the armed forces, and how this reasoning is developed within the context of Equal Protection analysis in America. In particular, I focus on one judgment which was particularly revealing in its justifications for upholding the military ban on gay personnel and which serves to highlight the overtly politicised role of the American judiciary in this context. I also will attempt to ground the analysis within a historical context by examining how the construction of gays and lesbians as the excluded outsiders from the military is a phenomenon which developed at a particular historical moment. At that point, the military shifted its focus from a sexual act to a sexual identity, and it is that identity – a lesbian or gay identity – rather than a same-sex sexual act which, under this mode of analysis, must be continually erased from the forces.

The policy of excluding lesbians and gay men, while not a recent innovation, first arose within the context of the Second World War.[2] Although the act of sodomy traditionally was prohibited and punishable when engaged in by military personnel (and, for that matter, civilians), the creation of a 'homosexual' identity was linked to the rise of psychiatry as a science and to the belief by some 'reform'-minded psychiatrists that homosexual *persons* should not be punished for their *acts*. They were, however, unfit for military service.[3] The focus thus shifted from the act of sodomy to the creation of an identity which, in fact, might only have a tenuous relationship with the prohibited sex act.[4] This change in emphasis resulted in a vast bureaucratic apparatus designed to eliminate gays from the armed forces:

> The new screening directives and procedures . . . though ineffective in excluding the vast majority of gay men, introduced to the military that homosexuals were unfit to serve in the armed forces because they were mentally ill. The military's more traditional means of handling homosexuality, which operated within its criminal justice system, was to define the sex act as the problem, for which the offender was tried and punished. The idea that homosexuals were mentally ill, on the other hand, defined the person, even when there was no sexual act, as disruptive of morale and unfit to serve. As psychiatrists wrote this idea into military regulations and directives, the belief that gay men and lesbians constituted a class of people who must be excluded from the armed forces became an important part of military policy.[5]

This policy has continued largely unchanged until very recently. Pursuant to the Uniform Code of Military Justice, acts of sodomy – regardless of whether engaged in by same-sex or opposite-sex partners – are outlawed.[6] Furthermore, under Department of Defense policy, anyone who engages in a same-sex sexual act or declares her or his homosexuality has been subject to discharge.[7]

In recent years, the judiciary has adopted a deferential approach to this military policy. Courts traditionally have held that lesbians and gay men do not constitute a category subject to strict judicial scrutiny and that the governmental justifications for the classification survive rational basis analysis. The decision of the District Court for the District of Columbia in *Steffan v. Cheney* exemplifies this reasoning.[8] Moreover, the language utilised by the Court deserves close attention because it masks another, more fundamental, rationale for the decision reached.

THE *STEFFAN* CASE

In March, 1987, Joseph Steffan, a midshipman at the United States Naval Academy, was informed that he was under investigation for allegedly being a 'homosexual'. Steffan was scheduled to graduate from the academy in a few months' time. Apparently, the Naval Investigative Service had been informed that Steffan had told another midshipman of his sexual identity. On 23 March 1987, Steffan was informed that he would not graduate because of Department of Defense regulations dealing with homosexuality.[9] On 1 April 1987, he submitted his qualified resignation to the Naval Academy Academic Board. This was accepted on 6 May 1987 by an Assistant Secretary of the Navy. A year and a half later, in December, 1988, Steffan requested that his resignation be withdrawn in a letter written to the Secretary of the Navy.[10] That request was denied and an action was launched seeking:

> his diploma from the Naval Academy, his commission as an Ensign in the United States Navy, a declaration that his resignation was null and void, and for a declaration that the Department of Defense Directives . . . are violations of the equal protection component of the fifth amendment to the Constitution'.[11]

Joseph Steffan's record in the Academy had been exemplary, a fact which is alluded to in the judgment.[12] As one commentator has described:

> Joseph Steffan was in the top ten of his class of approximately 4,500 midshipmen at the United States Naval Academy. He maintained straight A's in academic performance and in conduct. In his senior year, he was a battalion commander and was responsible for about 800 midshipmen. He was a star athlete in high school, and had twice sung the national anthem at the annual Army–Navy game.[13]

This factual background is crucial to an understanding of the paradox of the case and the decision of the District Court. Steffan had become the quintessential insider at the Naval Academy – an accomplished midshipman with the makings of an exemplary naval officer. He had successfully 'passed' into the confines of the military. Thus, he revealed that, by remaining in the closet, he could become an insider – a member of the military elite. In fact, absent a declaration (a 'coming out'), Steffan was indistinguishable from the norm. Moreover, he distinguished himself and set the standard for a midshipman. This made his presence within the Academy a threat to the military such that his expulsion not only was justified but essential. Steffan's accomplishments dangerously suggested, not that his sexual orientation within the military context necessarily defined him by a lack of subjecthood, but rather that he had to be *constructed* as possessing 'insufficient aptitude to become a commissioned officer in the naval service'.[14] That construction was engaged in because Joseph Steffan highlighted not the marginalisation of gays, but the *centrality* of same-sex bonds and desires within the boundaries of the military. Steffan's coming out publicised and articulated this paradox – that lesbians and gay men have been erased from the armed forces not because of an otherness, but rather due to the fear that the opposite might well be true.

This thesis is borne out by an examination of the District Court's analysis of the Equal Protection issue. First, Judge Gasch considered whether gay men and lesbians constitute a suspect classification demanding heightened constitutional scrutiny. The Court recognised that this inquiry was 'clouded' by the fact that there was no evidence suggesting that Steffan had engaged in any same-sex sexual acts while at the Academy.[15] Consequently, the issue revolved around his 'status as a homosexual',[16] and the Court resolved the question of the appropriate level of judicial scrutiny through the application of the test established in *Bowen v. Gilliard*[17]:

> the plaintiff must: 1) have suffered a history of discrimination; 2) exhibit obvious, immutable, or distinguishing characteristics that define him as a member of a discrete group; and 3) show that the group is a minority or politically powerless, or alternatively show that the statutory classification at issue burdens a fundamental right.[18]

As for the first issue, whether the group has suffered a history of discrimination, the District Court peremptorily concluded that the military's policy of excluding gay persons was not motivated by a discriminatory purpose nor could it be termed invidious. Although this reasoning was not further explained, it foreshadowed what is implicit throughout the judgment, namely, that the motivations of the military are not invidious because of the threat posed to it by gay persons. The nature of the threat was articulated in the consideration of whether a 'homosexual orientation' constitutes a 'distinguishing characteristic'.[19] The Court recognised that 'there is nothing obvious or distinguishing about plaintiff's homosexual orientation which sets him apart' and 'nothing in the record indicates that the plaintiff overtly "exhibited" such a characteristic'.[20] However, the Court did not find Steffan's apparent normalcy to undermine in any way the military's justifications for his personal erasure from the Academy. Indeed, it was because he was indistinguishable that the Court criticised Steffan for keeping his preferences secret (private) 'despite knowing all the while that the DoD [Department of Defense] and the Academy had regulations prohibiting homosexual orientation or conduct'.[21] Thus, the Court applied what Eve Sedgwick has referred to as the 'double bind': Steffan was under a positive *duty* as a member of the military to come out because his gay identity was otherwise undetectable but contrary to regulations. The result of his coming out, though, was his expulsion as unfit for service. Paradoxically, however, in going public he revealed that his sexuality had not rendered him incapable of service. He demonstrated, instead, that absent a public declaration, he remained completely undetectable on the inside of what is, in the end, an institution forged from same-sex bonds.[22]

The Court next considered whether the characteristic of sexual orientation is immutable.[23] Concluding that 'homosexual orientation is neither conclusively mutable nor immutable', the Court held that a gay identity cannot be characterised as an immutable characteristic for the purposes of Equal Protection analysis.[24] Rather, Judge Gasch reasoned that, since sexual orientation 'sometimes is chosen', the closer analogy is to alien adults who are not considered a 'suspect classification'.[25] Once again, despite the conclusory approach of the District Court, the reasoning is far more revealing than was intended. The analogy to aliens is appropriate because the alien is the paradigmatic outsider who has 'passed' within the boundaries of the nation. The alien conjures up images of the foreign, the subversive, the exotic, and the tempting, against which precautions must be taken to ensure that the purity of the nation is maintained.

Similarly, in drawing the analogy between the alien and Steffan, the Court suggested that, like the alien, Steffan is the outsider. He is subversive, potentially seductive and, like the most dangerous alien, he is undetectable without a voluntary declaration of his status. Otherwise, he has the ability to pass undetected.

However, it was in the discussion of the relative political powerlessness of those included within the classification that the lengths to which a court will proceed to reach a result became apparent.[26] Once again, the Court's reasoning is extraordinary. Judge Gasch began with a judgment as to the political power of homosexuals as a group in American society: 'it is still very clear that homosexuals as a class enjoy a good deal of political power in our society, not only with respect to themselves, but also with respect to issues of the day that affect them'.[27] The Court pointed out, in a footnote, that the Aids crisis has demonstrated the political power of the gay community: 'homosexual groups have been well publicized, heard and heeded by the political branches of our federal, state and local governments when it has come to dealing with the HIV epidemic'.[28] The Court further reasoned that the political power of the gay community was apparent from the fact that 'references to sexual orientation, sexual preference and Aids show up from time to time in the law of the various states, localities, and in the federal law'.[29] Little if any evidence was provided as to whether and how such references are politically empowering to gays. Rather, the absence of a complete erasure of identity became sufficient to constitute political power for the purposes of Equal Protection analysis. Power is thereby equated with the ability to gain attention. Of course, this ignores, first, the question whether the gay community as a practical matter could have exerted any political pressure on the military in its formulation of the regulations. Second, as a historical issue, the proposition is open to scepticism. In the military context, the recognition of a homosexual identity in the public sphere was not a result of political power, but instead was a deeply oppressive means of expelling lesbians and gay men from the armed forces. During the Second World War, the presence of the homosexual within political discourse had harshly negative results for gay military personnel:

> When previously only those men who had been caught in the sexual act and convicted in court were punished, now merely being homosexual or having such "tendencies" could entrap both men and women, label them as sick, and remove them from the service with an undesirable discharge . . . Their new "crime" was belonging to a class of people that the discharge policies deemed "undesirable" while denying them the rights to which they would have been entitled had they been defendants formally charged with a criminal act.[30]

The extent of discrimination and oppression against lesbians and gay men during the Second World War, when the precursor to the regulations at issue in the *Steffan* case first appeared, was extraordinary and demonstrated a virtually complete lack of political power to remedy the situation. This was precisely because of the diffuse and anonymous composition of the group. Classification by government allowed for the identification and oppression of lesbian and gay persons, and the bureaucratic creation of a homosexual identity was the means whereby an unsuccessful attempt was made to remove individuals from the military establishment.

The Court, though, ignored this history of powerlessness by instead drawing a revealing analogy between homosexuals and the aged. The Court reasoned that as heightened scrutiny was not extended to the 'aging and the mentally retarded'[31], so too there was no justification for heightened judicial scrutiny with respect to classifications based upon sexual orientation:

> nothing has been presented . . . which suggests a difference relevant to an equal protection analysis between those with a homosexual orientation and the aging, for example. Both classes have suffered historical discrimination on a variety of levels in society and in many forms. Both characteristics which define the class are arguably immutable. And it is argued that both groups suffer from underrepresentation in Congress and general political powerlessness.[32]

The analogy between gay persons and the aged merits scrutiny. The glaring flaw is that the status of being aged is one that, although not everyone will experience, everyone is *capable* of experiencing, assuming that a premature death does not intervene. On the other hand, only a minority of persons come to identify themselves as lesbian or gay in our culture. Consequently, while everyone has some stake in securing political rights for the aged, there is no analogous degree of political power for lesbians and gay men.

However, on another level, the Court might well be correct in how it draws the comparison. For the analogy to hold, it becomes necessary to argue that the potential exists for everyone to experience the status at issue. While not everyone will be an aged person, any individual *might* some day find her or himself in that role. By analogy, presumably everyone must have the capacity and the potential to be cast in the role of the homosexual or, at a minimum, to engage in same-sex sexual acts. If this is what underpins the argument, then Steffan's expulsion is far more understandable. If everyone has the capacity to engage in same-sex acts, the rigorous separation of act from identity becomes crucial.[33] Otherwise, the assumption of a gay identity would assume a naturalness analogous to ageing (or, alternatively, would reveal that all '"classifications" are highly contingent products of social relations').[34] As Bérubé has thoroughly documented, in the military context of the Second World War, same-sex(ual) activities were prevalent amongst military personnel, which underscored the nexus between the same-sex environment of the military and homosexual acts. To the extent that the presence of Steffan within the Naval Academy provided a bridge between act and identity, he revealed the social contingency of all identity concepts.

Thus, the District Court's analogy has an unintended persuasiveness. If the potential for assuming a gay identity is ever present, then the question of mutability of the characteristic assumes a new valence. The issue no longer is the immutability of homosexuality. It becomes instead the mutability of heterosexuality:

A key rationale for antihomosexual discrimination, then, is anxiety about the ambiguity of heterosexual interactions, about a potential for mutability that undermines heterosexual identity. Lest the change actually take place, "known" homosexuals must be segregated.[35]

Having made his identity known, Steffan's 'outness' demanded that he be put out of the military because his status revealed the extent to which he had been inside all along. His infiltration was demonstrated not only by his accomplishments, but also by the degree to which his identity, rather than being a minority one, assumed a centrality – an identity to which anyone potentially might be seduced simply by its articulation. Thus, the Court inadvertently makes its case against heightened scrutiny through the inside–outside dichotomy. The extent to which Steffan proved himself an insider, despite the construction of his status as outsider, demonstrated that his identity, rather than being marginal, was silenced because it was central to the military establishment. That centrality must be decentred by the Court in order to reestablish the separation between the homo-social environment of the military, same-sex sexual acts, and a gay identity.

In fact, this explanation underscores the Court's consideration of whether a 'rational basis' exists for the exclusion of lesbians and gay men from the military. The Court focused, in its discussion of the rationality of the military policy, upon whether the presence of gays 'seriously impairs the accomplishment of the military mission', referring to the relevant Department of Defense Directives:

The presence of such members adversely affects the ability of the Military Services to maintain discipline, good order, and morale; to foster mutual trust and confidence among servicemembers, to ensure the integrity of the system of rank and command; to facilitate assignment and worldwide deployment of servicemembers who frequently must live and work under close conditions affording minimal privacy; to recruit and retain members of the Military Services; to maintain the public acceptability of military service; and to prevent breaches of security.[36]

As a factual question, it is highly doubtful whether the presence of gays in the military has done anything to undermine the military mission. As Bérubé has argued, lesbians and gay men performed a wide variety of tasks as military personnel during the Second World War and, indeed, the record of Steffan undermines the very argument that is made to justify his exclusion. Moreover, as for the maintenance of the public acceptability of military service, there are fundamental problems in upholding this rationale. The Court posited that 'if . . . many would find the Navy's approval of a homosexual orientation among its fighting forces to be morally offensive, then it is not prejudice which is re-sponsible for the regulations, but rather a standard of morality'.[37] However, as some commentators and courts have recognised, 'stripped to their core, the military's regulations do nothing more than allow societal prejudice against lesbians and gay men to dictate the exclusion of talented people from military service to their country'.[38] Furthermore, even under a rational basis level of scrutiny, prejudice is not, by definition, a rational basis upon which to create a classification for the purposes of decision-making.[39] Thus, as a doctrinal matter, the issue can be restated as whether:

> military necessity is so compelling that it requires permitting the military to make a classification using prejudice as the only justification. To permit such a result would be to legitimize the use of *irrational* relationships to military necessity to outweigh the equal protection rights of individuals.[40]

The failure of the District Court in *Steffan v. Cheney* to interrogate the rationality of the military classification is reflective of the Court's own irrationality in its approach to the issue. The tenor of the judgment focuses on the awesome, seductive power of Steffan's sexuality which demands his expulsion from the military. Throughout the judgment it is apparent that the seductive potential of Steffan to corrupt the purity of the military mission provides the 'rational' basis for the classification. The Court is explicit in its development of this justification. Although there is no evidence in the record that Steffan engaged in same-sex sexual acts while in the Naval Academy, he 'could one day have acted on his preferences in violation of regulations prohibiting such conduct'.[41] Of course, the regulations themselves provide that a same-sex sexual act in itself may not necessarily lead to discharge, which problematises that argument.[42] This reasoning implies that the danger rests, not so much in Steffan's seduction of a heterosexual soldier into a same-sex sexual *act*, but lies instead in the seductiveness of his identity as a gay man.

Moreover, a gay identity comes to be described in the language, not only of seduction, but also of infection. The Court reasoned that a rational basis for expulsion could be traced to the danger of HIV infection from gay to heterosexual soldiers:

> To be sure, there is no evidence in this case about the plaintiff having had sex with anybody, male or female. But the defendants' policy of excluding homosexuals is rational in that it is directed, in part, at preventing those who are at the greatest risk of dying of AIDS from serving in the Navy and other armed services. This is understandable in light of the overall military mission of defending the Nation. The interest we as a Nation have in a healthy military cannot be underestimated or discounted.[43]

The implications of this statement far exceed its literal meaning. First, as a factual matter, the Court makes no distinction between gay men and lesbians, who belong to completely different risk groups for HIV. Second, the creation of the category is unnecessarily over-inclusive because, even assuming the Court's premise that there is a rational interest in excluding HIV-infected persons from the military (itself a highly dubious proposition), the alternative is to classify all military personnel based upon HIV status, rather than upon sexuality. On a metaphorical level, however, the argument takes on a far more provocative logic.

The metaphor of disease and infection is an often used means of creating the image of the polluted outsider waiting to infect the inside of the body politic: 'the metaphor implements the way particularly dreaded diseases are envisaged as an alien "other", as enemies are in modern war'.[44] As Mary Douglas has argued in a different context, 'physical crossing of the social barrier is treated as a dangerous pollution . . . The pollution becomes a doubly wicked object of reprobation, first because he crossed the line and second because he endangered others'.[45]

It is worth noting how the language of the court takes on a tone of nationalism and boundary-crossing in its discussion of HIV and gays. The infection, though, must be read not simply as a fear of Aids, but as a fear of infection of the atmosphere of the military with the spectre of a gay identity. The underlying concern, then, is that the homosocial bonds of military service might be *read* as, in some sense, 'homoerotic' or worse, gay. The metaphorical use of disease provides the means to create an image of the outsider, and the language of the Court alternates between military and national outsider – which further enhances Steffan's subversiveness. A gay identity thus is inscribed with an otherness through its equation with the diseased body, which itself is constructed as other to the healthy American body. The sexual subject, the national subject and the healthy subject all come to be assimilated with each other and Joseph Steffan (who earlier in the judgment was described in terms suggesting the quintessential insider) is constructed as foreign to any and all of these subjectivities.

The rationality of the classification of gays as unfit for military service stems precisely from their lack of the qualities of subjecthood. That otherness must be continually constructed in opposition to a universal subject because of the threat posed by lesbians and gay men to the boundaries through which the sexual subject, the military, and the body politic are constituted. Joseph Steffan was defined as the outsider because of his ability to pass – to reveal, through the articulation of a gay identity, that he was an insider all along. However, in assimilating the military with the nation, Steffan is further constructed, not as *being* an insider but as performing the role of the insider – as an espionage agent might perform a role to undermine national security.[46] The underlying concern, then, is not simply that Steffan had successfully performed the role until his own revelation, but that his success revealed the performativity of the military subject.[47] That is, the military subject, like all subjectivities, is established and maintained through its repetition. It thus became essential for the military and for the Court to restore the naturalness and coherence of the subject and to expel Steffan from the inside out. In the process of coming out, Steffan revealed not only that he had been acting the role of insider all along, but that, as a gay man, he had proved a better actor than many others. Finally, Joseph Steffan forced the Court itself to come out actively to engage in the ongoing constitution of the military subject as heterosexual, healthy, and American.

AFTERWORD

Since the decision of the District Court in *Steffan v. Cheney*, much has happened. The election of the Clinton Administration put the 'gays and the military' issue squarely on the political agenda. Despite his pledge to remove the ban on lesbians, gay men, and bisexuals from serving in the armed forces, political, military, and public pressure forced the administration to adopt the now famous 'don't ask, don't tell' policy.[48] Under this policy, presumably, Joseph Steffan would not have been asked about his sexual orientation by commanding officers. Moreover, he would be expected to refrain from divulging it in the military context.

The constitutionality of the policy even after the change in direction implemented under President Clinton, remains a contentious legal issue.[49] In November, 1993, the United States Court of Appeals reversed the decision of Judge Gasch. Mikva C.J., writing for a three-member panel, held that the Department of Defense directives were unconstitutional.[50] The Court avoided the issue of whether sexual orientation amounts to a suspect or 'quasi suspect' legal classification, finding instead that the regulations could not withstand rational basis review. Mikva C.J. reasoned that from a person's status alone, sexual misconduct could not be imputed and to do so would be 'illegitimate as a matter of law'.[51] Second, concerns about morale, discipline, and recruitment could not justify the policy, since these reasons all were based upon prejudice: 'a cardinal principle of equal protection law holds that the government cannot discriminate against a certain class in order to give effect to the prejudice of others'.[52] The Court also dealt summarily with the HIV justification which had been raised by Judge Gasch, finding it an 'illegitimate assumption'.[53] Finally, the threat of blackmail of lesbian and gay members of the forces was rejected, Mikva C.J. concluding that the directives themselves created such a risk.[54]

That judgment of the panel of three subsequently was 'vacated' and the case was reheard by the entire Court of Appeal bench for the District of Columbia circuit. By a majority of seven to three, the Court affirmed the original judgment in the District Court which upheld the constitutionality of the government regulations pursuant to which Steffan was dismissed from the Naval Academy.[55] Judge Silberman, for the majority, began from the assumption that the 'regulations would be serving a legitimate purpose by excluding those who engage in homosexual conduct or who intend to do so'.[56] The question of law then becomes whether the discharge of a midshipman who describes himself as a 'homosexual' is rational in constitutional terms.[57] The majority answered in the affirmative that an inference could reasonably be drawn 'that when a member states that he is a homosexual, that member means that he either engages or is likely to engage in homosexual conduct'.[58] A statement of (homo)sexual identity thus can be used by the military as a 'proxy' for (homo)sexual conduct.[59]

In dissent, Judge Wald framed the issue as the constitutionality of excluding a class of individuals from the services defined by homosexual orientation, rather than conduct.[60] She found the 'transforming' of a statement of orientation into a declaration of past or future conduct to be constitutionally impermissible.[61] Judge Wald held that 'since a decision not to act is within the control of the individual servicemember . . . it is not rational to assume that he will choose to engage in conduct that would subject him to discharge or even incarceration'.[62]

Joseph Steffan chose not to launch a bid to appeal against the decision to the United States Supreme Court, thereby ending this particular judicial saga.[63]

6

EQUALITY RIGHTS, IDENTITY POLITICS, AND THE CANADIAN NATIONAL IMAGINATION

In this chapter I continue to focus upon the issue of lesbians and gay men in the armed services and the connections between that policy issue and the construction of national identity. In the 1990s, identity has become the centrepiece of theoretical work in a variety of disciplines. We now know that, in the conditions of late modern (or postmodern) society, identity is complex – it is fragmented, intersected, subject to alteration, socially constructed, and it exhibits only a partial fixity at any moment. Most important, identities are to be valued, respected, and understood on their own terms. However, we also have relearned (if we ever forgot) that identities can be dangerous and fatal, especially when they coalesce in the form of nationalism. My focus thus remains on nationalism and sexuality. In particular, I explore the intersection of nationalism and identity in the Canadian context and will use as an example to explore these broad issues the constitutional recognition of 'sexual orientation' as a prohibited ground of discrimination. The Canadian context thus highlights a very different approach from that of America in terms of how sexual orientation is treated in constitutional law. Unlike America, where distinctions in law based on sexual orientation in general have been upheld as 'rational' and not subjected to rigorous judicial examination, in Canada the trend in recent years has been to find such distinctions to amount to constitutionally impermissible discrimination.

My reasons for focusing on sexual orientation in this particular legal context are twofold. First, it is interesting because of the relatively recent fairly broad acceptance within legal discourse of sexual orientation as a protected category under the Canadian *Charter of Rights and Freedoms*. I will argue that the Charter itself, and particularly its equality provisions (section 15), ensures the protection and development of newly emerging identities. The Charter can be viewed through the lens of postmodernism, and specifically, postmodern notions of identity. Sexual orientation represents an identity which has come to be legally recognised despite the fact that it is not an explicitly prohibited ground of discrimination under section 15.

Second, I focus on sexual orientation because, as an amalgam of identities, it presents a study in the transgressive power of 'new' identities to shift the frontiers and borders of citizenship and nationalism. If the Western nation has been defined and maintained by the creation of a devalued other placed outside the boundaries of the state, then one such expulsion, as I have argued earlier, traditionally has been the 'homosexual'. Once sexual orientation is accepted as an illegitimate basis of discrimination and recognised as a legal, political, and cultural identity worthy of protection, then the definition of citizenship (and correspondingly the composition of the nation) broadens and deepens along sexual lines.

I also will argue that Canada may be particularly situated to further the postmodern political agenda of facilitating democratic dialogue across an ever-expanding range of identities. This is because Canadian nationalism itself is signified in part by its own otherness – an absence of essential definition that creates space for identities which are articulated from the vantage point of social groups. Indeed, such group identities can come to be defined in nationalistic terms. Thus, 'Canadian' becomes an identity open to resignification and inter-section through an ever-increasing variety of perspectives engaged in a dialogue guaranteed by the Canadian *Charter of Rights and Freedoms*.

In the end, this openness of the Canadian identity leaves it both a source of great potential and peril. Ultimately, the issue is whether Canada can survive given its awareness of a lack of essence. In other words, is a sense of oneself as multiplicitous and provisional sufficient to provide the centrifugal force to prevent complete fragmentation along the lines of the various identities of which the state is composed? The postmodern option of democratic dialogue, I will argue in conclusion, may provide the only alternative to the violence of rupture that today is so readily associated with the disintegration of states in the name of national aspiration.

A POSTMODERN IDENTITY POLITICS

Throughout this chapter, I focus upon an identity politics which I label 'post-modern'. In so doing, I synthesise a cluster of ideas concerning identities, politics and rights which increasingly are applied within legal discourse.[1] The premise is that the process of identity formation is continually engaged by the individual subject and moreover is politically charged. Thus, there is a politics of identity which centres upon the plurality of subject positions through which each indi-vidual is constituted. Identity politics focuses on 'the fields in which power is thought to operate, and critically analyses in terms of domination the various universal identities now associated with modernism'.[2] The universal standpoint is rejected in favour of the multiplicity of viewpoints and intersections of dif-ference that better reflect the conflictual nature of identity and 'highlights that each person is embedded in a matrix of social and psychological factors that interact in different contexts'.[3] Identity necessarily is contingent, shifting, open to revision, unstable, and dependent upon the relationship of current and future political allegiances. Identity politics also is identified with the 'project of building new political groupings with categories neglected in previous modern politics . . . identity politics attempts to mobilize a politics based on the construction of political and cultural identities through political struggle and commitment'.[4] Law and the legal discourse of equality rights provides a forum in which that political struggle involving newly emerging identities and social movements can occur.[5]

Much of the theoretical grounding for this postmodern explication of identity and subjecthood has been undertaken by Laclau and Mouffe.[6] As I discussed in Chapter 1, they argue not only that identities are formed by the exercise of power in oppressive ways, but also that the formation of new identities can be undertaken by oppressed groups. If subjecthood is plural – a point of merging of a variety of subject positions which come to be articulated through discourse – then it is only through the conditions of political struggle that identities are established in any particular configuration. Crucially, Laclau and Mouffe argue that the political system never achieves a total closure that prevents the development of new and politically resistant identities articulated in the social arena.

The analysis has implications for a progressive political project, the goal of which becomes the establishment of a precarious and constructed unity amongst the constantly emerging partial identities of social subjects. This approach claims an anti-essentialist stance in its articulation of the 'precarious character of every identity and the impossibility of fixing the sense of the "elements" in any ultimate literality.'[7] At the same time, articulation of identities itself organises and constitutes social relations 'as a means for refusing the acceptability of any pre-existing notion of the social totality'.[8]

Under a postmodern interrogation, then, identity ceases to hold any 'naturalness' or essence:

the appearance of a new identity is not inevitable or determined, not something that was always there simply waiting to be expressed, not something that will always exist in the form it was given in a particular political movement or at a particular historical moment.[9]

The subject also is capable of intervention in the process through self-definition and articulation. As Judith Butler has recognised, the 'subject is neither a ground nor a product, but the permanent possibility of a certain resignifying process'.[10] This openness to resignification is explained in terms of the necessity of a devalued other against which identities are constituted and continually maintained, and the other in turn may subvert the identity through its own articulation. This relationship of mututal dependence results in instability.

CANADA: THE FIRST POSTMODERN STATE?

Having examined the construction of individual and group identities within the conditions of postmodernity, I turn now to the construction of the national identity. Specifically, I examine why it may be appropriate to draw upon post-modern theories of identity within the context of the *Canadian* identity. What is particular about Canada that might facilitate the articulation of identities and the development of Laclau and Mouffe's radical democratic pluralism? The answer might be found in the construction of the *national* identity. To the extent that a Canadian national identity is recognised as socially constructed, contingent and transformable, Canadian society may assume an openness to new identities. In other words, if the Canadian identity has been less than successful in fixing upon an other, there may be a greater openness to the articulation of many conflicting identities defined by membership in the Canadian community. Identity thus becomes an open site for the contestation over the national imaginary.

Like all processes of identity formation, the construction of a national identity has been dependent upon the constitution of the coherent national subject. That subject must be continually recreated to prevent the erosion of its essential appearance. Its construction is dependent upon the other and yet, because the construction of identity is never total, national identity also is under constant threat from the appearance of the other within its own borders.[11] Yet, there is no single element against which nationality is defined.[12] The maintenance of national identity demands an obsessive focus upon the essence of nation.[13] It requires the creation of national boundaries against which one may be inside or out depending upon the location of an identity within the grid of nationalism. Through the narrative trope of nationalism, a disembodied and abstract national subject is maintained with varying degrees of success.[14] Those others within the physical borders of the nation, but defined as outside its social construction, thus are alien to the nation and disenfranchised from the national identity. As Donald Pease has argued, the success of the construction of nationhood depends upon the ability to take on this essentialist tone:

> When understood from within the context of the construction of an imagined national community, the negative class, race, and gender categories of these subject peoples were not a historical aberration but a structural necessity for the construction of a national narrative whose coherence depended upon the internal opposition between Nature's Nation and peoples understood to be constructed of a "different nature".[15]

Of course, the boundaries of nationality and citizenship retain a measure of openness to the incorporation of new citizens. The nation thus is in a 'process of hybridity' by which new peoples are integrated while the nation maintains an essential appearance.[16] The frontiers of nationhood thus are capable of fluctuation as new identities are allowed space within the narrative of nationalism.

Postmodern theory has responded to this construction of national boundaries. Instead of fixed borders through which new identities may be permitted to enter and assume the badge of nationalism, postmoderns seek to reveal the national identity as a permanent site of contestation over content. The nation thus is exposed as provisional and subject to redefinition:

> the national subjects, who had previously derived their sense of identity

from incomplete identification with the meta-social subject of the national narrative, could become dislocated from this structure and could rediscover national identity itself as a permanent instability, an endless antagonism between figures integrated within ever changing social imaginaries and singularities forever external to them.[17]

The nation becomes a site of potential antagonism between competing social imaginaries emerging from the 'cultural difference and the heterogeneous histories of contending peoples, antagonistic authorities, and tense cultural locations'.[18] Under this pluralistic approach, narratives from new, previously unheard voices appear, articulating: 'counter-narratives of the nation that continually evoke and erase its totalizing boundaries – both actual and conceptual – [and] disturb those ideological manoeuvres through which "imagined communities" are given essentialist identities'.[19] The borderland between the national self and the other thus is wrenched open, undermining the essence of nationhood. The narratives of nationalism that emerge, for example, from some new social movements may challenge the unitary and totalising voice of 'the people'. Within the conditions of late modern society, a shift may be experienced away from the homogeneity of the discourse of nationalism towards a politics open to non-assimilationist claims of difference. These claims redefine the national subject itself, as the nation becomes a performative space for the articulation of competing visions.

A postmodern nationalism, then, is cognisant of its social construction and the contingency of its identity. The rigidity of the borders between the self of a nation and its others is relaxed. The focus shifts from the inside/outside dichotomy to the relationship of social subjects articulating different visions in an ongoing dialogic relationship. Cultural specificity thus is not surrendered through assimilation.[20] From this reworking of nationalism emerges a new vision of citizenship which is not dependent upon the exclusive identification of the subject with the nation. Instead, a shared notion of citizenship could develop based upon the articulation of competing identities.

Postmodern national identity has a particular relevance to Canadian nationalism. The success of Canada as a postmodern state is tied to its failure as a modernist nation. If a nation is ineluctably shaped by what it opposes, then, for example, English-speaking Canadian identity now may be shaped most strongly in opposition to the American national identity. However, English-speaking Canadians are aware of themselves as other to what appears a stable, totalising American nationalism. At the same time, the relationship of English-speaking Canadian and Quebecois identity depends upon each as other. Thus, it is difficult to speak of a Canadian national identity if it is composed of at least two different *national* imaginaries. Quebec, as the focus of a Francophone identity, understandably has a more fixed political identity given the clearer contrast to an other – namely, English-speaking Canada.

From this provisionality in the Canadian identity there may be found within the fabric of Canadian life a greater willingness to incorporate new social movements and identities in terms of national citizenship. The signifier 'Canadian' displays a greater openness to reworking as a result of an awareness that it is highly contingent and socially constructed. I fully accept that Canadian history is replete with examples of the oppression of identities which have been defined as outside the Canadian national community. The aboriginal peoples provide a stark example of how the rights of citizenship in both a formal and substantive sense have been denied. My claim, however, is that the Canadian national imaginary displays an instability which leaves it particularly open to contestation. The contingency of the national sign facilitates the articulation of competing identities deploying the language of nationalism. The use of the term 'First Nations', the existence of a Quebec national identity, or other regional/provincial identities which come to be articulated in nationalistic terms, exemplifies this phenomenon. Nationalism thus can be appropriated and is never essentially fixed. This is the symptom of politics in late modern society: 'a politics in which no political subjects are privileged, identities are never essentially fixed (or fixed by any essence), and the signifiers mobilized to achieve recognition have no intrinsically progressive or reactionary character'.[21] No nation can ever completely close its borders and achieve a 'holistic, representative vision of society' by denying the incorporation of new people into the field of citizenship.[22] Yet, there appears to be a 'difference' within the Canadian context. As Rosemary Coombe has argued, it is from 'the original "lack" (of meaning) which underpins the identity "Canadian" [that] is the source and the site for hegemonic articulations'.[23] Identity thus not only is defined by an otherness, but more generally by an absence. Thus, while there may be an obsession with national boundaries within the Canadian psyche, it stems from a self-reflexive awareness of the provisionality of national identity within our cultural and political conditions.

RETHINKING CANADIAN EQUALITY LAW

In this section, I apply this postmodern framework to the interpretation of the equality provisions of the Canadian *Charter of Rights and Freedoms*. Canadian equality law is specifically aimed at those groups who have suffered historical or social disadvantage. Indeed, I want to suggest that the focus is on those defined as other to the universal subject. What do the political conditions of postmodernity imply then about how a right to equality is conceived within Canada? In answer, I argue that they provide a political and cultural explanation for why Canadian equality rights are interpreted in an open-ended fashion, and provide the basis for a broader understanding of equality in terms of the contestation of identities. A recognition that all identities, including the national identity itself, are socially constructed suggests a conscious openness to the interpretation of rights within the Canadian constitutional framework. As Nitya Duclos has argued, 'quests for essences and identities, for simple universal rules, for tidy labels and determinate definitions (of equality or feminism or Canada) grounded in a fixed and finite (constitutional) set of ideals must be relinquished.'[24] If there is relatively little closure of the Canadian national identity, so too there can be no essential determinate definition of what constitutes equality, no universal rules that are applicable devoid of context. The grand narrative of equality or nationhood gives way to the ongoing revision of the national identity through numerous (and sometimes antagonistic) local discourses of what constitutes Canada.[25]

By way of background, it is important that the equality guarantees within the Charter have facilitated an open-ended interpretation by which individuals, as members of groups not explicitly recognised within the Canadian Constitution, can claim rights to equality before and under the law. The wording of section 15 of the Charter allows for this interpretation.[26] From the outset, the Supreme Court of Canada has interpreted the equality guarantees in what it has called a purposive fashion. In *Andrews v. Law Society of British Columbia*,[27] the first case in which section 15 was interpreted, Justice MacIntyre, for the Court, elaborated upon the meaning of discrimination for the purposes of Charter interpretation:

> I would say then that discrimination may be described as a distinction, whether intentional or not but based on grounds relating to personal characteristics of the individual or group, which has the effect of imposing burdens, obligations, or disadvantages on such individual or group not imposed upon others, or which withholds or limits access to opportunities, benefits, and advantages available to other members of society.[28]

From this definition of discrimination, the Supreme Court developed an approach to section 15 which turns on whether the claim rests upon grounds either enumerated within section 15 or analogous to those enumerated grounds (race, national or ethnic origin, colour, religion, sex, age, or mental or physical disability). Thus, an analogy must be drawn between the enumerated ground and the unenumerated basis in terms of the historical or social disadvantage due to discriminatory treatment which has been suffered by individuals because of membership in the group.

The focus on analogous grounds leaves open the expansion of the bases upon which unconstitutional discriminatory treatment may be found. This was explicitly recognised by Justice Wilson of the Supreme Court, writing in the *Andrews* case:

> I believe also that it is important to note that the range of discrete and insular minorities has changed and will continue to change with changing political and social circumstances . . . It can be anticipated that the discrete and insular minorities of tomorrow will include groups not recognized as such today. It is consistent with the constitutional status of s.15 that it be interpreted with sufficient flexibility to ensure the 'unremitting protection' of equality rights in the years to come.[29]

As Justice Wilson described, the question whether a group qualifies as analogous depends upon 'the context of the place of the group in the entire social, political and legal fabric of our society'.[30] Thus, disadvantaged groups, whose basis of identification is not explicitly recognised in section 15, may still have recourse through the courts.

For example, the question whether sexual orientation constitutes a recognised basis of discrimination for the purposes of section 15 provides a clear case of some courts' willingness to expand the range of protected grounds pursuant to which governmental discrimination is unconstitutional. After some initial hesitation, the uncontroverted trend in the law has been to hold that sexual orientation provides an analogous ground included within the rubric of section 15. The Supreme Court of Canada has now, in fact, confirmed this view as correct. In *Haig v. Canada (Minister of Justice)*,[31] the Ontario Court of Appeal considered whether the absence of sexual orientation from the list of proscribed grounds of discrimination in section 3 of the Canadian *Human Rights Act* was discriminatory as contrary to section 15. The factual context of the case concerned the dismissal of a Canadian Armed Forces officer on the basis of his sexual orientation. The Ontario Court of Appeal held, first, that the requisite degree of social disadvantage to justify inclusion within section 15 was met by the category of sexual orientation:

> The social context which must be considered includes the pain and humiliation undergone by homosexuals by reason of prejudice towards them. It also includes the enlightened evolution of human rights social and legislative policy in Canada, since the end of the Second World War, both provincially and federally. The failure to provide an avenue of redress for prejudicial treatment of homosexual members of society, and the possible inference from the omission that such treatment is acceptable, create the effect of discrimination offending s. 15(1) of the Charter.[32]

The Court held that the Canadian *Human Rights Act* must 'be interpreted, applied and administered as though it contained "sexual orientation" as a prohibited ground of discrimination'.[33] Thus, by virtue of the analogous grounds approach, sexual orientation comes to be 'read in' as a prohibited ground of discrimination under federal human rights law.

The general approach adopted by the courts and its specific application to discrimination on the basis of sexual orientation suggests a willingness to recognise emergent identities within constitutional discourse and to protect those who so identify themselves through the equality guarantees of the Charter. While not all judges are sympathetic to this approach, significant legal advances have been made. As Justice Wilson suggested in *Andrews*, the adaptability of what constitutes a 'discrete and insular minority' leaves section 15 open as an avenue of action for some new social movements as they coalesce and articulate demands. However, within the interpretation of section 15, a tension exists between the capacity for growth and development of grounds for discrimination and a fixity or 'immutability' demanded of the group. That is, the 'personal characteristic' to which equality rights attach sometimes is explained and justified on the basis of the difficulty of altering the characteristic. For example, in *Veysey v. Commissioner of the Correctional Service of Canada*,[34] a case which involved an application by an inmate of a correctional facility to participate in a family visitation program with a same-sex partner, the Federal Court Trial Division held that sexual orientation satisfied the test of analogous grounds. The Court relied in part upon the fact that sexual orientation was found sufficiently *immutable* to constitute a characteristic analogous to the enumerated bases of discrimination.[35] Thus, while the categories of discrimination are never closed, they might be limited to the extent that the characteristic must be found unalterable. It may be that the analogous grounds test demands that a characteristic cannot be described as assumed at will. Rather, the fact that sexual orientation, in the eyes of the judiciary, appears unalterable, fixed and central to identity, likely is foundational to the willingness to accept it as a prohibited ground of discrimination. This approach can be contrasted to the American Equal Protection jurisprudence, which I described in Chapter 5. American courts in general have displayed a reluctance to find governmental classifications based upon sexual orientation to be subject to heightened judicial scrutiny, reasoning that the characteristic is not necessarily immutable.

Furthermore, Canadian courts have been impressed with arguments relating to a historical pattern of discrimination. For example, in *Veysey* the Court reasoned that a history of prejudice was of particular relevance:

> Another characteristic common to the enumerated grounds is that the individuals or groups involved have been victimized or stigmatized throughout history because of prejudice, mostly based on fear or ignorance, as most prejudices are. This characteristic would also clearly apply to sexual orientation, or more precisely to those who have deviated from accepted sexual norms, at least in the eyes of the majority.[36]

This appeal to history may provide a further limitation upon the availability of the protection of the equality guarantees. A focus on historical disadvantage obviously demands that the characteristic has some historical grounding. In other words, if one is dealing with a new social movement, the reasoning suggests that the characteristic must have some historical recognition as a feature central to identity and that it has been socially disadvantaged. In terms of the postmodern focus on the provisionality and contingency of identities, the emphasis upon both history and immutability is problematic. It seems to demand a transhistorical and unalterable essence.

Despite these tensions, in my view the postmodern conception of identities can assist in understanding the goals of equality rights in Canada. This re-examination of equality through the lens of postmodernism leads to an understanding of rights that focuses on dialogue and the articulation of shifting and emerging identities. As I argued in Chapter 1, in the context of speech rights in America, that dialogue dispels, to some extent, the dichotomy of self–other which is the basis upon which identities have been maintained. Through a communicative ethics that demands a responsibility to the other, a politics of difference and multiplicity may replace a vision of rights that is reproduced from a universal standpoint. The emphasis of equality rights, then, is on the expression of identities defined in terms of difference. Moreover, a community can envision rights as a means to nourish the development of newly emergent group identities. A common communal identity thereby comes to be centred on differences within and amongst the membership – on the multiplicity of subject positions that make up the community and the individuals within it.

This relationship of identities has ramifications for our understanding of a sexual identity. In particular, the debate between social constructionist and essentialist theories of sexuality can be addressed.[37] The focus on difference, contingency and redefinition suggests that a sexual identity, like all other identities, has a constructedness that is open to alteration. Homosexuality as an identity concept thus can be taken 'into the realm of social and discursive formations'.[38] Many theorists of sexuality have argued that the 'homosexual' identity is a product of a particular historical period and its coherence is undercut by the postmodern challenge to the stability of all identity categories. Indeed, we have entered a period in which a gay identity increasingly is given articulation and is open to expression in new forms. A gay identity may become unstable and provisional, and it may prove to be the paradigmatic postmodern identity:

> Framing gay identity as an emerging sociohistorical event, as an unstable contestable institutional/discursive production and strategy, provided gays with a rationale to begin seeing themselves as having multiple identities, recognizing multiple, sometimes contradictory positions of social power and oppression, and seeing their own fight for sexual/social empowerment as connected to struggles around gender, race, ethnicity, class, and so on.[39]

Through a focus on contingency, one can avoid the totalising of sexuality and sexual practices as identity categories. As Steven Epstein has argued, 'deviant identities are particularly likely to assume totalizing dimensions: all behavior of persons so categorized becomes interpreted by others through the prism of the perceived difference'.[40] In other words, a social constructionist understanding of sexuality contests the singularity of sexuality as an identity category. This is closely related to the postmodern focus on identity as multiplicitous, constructed, and a product of discourse.

If this framework demands that 'we must be able to speak of sexually based group identities without assuming *either* that the group has some mystical or biological unity, or that the "group" doesn't exist', then a focus on immutability in the analysis of sexual orientation is theoretically misplaced.[41] On the other hand, the willingness of social actors to accept discrimination on the basis of sexual orientation as illegitimate in part results from the acceptance of essentialist arguments concerning the 'nature' of homosexuality. Specifically, lesbians and gay men 'deserve' legal protection because of the immutability of the identity category (i.e. 'we can't help who we are') and the history of prejudice and discrimination (i.e. 'homosexuals have been persecuted'). While I fully accept

111

and experience the continued existence of prejudice against lesbians and gay men at all levels of society, a focus on history reinforces the category of the homosexual as unchanging, static and historically and culturally invariant. In other words, it reproduces a totalising, and essentialist conception of identity.

At the same time, the use of essentialist arguments continues to have a resonance and persuasiveness. Moreover, reliance upon essentialist claims of sexuality may lead to legal advances. Carole Vance has identified this phenomenon in the American legal and political context:

> gay politicos and lobbyists find it helpful in the short run to respond with assertions about gays through the ages, to assert a claim to a natural group status, and to insist that being gay is an essential, inborn trait about which there is no choice . . . By dint of repetition, ideas about gay essentialism were reinforced in the contemporary gay movement (though they were hardly unknown in American culture) and, more importantly, linked to group advancement, success and self-affirmation.[42]

The tension between constructionist and essentialist understandings of sexuality in legal discourse is understandable. By articulating a group identity – a difference from the background norm – a partial fixity in the category is necessary to provide coherence. At the same time, postmodern theory suggests that identities are inherently unstable. Yet, as a strategic matter, it may be advantageous to describe identities in essentialist terms. Indeed, in the American context, difficulty in achieving legal protection for lesbians and gay men under the Equal Protection clause of the Constitution in part can be traced to the failure of essentialist notions of the immutability of sexual orientation. Epstein has referred to this conundrum as the 'paradox of identity politics'[43] because of the difficulty of asserting an identity without assuming a '"totalising" sameness within the group.'[44]

That tendency towards totalisation is problematic, because it replicates the boundaries through which a dichotomy of inside/out is structured around the identity concept. One of the focal points of identity theory, as I suggested in Chapter 1, is the way in which the universal subject position has been constructed through the erection of boundaries. For example, the establishment of a universal sexual subject was dependent upon the denial of sexual subjectivity to lesbians and gay men. To prevent the erosion of the stable heterosexual subject, the creation of a negative image of the outsider must be attached to the homosexual. The need to maintain boundaries is not unique to the sexual subject. The individual associates herself with numerous identity categories. She therefore may be located both at positions of privilege and otherness, which in turn may be subject to change over time. Subject locations compete within this framework for status, revealing the provisionality of a subject position. The emptiness of the signifiers of identity means that they can be essentialised by the construction of a subject position in contradistinction to an other. However, it is 'more than a simple boundary marking the outer limits of the centred term because it functions as a supplement, marking what the centre lacks but also what it needs in order to define fully and confirm its identity'.[45]

It is through a partial fixity of identity that new social movements emerge and make claims to rights. The acceptance of these claims expands the frontiers of the universal subject position as the group is accommodated. For example, a claim to rights for a minority sexual identity does not simply expand the realm of the universal sexual subject. It also 'decentres the dominant discourse and identities that have suppressed it'.[46] Sexual subjectivity is redefined in the process.[47] Indeed, subject positions inevitably are open to decentring by the other against which they have been constituted. Consequently, the articulation of a newly emergent identity must be made with an awareness of its own provisionality. As Joan Scott argues, 'the project of history is not to reify identity but to understand its production as an ongoing process of differentiation, relentless in its repetition, but also . . . subject to redefinition, resistance, and change'.[48] This contingency in our conception both of equality and of nationhood can provide fresh insights into a consideration of Canadian equality jurisprudence dealing with sexual orientation as an analogous ground of discrimination. In particular, the decision in *Haig*, that I referred to earlier, assumes a new significance. The facts concerned the application of the Canadian Armed Forces' policy directive relating to homosexuals in the forces. Haig was told, upon informing his commanding officer of his homosexuality, that he would 'cease to be eligible for promotions, postings or further military career training'.[49] While the legal question was the constitutionality of the absence of protection against discrimination on the basis of sexual orientation in the Canadian *Human Rights Act*, the substance of the case raised the issue of lesbians and gay men in the military. Subsequently, the government lifted the policy as a result of a settlement reached in litigation brought by a member of the Canadian Armed Forces, Michelle Douglas, who had been released because of her sexual orientation.[50] The decision of the government speaks not only to identity in relation to sexual orientation, but also is relevant to how the Canadian national identity is imagined. While the power of law to shape the national imaginary at best is partial, the presence of openly lesbian or gay members in the armed services is significant. The military is an important signifier of national identity in many states. As I argued in Chapter 5, it is linked to the boundaries of national identity, for it is charged with protecting the literal, physical boundaries by providing protection against invasion by the outsider. Thus, the military is a powerful, central signifier of nationalism and can be expected to reflect the national identity. The relative readiness of the Canadian government and society to open up this national sign to resignification (albeit with some dissent) along the lines of sexual orientation consequently is noteworthy and can be contrasted to the American experience. To reiterate, in the United States, the courts traditionally have rejected the substance of the claim that the ban on lesbians and gay men in the American forces is contrary to the Equal Protection clause of the United States Constitution. This can be explained in part by the importance that America attaches to the maintenance of the separation of a military identity from a gay identity. It is interesting, moreover, that the recent judicial and political changes in position on this issue have occurred in the post-cold-war period, as America undergoes a period of confusion as to the ideological bases of the boundaries of national identity. The naturalness and essentialism of the signifiers of the American military machine in the mid-1990s may be showing some signs of weakness, which may leave them open to rearticulation in a new, unauthorised manner.

In the Canadian context, the military has served neither the same literal function of constant safeguarding of the national borders, nor does it appear to serve the same metaphoric function of border patrol. Indeed, the military simply may be a weak signifier of national identity, which in itself is noteworthy. The Canadian Armed Forces can accommodate lesbian and gay identities, which, in turn, may redefine the military subject. The national imaginary thus has an openness to difference and the armed forces in Canada have become a site for the contestation of images of national identity. In other words, the fact that the national identity is socially constructed and defined by the articulation of numerous, shifting identities, facilitates the expression of a gay identity within national institutions. In the course of the ongoing dialogue over equality rights, the Canadian military comes to be reworked. In this respect, it may be significant that today the primary role of the Canadian Armed Forces is in peacekeeping operations abroad. One of the goals of the intervention of peacekeeping troops is to facilitate dialogue and *rapprochement* between opposed parties, rather than to police the boundaries of the Canadian nation. Finally, the fact that a gay identity can be articulated in military terms serves to redefine the meaning of that identity as well, demonstrating once again its social construction.

Nationalisms and sexualities thus meet and, in the Canadian context, a sexual identity is openly allowed to cross into the borders of the national imaginary, which in turn redefines the scope of citizenship. The consequences of a new identity within the national discourse are unpredictable. While I would hope that the emergence of a gay identity within Canadian national institutions might give the signifiers of nationality a new 'queer' inflection, such a result cannot be predicted.[51] Moreover, given the ability of the Canadian national identity to incorporate subjects defined in diverse nationalist terms, Canadian social and political discourse might be conducive to the articulation of *new* sexual identities, such as Queer Nationalism.[52] Like the aims of queer nationals, Canada might be a space where 'the boundaries between what constitutes individual and what constitutes national space are explicitly blurred'.[53] This process is facilitated by the emergence of new voices articulating demands for inclusion in the national imaginary in the name of equality rights.

CONCLUSION: THE FUTURE OF A POSTMODERN NATIONAL IDENTITY

The characterisation of Canada as a postmodern state begs the question whether such a nation ultimately can survive. If a postmodern national identity is one in which its citizens are aware of the contingency of nation and the multiplicity of their own identities, to what extent can national identity alone bind the members together? How are the various identities with which citizens identify prevented from redefining themselves in nationalistic terms to the exclusion of a Canadian national identity? This raises whether there is an inevitable process of disintegration and fragmentation of the nation in the conditions of postmodernity. Thus, if Canada is the first postmodern state, will it also be one of the first to dissolve in this current political situation?

Of course, the answers to these questions are beyond the scope of this chapter. However, an awareness of the constructed character of nationhood may render more problematic the maintenance of the bonds of citizenship through which the integration of a nation is maintained. The openness of the signifiers of Canada suggests that emotional appeals to nationhood may prove unsuccessful. The sentimental deployment of nationalism is futile if the mysteries and essentialism of the nation are stripped away. While demands of undivided loyalty to the state are incompatible with the multiplicity of identifications of the citizen, some conception of loyalty might still prove necessary to prevent the rupture of the nation into its various component parts. Loyalty, however, must be broadened to encompass the loyalty of the subject to a variety of communities and subcultures. It may well be that loyalty now only can be expected and only will be forthcoming in those circumstances where the individual is convinced that through membership in the postmodern state, the right to identify variously and to express her identities will best be secured. Loyalty thus stems precisely from the values which underpin the equality guarantees of the Canadian Constitution. A commitment to equality of participation within a dialogic community is a precondition to loyalty to the state. In other words, it is only through a commitment to the security and flourishing of difference that loyalty will be forthcoming.

The self-reflexivity of the individual leads to an awareness that the alternatives facing the social order when confronted with difference are dialogue between and among those different identities and the violence (metaphoric and literal) of separation and disintegration. An irreconcilable tension necessarily exists between these two forces, which cannot be transcended. Loyalty to the dialogic community in principle and in operation thus depends upon the success of the state in controlling the impulse towards complete fragmentation and its accompanying psychic and physical pain. This definition of loyalty never claims to be totalising for it emerges out of the complexity of allegiances of citizens, rather than from the essentialism of a homogeneous nation. Finally, it is through a dialogic relationship that moments of crisis, communal and personal, can be resolved through communication. These moments emerge when identities conflict and loyalties collide. These crises must be dampened by the larger community to control the instinct towards exit from the state.

Thus, in conclusion, I have argued in this chapter that through a postmodern understanding of identity and a postmodern identity politics we can deepen and broaden the conception of equality within Canadian law and society. I advocate an anti-essentialist approach that reflects the fragmentation of the Canadian national identity. The recognition of sexual orientation as a prohibited ground of discrimination exemplifies this vision, which centres upon an ideal of equality based on the right to articulate an identity in the public sphere. It represents a different interpretation of equality rights in which the protection of newly emergent identities is ensured and participation in a democratic dialogue of rights is guaranteed. This approach ultimately demands a rethinking of rights such that they no longer depend upon a universal standpoint which has denied to some the articulation of subjecthood. Instead, in the place of universality, there emerges a focus on difference and a communal and national identity forged from difference. To this end, an attempt is made to minimise the exclusionary power of communities as an appropriate model of equality rights in Canada. The national identity thus is revealed as a permanent site of contestation over the meaning of nationhood. The nation comes to have a heightened capacity for redefinition and thus is explicitly constructed through an ongoing dialogue involving competing social imaginaries. Such a vision of nation may be more open to the intersection of different identities and facilitates the development of a liberatory imagination of rights, based on a multiplicity of identities, as an alternative to universal rights and a totalised, one-dimensional subjectivity.

7

UNMANLY DIVERSIONS

The construction of the homosexual body
(politic) in law

In this chapter, my focus returns to the British context. I examine two events concerning the relationship of gay men to crime that attracted media and public attention in 1993 in Britain. Perhaps not surprisingly, neither occurrence centred on the gay man as victim of heterosexually-imposed violence or on the perpetuation of state violence upon gays.[1] Rather, these occurrences were employed to construct the gay man as lacking in self-control, as violent, and, ultimately, as murderous. The 'homosexual' becomes one who has transgressed the boundaries not only of the sexual, but also of the civilised, through acts of depravity that require the reaffirmation of social norms. The events are symbolic in that they reaffirm definitions of normalcy, and are designed to expurgate the gay man from the realm of the social to a pathologised sphere of decay, illness, and to an unavoidably brutal, and, ironically, seductive death. Thus, these narratives link sex to death and serve as modern parables about homosexuality and the threat of epidemic.

While the two stories that I focus upon may seem disparate, I argue that on many different levels there are connections in how they have been interpreted within dominant culture and the performative role they play in constituting a social reality. Each is concerned with the relationship of sex and violence. Moreover, both are narratives about homosexual men and, in different ways, they are about death and destruction. These are stories of sadomasochists and serial killers.

SADOMASOCHISM, CONSENT, AND THE BOUNDARIES OF MASCULINITY

R. v. Brown

In *R. v. Brown*, the House of Lords decided, by a majority, that consent is no defence to an assault causing actual bodily harm within the criminal law.[2] The simplicity of that holding disguises both the unusual character of the facts as well as how the judgment participates in the construction of gay male sexuality. The five appellants to the House of Lords were convicted of assaults occasioning actual bodily harm contrary to section 47 of the *Offences against the Person Act 1861*. Three of the appellants were also convicted of wounding contrary to section 20. Those convictions were upheld by the Court of Appeal and by the House of Lords. There was no question that the appellants 'intentionally inflicted violence upon another' and thereby caused actual bodily harm and, in some instances, wounding.[3] However, the unique nature of the case stemmed from the fact that there was no complainant, for the so-called 'victims' consented to the assaults, which were committed in the course of homosexual sadomasochistic sex. The only issue, simply put, was whether the consent of the victim operated to negate the commission of the offence or as a defence to the charge of assault. The assaults themselves were described in some detail by Lord Templeman:

> The evidence disclosed that drink and drugs were employed to obtain consent and increase enthusiasm. The victim was usually manacled so that the sadist could enjoy the thrill of power and the victim could enjoy the thrill of helplessness. The victim had no control over the harm which the sadist, also stimulated by drink and drugs, might inflict. In one case a victim was branded twice on the thigh and there was some doubt as to whether he consented to or protested against the second branding. The dangers involved in administering violence must have been appreciated by the appellants because, so it was said by their counsel, each victim was given a code word which he could pronounce when excessive harm or pain was caused. The efficiency of this precaution, when taken, depends on the circumstances and on the personalities involved. No one can feel the pain of another. The charges against the appellants were based on genital torture and violence to the buttocks, anus, penis, testicles and nipples. The victims were degraded and humiliated, sometimes beaten, sometimes wounded with instruments and sometimes branded. Bloodletting and the smearing of human blood produced excitement.[4]

These events occurred over a ten-year period and came to light as a result of a police investigation concerning an unrelated matter. There had been no complaints to the police nor had there been permanent injury suffered. However, a number of the encounters had been videotaped for the benefit of members of the group. These videotapes formed the basis of the case against the appellants.

In his judgment, Lord Templeman characterised the issue as whether the prosecution must prove a lack of consent in order to establish guilt. In answering that question, he recognised, first, that consent does preclude a complaint when no actual bodily harm has occurred. Moreover, even where actual bodily harm, wounding, or serious bodily harm results, an acquittal will be forthcoming 'if the injury was a foreseeable incident of a lawful activity in which the person injured was participating'.[5] A limited range of events were cited as falling within this category: surgery, ritual circumcision, tatooing, ear-piercing, and violent sports such as boxing. The issue, then, was 'whether the defence should be extended to the infliction of bodily harm in the course of sadomasochistic encounters'.[6]

For Lord Templeman, this case was to be decided on the basis of public interest and policy, both of which led inexorably to conviction. First, he responded to the argument raised by the appellants that the defence of consent should be extended to the offence of occasioning actual bodily harm but not to charges of serious wounding and the infliction of serious bodily harm. Such a differentiation was held impracticable as 'sado-masochistic participants have no way of foretelling the degree of bodily harm which will result from their encounters'.[7] Moreover, this was not a case about freedom of sexual satisfaction. Rather, the acts were portrayed as primarily violent:

> In my opinion sado-masochism is not only concerned with sex. Sado-masochism is also concerned with violence. The evidence discloses that the practices of the appellants were unpredictably dangerous and degrading to body and mind and were developed with increasing barbarity and taught to persons whose consents were dubious and worthless.[8]

The last comment referred to the finding of the Court of Appeal that the participants were involved in the corruption of youths and employed alcohol and drugs as a means of obtaining consent.

Lord Templeman also focused on the potential dangers arising out of these sexual practices. The trial judge had been informed by the Crown prosecutor (over the objection of defence counsel) that two members of the group had died of HIV-related illnesses and that one other had contracted HIV infection (although it was conceded that this was not necessarily as a result of participation in this group). In response, the appellants asserted that steps were taken to reduce the risk of infection, including the sterilisation of instruments of torture. Lord Templeman rejected this argument, finding that such measures could not remove the danger, and he concluded that 'it is fortunate that there were no permanent injuries to a victim though no one knows the extent of harm inflicted in other cases'.[9] As an aside, he noted that 'cruelty to human beings was on occasion supplemented by cruelty to animals in the form of bestiality'.[10] For Lord Templeman, such activities were 'unpredictably dangerous'[11] and although sexually motivated, 'sex is no excuse for violence'.[12] In the end, he upheld the convictions, concluding that 'society is entitled and bound to protect itself against a cult of violence. Pleasure derived from the infliction of pain is an evil thing. Cruelty is uncivilised'.[13]

Lord Jauncey, in concurring reasons, emphasised that 'none of the appellants had any medical qualifications and there was, of course, no referee present such as there would be in a boxing or football match'.[14] For Lord Jauncey, the public interest demanded recognition of the possibility of serious injury arising out of sadomasochistic activities, particularly by practitioners less 'controlled or responsible' than the appellants:

> it would appear to be good luck rather than good judgment which has prevented serious injury from occurring. Wounds can easily become septic

if not properly treated, the free flow of blood from a person who is HIV positive or who has Aids can infect another and an inflicter who is carried away by sexual excitement or by drink or drugs could very easily inflict pain and injury beyond the level to which the receiver had consented. Your lordships have no information as to whether such situations have occurred in relation to other sado-masochistic practitioners.[15]

In addition, the public interest in avoiding the 'proselytisation and corruption of young men' was a relevant issue.[16] Lord Jauncey also questioned the actual secrecy of the activities in light of the creation of video recordings: 'if the only purpose of the activity is the sexual gratification of one or both of the participants what then is the need of a video-recording?'[17]

In conclusion, Lord Jauncey graphically asserted that if sadomasochistic homosexual activity is to be legal, then decriminalisation is a matter for Parliament and not for the courts:

> If it is to be decided that such activities as the nailing by A of B's foreskin or scrotum to a board or the insertion of hot wax into C's urethra followed by the burning of his penis with a candle or the incising of D's scrotum with a scalpel to the effusion of blood are injurious neither to B, C and D nor to the public interest then it is for Parliament with its accumulated wisdom and sources of information to declare them to be lawful.[18]

Lord Lowry, concurring with Lords Templeman and Jauncey, focused on the public interest. In so doing, he sought to distance sadomasochistic sexual encounters between men from both the 'normal' sexuality of 'family life' and from the 'manly diversions' of sport where consensual assaults do not run contrary to law:

> What the appellants are obliged to propose is that the deliberate and painful infliction of physical injury should be exempted from the operation of statutory provisions the object of which is to prevent or punish that very thing, the reason for the proposed exemption being that both those who will inflict and those who will suffer the injury wish to satisfy a perverted and depraved sexual desire. Sado-masochistic homosexual activity cannot be regarded as conducive to the enhancement or enjoyment of family life or conducive to the welfare of society. A relaxation of the prohibitions in ss 20 and 47 can only encourage the practice of homosexual sado-masochism, with the physical cruelty that it must involve, (which can scarcely be regarded as a 'manly diversion') by withdrawing the legal penalty and giving the activity a judicial imprimatur.[19]

In dissenting reasons, Lord Mustill framed the issue as a 'case about the criminal law of private sexual relations'.[20] After reviewing numerous categories of cases where the infliction of actual bodily harm does and does not give rise to an assault in law, Lord Mustill concluded that:

I cannot accept that the infliction of bodily harm, and especially the private infliction of it, is invariably criminal absent some special factor which decrees otherwise. I prefer to address each individual category of consensual violence in the light of the situation as a whole. Sometimes the element of consent will make no difference and sometimes it will make all the difference.[21]

Lord Mustill emphasised that in this category of case the importance of individual autonomy weighed in favour of interpreting the 1861 Act narrowly: 'the state should interfere with the rights of an individual to live his or her life as he or she may choose no more than is necessary'.[22] In addition, Lord Mustill questioned the health risks cited by the majority and, in particular, the threat of transmission of HIV:

the consequence would be strange, since what is currently the principal cause for the transmission of this scourge, namely consenting buggery between males, is now legal. Nevertheless, I would have been compelled to give this proposition the most anxious consideration if there had been any evidence to support it. But there is none.[23]

Furthermore, in answer to arguments about the corruption of youth, Lord Mustill pointed out that existing legislation already covered that field. Finally, as for the danger of proselytisation, he underlined the circularity of the argument: 'if the activity is not itself so much against the public interest that it ought to be declared criminal under the 1861 Act then the risk that others will be induced to join in cannot be a ground for making it criminal'.[24]

Sadomasochism and the construction of sexuality

The reasoning of the majority in *Brown* can be analysed on a number of different levels for what it reveals about the construction of sexuality, violence, Aids, and moreover, how the case functions symbolically to reaffirm social definitions of sanctified sexual norms. First, the judgment exemplifies what Gayle Rubin has described as the characterisation of 'sex acts according to a hierarchical system of sexual value' in which sadomasochists constitute a 'despised sexual caste'.[25] Consequently, those sex acts revealed by the House of Lords in *Brown* are constructed as 'utterly repulsive and devoid of all emotional nuance . . . a uniformly bad experience'.[26] The issue of consent thereby ceases to be of overriding or even of primary importance: 'some sex acts are considered to be so intrinsically vile that no one should be allowed under any circumstances to perform them. The fact that individuals consent to or even prefer them is taken to be additional evidence of depravity'.[27] The presence of consent to sexual acts thereby demands 'the need to find someone who has been hurt' in order to justify the imposition of criminal penalties.[28] That injured party or victim may be the individuals involved, others who may be proselytised, or the general public. In other words, the hurt is inflicted both upon the individual body and upon the body politic.

Indeed, a discourse of harm operates on a number of different fronts through- out the judgment. The threat of permanent injury to the individuals directly involved as recipients of sadomasochistic sex is reiterated throughout the majority reasons. Sadomasochistic sexual practices are 'unpredictably dangerous'[29]; 'developed with increasing barbarity';[30] and probably 'will get out of hand and result in serious physical damage'.[31] Consent thus becomes overriden by the likelihood of physical harm to participants. Although permanent physical injury did not occur on the facts of the case, the potential is ever present and looms large.

The spectre of serious injury – of sexual acts out of control that lead to harm – is contradicted by some sociological research on sadomasochistic sexual practices. As Weinberg argues, reviewing the literature in the field, if sadomasochism is viewed sociologically, its meaning is tightly controlled and actions are a product of an agreed set of terms:

> The meaning of what is happening is shared, and a variety of "keys" are used to cue participants into what is "really going on". Frames not only define interaction, but they also control and restrict it as well. They set forth mutually agreed upon limits for behavior, which participants accept as inviolable. So, for example, what may appear to the uninitiated observer as a violent act may really be a theatrical and carefully controlled "perform- ance" from the perspective of the participants.[32]

These shared meanings are learned within the subculture, and the 'effect' of exclusive control by one party may be far removed from how the performance actually has been mutually planned: 'the action is often, but not always, scripted and therefore collaborative, so that neither the dominant nor the submissive usually has complete control'.[33] Although scripting may take place, a certain amount of room for improvisation may remain, allowing for divergence from the planned scenario.[34]

Trust thus may play a function in limiting the potential for uncontrolled violence. Trust arises both from the relationship created over time between the parties to the scene and from subcultural norms and values that are accepted by one who comes to self-identify as an s&m participant.[35] The construction of sadomasochistic sex as uncontrolled violence therefore may be misplaced. The performance of the sexual encounter suggests a high degree of predictability and a mutual awareness of limits and boundaries beyond which participants are socialised not to proceed. On this point, the appellants argued that the use of 'code words' by recipients ensured that limits would be respected. However, Lord Templeman's rejection of the effectiveness of code words to control the encounters demonstrates an unwillingness to recognise the possibility of negoti- ated limits to sexual acts.

The discussion of harm in the judgments also includes numerous references to the danger of transmission of HIV through sadomasochism. Although no evidence was presented of transmission between group members, the risk of HIV infection becomes a harm that justifies criminal sanctions. Lord Lowry is most forthcoming as to the relationship between the virus and the criminalisation of sexual activity. The danger of HIV is a direct result of the loss of control by participants in the sexual encounter. The threat of Aids becomes *the* logical outcome of sadomasochistic (or, perhaps, homosexual) sex:

> A proposed general exemption is to be tested by considering the likely general effect. This must include the probability that some sadomasochistic activity, under *the powerful influence of the sexual instinct*, will get out of hand and result in serious physical damage to the participants and that some activity will involve a danger of infection such as these particular exponents do not contemplate for themselves. When considering the danger of infection, with its *inevitable threat of Aids*, I am not impressed by the argument that . . . as long ago as 1967, Parliament . . . legalised buggery, now *a well-known vehicle* for the transmission of AIDS.[36]

This passage contains a complex matrix of the potential harms that stem from sadomasochistic gay sex. Sexuality is perceived as a powerful instinct that is not easily contained. Indeed, without legal constraints, it will wreak havoc. One result is infection and the *inevitable* outcome is transmission of HIV and, ultimately, death.

The distinction between normal and sadomasochistic sex is one which is firmly maintained in the judgments. In fact, for Lord Templeman, sadomasochism is at least as much about violence as it is about sex, while 'normal' sex presumably is a bounded sphere removed from violence. For Lord Lowry, sadomasochistic sex is the antithesis of normal, heterosexual family life and, consequently, it is not compatible with the social good. Nor is it analogous to those 'manly diversions' such as boxing where consent does provide a defence to a charge of assault. For the majority of the House of Lords then, the presence of negotiated limits and boundaries is what characterises the acts as the antithesis of the sexual, as it is commonly understood.

A manly diversion: *R. v. Aitken* and the limits of consent

One kind of assault – a 'manly diversion' – to which one can give meaningful consent was made clear in a case before the English Court of Appeal. In *R. v. Aitken et al.*, the central question was the effectiveness of consent to an assault that caused *grievous* bodily harm.[37] The appellants in the case were three Royal Air Force Officers who had attended a party where a large amount of alcohol was consumed. Some 'horseplay' ensued which involved the setting alight of some participants (who were wearing fire resistant RAF suits). These activities were viewed as pranks which led to no serious injury. Later in the evening, after the party disbanded, the appellants set fire to another participant (also wearing fire retardant clothing) using a considerable quantity of white spirit and a light. The victim, Gibson, resisted, but being severely intoxicated, that resistance was weak and ineffective. In this instance, the activity got 'out of hand' and flames flared up rapidly. According to one appellant, Gibson 'had gone up like a torch'.[38] Although the appellants, themselves intoxicated, took immediate steps to extinguish the flame, the victim suffered severe burns 'with 35 per cent of his body sustaining superficial burns of a life-threatening nature'.[39] The issue before the Court was whether the appellants had inflicted grievous bodily harm *unlawfully* and maliciously.

In particular, the Court of Appeal considered whether the judge advocate had failed to give the jury proper direction as to the meaning of the word 'unlawfully' in section 20 of the *Offences Against the Person Act 1861* ('unlawfully and maliciously inflicting grievous bodily harm'). In directing the jury on unlawfulness, the judge advocate had explained that it was up to them to determine whether this activity went beyond the bounds of horseplay:

> Was this no more than horseplay? Looking at it in the light of the Royal Air Force ethos, was this going far beyond normal horseplay, to such an extent that you can say, "no, this is way beyond those levels. It is not possibly lawful to behave in this manner".[40]

The Court of Appeal, quashing the convictions, held that this instruction was inadequate. In essence, the Court accepted the argument of the appellants that the events of the evening were not *per se* unlawful and the jury should have been instructed accordingly. The appellants had argued before the Court of Appeal that:

> in seeking to restrain him from leaving the room, grappling him to the ground and then, as he was getting up, trying to carry out the same type of burning incident as had happened earlier in the evening the appellants were acting in a manner consistent with what had been going on during much of the time. The fact that Gibson struggled, albeit weakly through drink, to avoid the attentions of the three during the incident in question should not, it was submitted on the appellants' behalf, be taken in isolation. The totality of the circumstances, his knowledge of the course which celebration evenings such as the one in question was likely to take and his continued presence with the others demonstrated an acceptance by him that horseplay of the nature perpetrated upon him might well take place.[41]

The Court of Appeal accepted that the issue of consent to the assault which caused *grievous* bodily harm ought to have been put to the jury. Thus, consent would render the assault no longer unlawful. Interestingly, the issue turned, not only on actual consent, but also on the subjective belief of the appellants:

> the judge advocate should then have directed the court as to the *necessity of considering whether Gibson gave his consent as a willing participant to the activities in question, or whether the appellants may have believed this, whether reasonably or not.*[42]

In this case, consent is assumed to operate as a defence to a charge of assault causing grievous bodily harm. Although the Court of Appeal never discusses which category of exception renders the physical assault lawful, the description of horseplay is similar to the manly diversions described by Lord Lowry in *Brown*. In *Aitken*, consent to the activity is comprehensible to the Court of Appeal and the jury therefore should have been instructed that a belief in the victim's consent – whether reasonably held or not – was sufficient to negate the commission of an offence.[43] By contrast, in *Brown*, the analysis of consent focuses solely on the victim. Consent is continually queried for its voluntariness and the potential for coercion frequently is cited.

In *Aitken*, consent to the brutalisation is plausible to the Court. Consequently, the activity can be reduced to mere horseplay. The use of that term demarcates a clear boundary between the homosexual practices of the defendants in *Brown* (which cannot be thought of as manly diversions) and the homosocial (albeit clearly not homosexual) activities in *Aitken*. The term horseplay conjures up innocent schoolboys – precisely the innocents who, according to the House of Lords in *Brown*, are in need of protection from the accused sadomasochists. Through this construction of the facts, any sexualised dimension to the activities in *Aitken* remains absent. The party itself took place in 'married quarters', a metaphoric safe haven for manly diversions, quarantined from the dangers of seduction lurking outside. The married quarters provide a realm of 'private and family life', to quote Lord Templeman in *Brown*. This creation of a metaphoric bounded space allows for the rigidity of the separation between the homosocial environment of the military with its friendly horseplay; and the spectre of the homosexual, removed and ostracised from the space of the homosocial and heterosexual male, and subjected to the judicial gaze.

However, the facts of *Aitken* highlight many of the dangers described by the House of Lords in *Brown*. The injuries suffered by Gibson were the result of a controlled activity that got out of hand. The rules of the game, if they ever existed, were transgressed as the thrill of victimisation caused the limits to be crossed. The Court was faced with the persistent problem of determining consent when excessive alcohol is involved with the attendant danger of an induced consent which is not truly voluntary. Moreover, the possibility existed that alcohol caused the aggressors to wrongly assume consent. This of course was one basis upon which the House of Lords questioned the reliability of the consents to sadomasochistic activities. Furthermore, unlike the case in *Brown*, in *Aitken* it is unlikely that limits ever were negotiated in any kind of shared conversation. Curiously, though, in *Brown* it is the presence of negotiated limits agreed upon in advance that undermines the case for the appellants. The absence of a shared conversation – of rational conversation – in *Aitken* strengthens the claim of the relevance of consent and the perception by the defendants that consent was given. The *absence* of agreement thus characterises the diversion as 'manly'. In other words, it is the giving of consent voluntarily and fully informed which undermines the manliness both of the victim and the aggressor. This distinguishes the facts in *Aitken* from the sadomasochistic behaviour in *Brown* and serves to separate 'normal' male sexuality from the homosexual.

SEDUCTION, CONTAGION, ADDICTION: THE PATHOLOGISING OF THE HOMOSEXUAL

Introduction: the gay man as sadomasochistic serial killer

The construction of the homosexual can be traced through the reasoning of the House of Lords in *Brown*. However, the construction of the homosexual as pathological is not unique to legal discourse. The creation of a pathological sadomasochistic identity, which becomes synonymous with the homosexual, occurs through a web of discourses. I will suggest in this section that three different techniques are commonly employed: the characterisation of the homosexual through the language of addiction, seduction, and contagion. Each deployment provides metaphoric and mythic power for the expurgation of the homosexual from the realm of normal society and assists in the consolidation of that normalcy. The normal thus is constituted as the non-addicted body exercising free will and immune from the threat of contagion. Lurking in the background will be another set of discourses – sometimes articulated and sometimes implicit – which focus on the threat of Aids and a death that *inevitably* results from the dangers of addiction, seduction, and, especially, contagion.

In June, 1993, the British media gave extensive coverage to a series of murders of gay men in London. An individual enticed five different men back to their homes after engaging in conversations in a London gay pub. Each man was found dead; four from asphyxiation and three of those from strangulation. All of the victims were discovered naked and in some cases there was evidence of sexual activity. An individual subsequently was arrested and convicted in connection with those murders. According to press reports, 'four of the five victims were homosexual and are believed to have had an interest in sado-masochism. Several of their homes contained bondage equipment.'[44]

The reporting of these events by the mainstream media provides as fertile a source for investigating the themes raised earlier as does the judgment of the House of Lords in *Brown*. In fact, the two events are not wholly disconnected. It has been argued that the murder investigations were impeded by the reluctance of practitioners of gay sadomasochistic sex to provide evidence, given that in so doing they might implicate themselves as having committed unlawful assaults through consensual sexual relations.

On a rhetorical level, the commonalities between the discourses surrounding both events also are readily apparent. The construction of the homosexual and his lifestyle as other than the normal, the familial, and the social, filters through the coverage of events. The 'gay world' is described as 'a mystery'; 'all but closed to outsiders'; 'where assumed names are common'; 'where young men appear and vanish in an endless stream'; and 'where violent assault is always to be feared'.[45]

126

The 'scene' is a 'predatory, risky and anonymous world of multiple sexual partners, rushed and often violent sex with strangers'.[46] The men who enter this world often lead 'a double life'.[47] The murdered men in this case were described as 'quiet', 'quiet-living', 'little', 'bespectacled', holding 'steady responsible jobs', and 'living in respectable areas'.[48] These descriptions highlight the difficulty of distinguishing the pathological from the normal – they could be anywhere, they could be your neighbours, they seem perfectly respectable. Public persona and private life are sharply differentiated and it is through the gay subculture – this 'twilight zone' – that the media can bridge the yawning gulf between public and private worlds. At the time of the media's interest, reporters were sent to investigate the gay subcultural scene and the descriptions conjure the image of explorers in a foreign land. Furthermore, from this terrain emerged the language of addiction, seduction, and contagion that also permeates the judgment of the House of Lords in *Brown*.

The language of addiction

The discourse of addiction and the creation of the identity of the addict are increasingly prevalent phenomena in late-capitalist society. As Eve Sedgwick has suggested in her recent exploration of the use of the language of addiction within a variety of sites, we are seeing the extension of addiction to a wide range of 'substances', rendering it devoid of any essential meaning:

> To the gradual extension of addiction–attribution to a wider variety of "drugs" over the first two-thirds of the twentieth century there has been added the startling coda of several recent developments: in particular, the development that now quite explicitly brings not only every form of substance ingestion, but more simply every form of human behavior, into the orbit of potential addiction–attribution . . . the locus of addictiveness cannot be the substance itself and can scarcely even be the body itself, but must be some overarching abstraction that governs the narrative relations between them.[49]

It is this 'narrative relation' between body and substance that structures the language of addiction and increasingly 'any substance, any behavior, even any effect may be pathologized as addictive'.[50] But as addiction comes to lack 'any necessary specificity of substance, bodily effect or psychological motivation'[51], the focus shifts from the substance of addiction to the subject of addiction – and, in so doing, addiction comes to be associated simply with individual free will. Thus, we are witnessing a 'pathologizing of addiction as a malady of the will'.[52] However, the relationship of addiction to the exercise of will is deeply problematic. On the one hand, discourses of addiction focus on the failure of individual will. To be hooked is to lose control, to fall victim to a compulsion which negates the exercise of choice. On the other hand, addiction is now structured precisely around those phenomena that are associated with personal freedom. The exercise of individual will therefore becomes a symptom and object of an addictive personality (the exercise addict being the obvious example). As Sedgwick has argued, this structuring of addiction around both compulsion and volition gives rise to a 'system of double binds', where claims of free will can be answered through the language of compulsion, and vice versa:

> where an assertion that one can act freely is always read in the damning light of the "open secret" that the behavior in question is utterly compelled – while one's assertion that one was after all, compelled shrivels in the equally stark light of the "open secret" that one might at any given moment have chosen differently.[53]

This relationship between compulsion and free will also has been described as 'self-destruction for fuller self-possession'.[54] It is the addictiveness of free will itself – a manifestation of the possession of the self – that leads, within this formulation, to the destruction of that same self.

The development of this discourse around addiction closely parallels the emergence of discourses of the homosexual, which makes it less surprising that the language of addiction was employed in the House of Lords decision in *Brown* and in the commentary on the serial killer case. The construction of the addict and the homosexual as identities, rather than acts, has 'historical interimplications':

> The two taxonomies of the addict and the homosexual condensed many of the same issues for late nineteenth-century culture: the old anti-sodomite opposition between something called "nature" and that which is *contra naturam* blended with a treacherous apparent seamlessness into a new opposition between substances that are *natural* (for example, "food") and those that are artificial (for example, "drugs"), and hence into the char-acteristic twentieth-century way of distinguishing desires themselves between the natural, called "needs", and the artificial, called "addictions".[55]

The discourse of addiction amounts then to a reification of the natural, which is contrasted to the artificially stimulating. Of course, this analysis reveals that the unnaturalness (or naturalness) of any desire is itself a social construction realised discursively.

This process of condensing the categories of addiction – of unnatural abuses – also is clearly at work in discourses surrounding HIV. The collapsing together of risk groups reaffirms the social construction of the natural and the artificial and provides a cautionary warning for the consequences of free will:

> one of the many echoes resounding around the terrible accident of HIV and the terrible nonaccident of the overdetermined ravage of AIDS is the way that it seems "naturally" to ratify and associate – as unnatural, as unsuited for survival, as the appropriate objects of neglect, specularized suffering and premature death – the notionally self-evident "risk group" categories of the gay man and the addict.[56]

The ways in which the discourse of addiction structures the discourse of the gay male are easily discernible. Most obviously, the gay man's sexuality is out of control. The exercise of free will (self-possession) necessarily and inevitably leads to his self-destruction. The artificiality and unnaturalness of desire thus becomes addictive and requires ever-increasing quantities to satisfy. Ultimately, the limits are reached only at the point of physical exhaustion:

> Homosexual desire symbolizes pure sexual lust or unrestrained desire, subject only to the quantitative limitations of physical exhaustion. It is this compulsive, hyperactive, insatiable desire that is thought to compel homosexuals to eroticize the forbidden and to transgress all moral boundaries, rendering them a profound social danger.[57]

In this regard, the homosexual possesses the same attributes as others who are portrayed as unregulated and devoid of self-control: 'Gays, prostitutes, and addicts are not in control of their desires or do not allow their desires to be controlled, and this makes them perverse and threatening agents of pathology'.[58]

Like other addicts, the gay man comes to be unable to control his desire for the artificially stimulating and is caught in the system of double binds. The exercise of a particular sexual choice leads to a compulsiveness – an addiction to sexual freedom. Once he enters this realm of the forbidden and the transgressive, the compulsion leads to ever-increasing heights of depravity of lust; an escalation that leads ultimately to his self-destruction.

Both the serial killer case and the reasoning in *Brown* utilise this discourse. The murdered victims of the serial killer often are described as victims of their own unnatural needs, which they are compelled to fulfil. As a result of their 'addiction' they 'strayed into the orbit of a man who had been long preparing to push the game of sexual pain beyond the final barrier'.[59] Murder, then, becomes the erotic limit for the addicted gay man, which is the logical end result of taking up such a dangerous 'habit'. Indeed, in the same article, one of the murdered men is described as 'cheerfully *addicted* to bondage sex', his good cheer no doubt reflecting an ignorance of the dangers that result from the exercise of his sexual will.[60]

A similar use of addiction is engaged by the Law Lords in *Brown*. Throughout the majority reasons, the appellants are characterised in terms of their uncontrolled and unregulated need for sexualised violence. Like other forms of addiction, their desire for stimulation escalates, which means that the addiction becomes uncontrollable. Once again, the relationship of free will and compulsion is paradoxical. In exercising a choice to engage in sadomasochistic sexual encounters, the appellants increasingly become addicted to their sexual proclivity, with necessarily dangerous consequences.

A discourse of addiction thus underpins the reasons of the majority. It explains why, in Lord Templeman's reasons, 'sado-masochistic participants have no way of foretelling the degree of bodily harm which will result from their encounters', despite any system of regulation in place during those sessions.[61] Ever-increasing degrees of stimulation are required to get a sexual fix. Similarly, Lord Jauncey conflated the addictions of the sexual with other addictions, which reinforces the uncontrollability of the situation: 'an inflicter who is carried away by sexual excitement or by drink or drugs could very easily inflict pain and injury beyond the level to which the receiver had consented'.[62]

The analysis of Lord Lowry, however, at first blush appears at variance with that of his brethren. Like Lords Templeman and Jauncey, he recognised the likelihood (perhaps inevitability) of a cycle of escalating violence resulting from addictive behaviour. He framed the analysis, though, not in terms of the artificiality and unnaturalness of the sexual pursuits, but in terms of instinct. Thus, he foresaw the '*probability* that some sado-masochistic activity, under the powerful influence of the sexual instinct, will get out of hand'.[63] Rather than structuring desire around the binary of the natural and the artificial, Lord Lowry suggested that the sadomasochistic sexual encounter will get out of hand because of its instinctive and presumably natural foundations. If we are engaged with a 'problem' of instinct rather than addiction, then the double bind of volition and compulsion seems resolved. The sex instinct, by virtue of its natural basis, cannot be described both as addictive and volitional in the way that addictions usually are constructed.

However, if the concept of addiction has been evacuated of any essential meaning, then presumably the sexual *instinct* itself can be the substance of addiction. In this way, Lord Lowry's reasoning is consistent with addiction analysis. Free will must control the instinctive in Lord Lowry's approach in order to prevent the spiral of addiction. If the instinctive is in some sense natural, then another discourse emerges within this judgment. The natural, rather than juxtaposed against the artificial, forms a binary relationship with the social. It is the natural which must be brought under control or 'harnessed' to the proper ends of society. The sexual instinct must be regulated to prevent a loss of control and utilised towards appropriate social ends. Despite his focus on the social as a contrast to the natural, Lord Lowry remains firmly entrenched within a discourse of addiction.

Furthermore, the phenomenon of addiction becomes problematic because of the way it is read as threatening to the bonds of society. In an interview, Jacques Derrida has explored the logic of addiction in relation to drug use and has suggested that the threat from addiction arises in relation to the perceived withdrawal of the addict from civil society: 'he cuts himself off from the world, in exile from reality, far from objective reality and the real life of the city and the community; that he escapes into a world of simulacrum and fiction'.[64] Addiction is a fictional world because of the inauthenticity of the stimulation of the drug, which contrasts to the genuineness of social life. A 'free and responsible subjectivity' depends upon a symbolic connection to that social life.[65] The normal, non-addicted, and engaged body thus is a prerequisite to the continued existence of the social bond:

this protection of the social bond, and thus of a certain symbolicity, indeed of rationality in general – this is almost always presented as the protection of a "natural" normality of the body, of the body politic and the body of the individual member.[66]

Addiction, as I have argued, is read as destructive of the self and, as well, as destructive of society by virtue of its power to desocialise. The indictment against drug use is designed to 'forbid a pleasure that is at once solitary, desocializing, and yet contagious for the *socius*'.[67]

Addiction, then, is devoid of the 'truth' of social life. It is constructed as a withdrawal of the body from the body social and from the 'authentic' life in favour of the simulacrum. Although Derrida's analysis is framed in terms of drugs, the analysis also applies to the deployment of the language of addiction in relation to a gay male sexuality. It explains why, for Lord Templeman, the fact that charges against the appellants were laid pursuant to the law of assault, rather than indecency, is perfectly comprehensible. As he posits, 'indecency charges are connected with sex. Charges under the 1861 Act are concerned with violence.'[68] The sadomasochistic encounters are an inauthentic form of sexual expression that ultimately need not even be characterised as sexual by the law. For the majority of the Law Lords, there is a truth and an authenticity to sex and the experience of sadomasochism is both inauthentic and artificial.[69]

Furthermore, the normal, non-addicted body becomes the precondition for the survival of the social body. It is the addict, no matter what the substance of addiction, who threatens society through his withdrawal from its reach. This desocialising effect of addiction can be reframed in terms of the public–private distinction. Addiction is constructed as a withdrawal from the public realm into a private world. Discourses surrounding both the serial killer case and the *Brown* decision are replete with references to the gay other world and the double life (public v. private) led by many gay men. The retreat from the social into an-other world renders a reading of the occurrences within that private realm particularly difficult for judges to decipher publicly.

Of course, the fact that the private world is itself a discursive sphere and a subcommunity means that its construction as contrary to the social is flawed. Rather, it presents an alternative social ordering. As Derrida has argued 'the act of drug use itself is structured like a language and so could not be purely private'.[70] So too, as I suggested earlier, the sadomasochistic community, instead of constituting a realm of privacy (in the sense of isolation from a social reality), creates a social world (and legal order) with its own language and regulatory codes of conduct. The lack of public fluency of the judiciary in that shared language renders them unable to interpret the limits and boundaries that may well be respected within the sadomasochistic sexual encounter.[71] It also explains how the serial killer episode can be characterised as the ultimate (and inevitable) step in a progression of violent acts. The justification for the prosecution of private sexual relations implicit in the judgment of the majority in *Brown* (and the public–private distinction forms the basis of the liberal critique of the decision), is that such activities are harmful to the body social because they represent a withdrawal from the dominant social order in favour of an alternative set of norms. It is the difficulty of monitoring that order (which, although private, is not solitary) which renders those activities particularly dangerous. Within this sub-culture, language itself has been reworked through the introduction of code words that provide the basis for the regulation of sexual conduct. The fact that judges are unable to read that language (or perhaps to comprehend the negotiation of a language of sexual limits) also 'speaks' to the construction of the sexual. The creation of a set of sexual rules through language suggests a subcultural exit from the dominant regime. This alternative, however, is construed by the Law Lords as inauthentic, unreal, and the product of a sexual addiction.

Thus, the public–private distinction, rather than foreclosing the prosecution of the defendants in *Brown, demands* that public order be protected from the emergence of an alternative set of norms. This is achieved in part through erecting borders against the other, constructed as outside the dominant order. As Beverly Brown has argued in the context of indecency law, we are witnessing the collapse of a private realm free of the penetrating gaze of the state. Of course, as Brown has noted, the Wolfenden strategy itself was designed to isolate homosexuality in a private realm, where it would not display itself or participate in dialogue within the public sphere.[72] Yet, ironically, the development of a 'private' subcultural world that has avoided the gaze comes to be the subject of condemnation and is found particularly dangerous. The home itself becomes a target of surveillance in order to detect 'an inherently dangerous, unpredictable, latent and punitive sexu-ality, a degenerate sexuality capable of extinguishing future generations'.[73]

The language of seduction

Seduction, like addiction, is a discourse that pathologises the homosexual. The power of the gay man to seduce the 'normal' male into both a sexual act and a sexual identity is frequently employed to expurgate the homosexual from the bounds of civil society. The seductiveness of the gay man (and of homosexuality) is constructed as threatening to the integrity of a heterosexual identity. It is a threat which has been cited as justification for the use of force in retaliation to the 'homosexual advance'. Such a response to the sexual advance stems not only from the fear of being seduced into an act, but more importantly, from the seductiveness of this alternative sexual identity:

> Of course, heterosexual culture in the West has long interpreted homo-sexuality as a threat to the security or integrity of heterosexual identity. In our dauntingly inconsistent mythology of homosexuality, "the love that dared not speak its name" . . . was so designated not only because it was seen as lurid, shameful, and repellent, but also, and contradictorally, because it was, and is, conceived of as being potentially so attractive that

even to speak about it is to risk the possibility of tempting some innocent into a fate too horrible – and too seductive – to imagine.[74]

The temptation that the gay man offers is so powerfully seductive as to be almost irresistible. Moreover, this seductiveness is linked to a discourse of youth and the potential corruption of the young. This connection has long had a resonance which functions to stifle dialogue. The gay male becomes a 'predatory, determined invert, wrapped in a Grand Guignol cloak of degeneracy theory, and casting his lascivious eyes – and hands . . . onto "our" children, and above all onto "our" sons'.[75] Most importantly, though, the danger of seduction lies not simply in the possibility of an *act* of same sex intercourse (which does not in itself create the homosexual), but the seductiveness of an *identity*, and an all-consuming sexual identity.

The spectacle of the homosexual as the source of erotic seductiveness is one means of pathologising the gay man. It provides a recurring image of child molestation which helps facilitate the social construction of homosexuality as 'intrinsically monstrous within the entire system of heavily over-determined images inside which notions of "decency", "human nature" and so on are mobilised and relayed throughout the internal circuitry of the mass media marketplace'.[76]

This discourse is employed by the Law Lords. The dangers of seduction of vulnerable and innocent youth into a degenerate (and all too appealing) lifestyle is a rationale for criminalising the consensual sadomasochistic sexual encounter. Lord Templeman is most expansive in employing this justification. He noted that 'the victims were youths some of whom were introduced to sadomasochism before they attained the age of 21'.[77] He then favourably cited at length the judgment of Lord Lane in the Court of Appeal, who described the degeneracy and seductiveness of the appellants. According to Lord Lane, two members of the group:

> were responsible in part for the corruption of a youth "K". . . . It is some comfort at least to be told, as we were, that "K" has now it seems settled into a normal heterosexual relationship. Cadman had befriended "K" when the boy was 15 years old. He met him in a cafeteria and, so he says, found out that the boy was interested in homosexual activities. He introduced and encouraged "K" in "bondage" affairs. He was interested in viewing and recording on video tape "K" and other teenage boys in homosexual scenes.[78]

Fortunately, the awesome seductive power of the homosexual was not overwhelming in the case of 'K', who managed to resist and, in a move that provided some solace, entered the domain of normal sexuality. Presumably, 'K' left behind a life of degeneracy and assumed a thoroughly heterosexual (and non-sadomasochistic) identity. Like Lord Templeman, Lord Jauncey also recognised that 'the possibility of proselytisation and corruption of young men is a real danger', thereby justifying a dismissal of the appeals.[79]

The pathologising of the gay man through an association with the seduction of the innocent extends to media representations in the gay serial killer case. In this example, the seductiveness of the sex act stems from its connections with danger and the possibility of death. In other words, the *addictiveness* of gay sex contributes to its *seductive* potential and heightens its attractiveness.

The seductiveness of homosexuality then is a siren song that leads the unwary into the clutches of the pathological. It is irresistable, despite the victim's awareness of its dangers and the perhaps fatal outcome. This in turn contributes to the seductiveness of the sexual encounter – the linking of pleasure and danger – and leads to a powerful seduction into a lifestyle that is both all consuming and usually irreversible.

Contagion

Like the discourses of addiction and seduction, the construction of homosexuality as a deviant sexual practice consistently has been realised through a discourse of contagion. As I discussed in Chapter 5, while the association of disease and its contagiousness with sexual practices is not new, the present climate has facilitated a renewed vigour in the deployment of the language of contagion and disease within an analysis of gay male sexuality.

The linking of the dangers of disease with transgressions of the dominant moral code is hardly unique to our current cultural conditions. Mary Douglas argued that 'danger-beliefs' centring upon disease and pollution resulting from socially transgressive behaviour is one means of maintaining social norms. The language of disease employs 'nature' and the consequences of disobeying the laws of nature as a means of social control:

> the laws of nature are dragged in to sanction the moral code: this kind of disease is caused by adultery, that by incest . . . The whole universe is harnessed to men's attempts to force one another into good citizenship. Thus we find that certain moral values are upheld and certain social rules defined by beliefs in dangerous contagion.[80]

Thus, morality is reinforced by apparently universal rules deriving from nature which 'make judgment on the moral value of human relations'.[81] Moreover, for the morally transgressive citizen, protection from the wrath of nature may come only from the social body, because the individual is unable to resist the danger himself.[82] The figure of the transgressor comes to be seen as blameworthy. He is a polluted figure; 'he has developed some wrong condition or simply crossed some line which should not have been crossed and this displacement unleashes danger'.[83]

The transgression that leads to danger and exposes the individual to the contagiousness of disease, centres upon the body. Transgression is a violation of social norms because it is a crossing of boundaries which must be protected and the body serves as a metaphor for this space. Boundaries symbolised by the body must be reinforced through their social construction as impermeable. That norm is undermined by morally deviant behaviour. The language of pollution accentuates and reinforces moral indignation at the undermining of the structure of boundaries for:

> when action that is held to be morally wrong does not provoke moral indignation, belief in the harmful consequences of a pollution can have the effect of aggravating the seriousness of the offence, and so of marshalling public opinion on the side of right.[84]

The association of homosexuality with pollution, disease and contagion has been exacerbated in the age of Aids. Homosexuality long has been the target of the metaphors of pollution and fatal illness. The homosexual has been constructed as a 'vessel holding disease and, therefore, an extension of the disease'.[85] The Aids pandemic, however, 'has been invoked as proof of the diseased, contagious and dangerous nature of homosexuality'.[86] As a consequence, the association of Aids and the gay man has facilitated a discourse of contagion, disease, and decay leading to an inexorable death.

This linkage between sexual act, sexual identity, and destruction (both of the body and the body social) is maintained through the connections between the discourses of addiction, seduction, and contagion. In fact, the construction of the homosexual as an identity in the nineteenth century emerged precisely 'at the interstices of a host of overlapping discourses concerning sickness, contamination and genetic throwbacks, and was regarded as the most concrete evidence of the results of indecency, depravity and uncleanliness'.[87]

The homosexual as personification of disease has been reinforced through the social response to Aids. The 'disease' of homosexuality – which has been utilised to collapse an identity into an immune deficiency syndrome – demands the creation of a heterosexual sphere protected against the destructiveness of this 'other'. Through the discourses surrounding Aids, a literal and a metaphoric illness are joined together and the contagiousness of both demands a social response. Homosexuality thus becomes a hazard for individual and social life because 'the mere fact of gay sex is held to be dangerous for other people'.[88] In developing these connections within dominant discourses, there emerges a 'moral etiology of disease that can only conceive homosexual desire within a medicalized metaphor of contagion'.[89] Combined with the association of homosexuals with corruption, the connections between homosexuality (and its seductiveness) and individual death, social disorder, and decay are further strengthened. To reiterate, this social construction of the contagiousness of a sexual disease and the disease of a sexuality is far from historically specific:

> And it is no surprise to any gay person that death holds down the center around which the sliding signifiers of AIDS discourse swirl; for centuries in the West, death has been held out as the penalty for homosexual acts. All of the discourse of AIDS has encoded the homosexual Other . . . In fact, no event in the AIDS crisis has been a surprise – not the relentless deaths, not

the years of invisibility, not the sudden and promiscuous speaking about AIDS once sexual anxiety could be repressed and rearticulated as "public health".[90]

Thus, the discourses surrounding the Aids pandemic must be understood as a 'powerful condensor for a great range of social, sexual and psychic anxieties'.[91] The reaction to these anxieties leads to the reinforcement of the boundaries that mark off risk groups, whereby 'the innocent victim is bounded off from the guilty one, pure blood from contaminated, the general population from the Aids populations, risk groups from those not at risk'.[92] Through the reinforcement of these boundaries, heterosexuality and the family become a protected sphere that forms the foundation of the social order that is under continued threat from outside.

Epidemic conditions also can be employed to justify public intervention. As Linda Singer argued, the construction of disease as an epidemic creates the social conditions not simply for repression, but more importantly, 'the epidemic provides an occasion and a rationale for multiplying points of intervention into the lives of bodies and populations'.[93] Moreover, the current pandemic has been inscribed as profoundly sexual, which facilitates connections between disease, contagion, and the transgression of the boundaries demarcating the limits of social propriety. It is this fusing of disease and moral transgression that fuels the perceived threat to the body politic arising from the contagiousness of the disease of transgression. The deployment of power thus becomes justifiable given the danger to the social order:

> The establishment of a connection between epidemic and transgression has allowed for the rapid transmission of the former to phenomena that are outside the sphere of disease . . . The use of this language marks all of these phenomena as targets for intervention because they have been designated as unacceptable, while at the same time reproducing the power that authorizes and justifies their deployment. According to this discourse, it is existing authority that is to be protected from the plague of transgressions.[94]

Transgression itself becomes a plague which must be eradicated to protect the viability and continued existence of society. Unsafe activities which may lead to HIV transmission thus are judged as 'indulgence, delinquency – addictions to chemicals that are illegal and to sex regarded as deviant'.[95]

Transgression of the moral boundaries of society is perceived as leading to fatal consequences, which provides the ideal precondition for the reinforcement of the naturalness of those boundaries. Activities though must be continually monitored and regulated because, despite the consequences of crossing the moral divide, the addictiveness and seductiveness of sexual transgression will lead many into peril. The transmission of HIV is caused by the contagiousness of homosexuality which is particularly dangerous for the innocent and vulnerable. Homosexuality thus becomes a 'death wish' and the homosexual body is rendered a contagious vessel, threatening to infect the body politic.

It is this destructive potential – and the destruction not only of the self but also of society – which provides the justification for the intervention in the lives of citizens. This is particularly apparent in the reasoning of the House of Lords. The impossibility of the homosexual body and the inevitability of its death weaves its way throughout the judgments of the majority. Lord Lowry, for example, was most forthright in his determination that:

When considering the danger of infection, with its *inevitable* threat of AIDS, I am not impressed by the argument that this threat can be discounted on the ground that, as long ago as 1967, Parliament, subject to conditions, legalised buggery, now a *well-known vehicle* for the transmission of AIDS.[96]

The gay male thus becomes firmly tied to the transmission of HIV. Infection is the inevitable result of sexual contact and death is the consequence of a sexual identity. The fact that no evidence was presented linking the particular sexual practices of the appellants to HIV infection does not dispel the inevitability of the consequences of gay sex, whether sadomasochistic or not. Lord Jauncey described as 'good luck rather than good judgment' that injury did not occur.[97]

In fact, Lord Templeman questioned whether any action to reduce or eliminate the possibility of the transmission of HIV through a gay male sexual act could be successful. At one point it appears that the impossibility of the homosexual body ultimately will triumph over safe sex practices. Lord Templeman argued that '*the assertion that the instruments employed by the sadists were clean and sterilised could not have removed the danger of infection*, and the assertion that care was taken demonstrates the possibility of infection'.[98] Thus, safer sex techniques cannot counter the threat of contagion and the fatal disease of homosexuality cannot be eliminated from the sex act. Rather, safer sex itself becomes the proof of contagion. It is only by regulatory surveillance through the state that the body and the body politic can be protected *from* the homosexual male's inevitable drive towards death.

Within the judgment in *Brown*, this characterisation of the diseased and contagious body is realised in large measure through the frequent mention of blood as an agent of contagion. The preoccupation with blood is explicit in the judgment of Lord Templeman, who explained that 'bloodletting and the smearing of human blood produced excitement. There were obvious dangers of serious personal injury and blood infection.'[99] Interestingly, Foucault argued that historically 'blood was a reality with a symbolic function',[100] and, moreover, 'the preoccupation with blood and the law has for nearly two centuries haunted the administration of sexuality'.[101] In *Brown*, blood continues to carry this symbolic function, operating to further reinforce the proposition that, in this case, 'sex is indeed imbued with the death instinct'.[102]

In engaging in this process of medicalisation, the House of Lords transformed the 'symptoms' of sadomasochism – the letting of blood, the penetration of skin, the imposition of pain generally – into the signifiers of the disease of homosexuality and the end result of that disease, a gruesome death. The Law Lords operate a 'clinical gaze' that reveals the truth of the sadomasochistic acts – they 'discover its secrets'.[103] Indeed, the literal secrets of the appellants are revealed and the 'truth' of those acts is discerned by the Law Lords. Ultimately, the gaze reveals, as Foucault described so eerily in reference to the development of the clinic, that 'the idea of a disease attacking life must be replaced by the much denser notion of pathological life'.[104] This gaze that reveals the pathological life of the homosexual body condemns the lives of the appellants and ultimately the lives of all gay men, for within the judgment it is apparent that death becomes the 'invisible truth' of the body rendered visible.[105]

The reporting of the serial killer case also uncovers this truth. When newspaper reports disclosed that all five men died 'as a direct result of cruising',[106] the truth of homosexuality as death wish is brought to light, which also is explicitly linked to the threat of HIV. For example, the reports speculated that the motive for the murders 'could be revenge for an HIV infection or a desire to destroy homosexuals'.[107] The self-destructiveness of the homosexual thus forms the basis of an urban myth of the HIV-positive serial killer seeking vengeance. The gaze also is employed within this narrative. The 1993 London Gay Pride March itself, which occurred in the midst of the serial killings, was described as overshadowed by the *literal* gaze of the killer: 'they [the marchers] knew it was almost certain that a murderous psychopath was either walking alongside or watching closely'.[108] Such narratives ultimately serve as Aids parables through a process of 'project[ing] upon the living body a whole network of anatomo-pathological mappings: to draw the dotted out line of the future autopsy'.[109] They also serve to eroticise sadomasochism for the general public.

In both the *Brown* decision and in the events surrounding the serial killer case, the contagiousness of disease and the polluted body of the homosexual serve as reminders of the outcome of sexual transgression. Thus, homosexuality itself becomes a contagious condition which requires a sharp protective boundary between heterosexuality and its other, for transgression of that boundary leads to a brutal and inevitable death.

CONCLUSION

In this chapter, I have interrogated two examples of the relationship between law and a deviant sexuality as a means of illustrating how law, as a set of discourses, works to pathologise gay male sexuality. The operation of power through law and the discourses that surround law are not simply prohibitive. Law also constitutes sexuality as deviant and seeks to regulate what is defined as beyond normality. The pleasure of sex and the power of law thus exist in a complex relationship. In *Brown*, for example, a sexual proclivity is tranformed into legal discourse. In so doing, the law operates to intensify the body and to exploit it as an object of knowledge. Through its gaze, law is engaged in 'penetrating bodies in an increasingly detailed way, and in controlling populations in an increasingly comprehensive way'.[110] As the Law Lords recognised, the pleasure of power and powerlessness is realised only through an escalation of relations of dominance and submission. However, it is the intensity of the deployment of sexuality within legal discourse which is escalating; highlighting the power imbalances that operate between the appellants and that discourse.

However, the relationship of pleasure and power is far from straightforward. The exercise of power does not simply act in response to sexual pleasure, but power also is constitutive of pleasure. The attempt to prohibit erotic pleasure through law thus may operate as a precondition to the erotic fantasy itself. As Judith Butler has argued so persuasively, 'the very rhetoric by which certain erotic acts or relations are prohibited invariably eroticizes that prohibition in the service of a fantasy'.[111] The sadomasochism of the encounters in *Brown*, then, must be understood as produced and sustained by the discourses of prohibition that already have conditioned it in advance.

In conclusion, both the decision of the House of Lords in *Brown* and the serial murders in the summer of 1993 highlight a sadomasochistic relationship. However, it is the production through discourse of the figure of the homosexual – sadomasochistic, polluted, addicted to his desires, self-destructive, and yet terrifyingly seductive – which itself constitutes that relationship. What is achieved is 'a vehement and public way of drawing into public attention the very figure that is supposed to be banned from public attention'.[112] In the end, then, it is law itself which acts sadomasochistically – engaged in 'a public flogging and debasement of the homosexual',[113] brought under its gaze in order to be denigrated and reviled.

8

TOWARDS A QUEER LEGAL THEORY

It is appropriate to conclude this book with an intervention on the emergence of 'queerness' in the 1990s. We have recently witnessed the growth of 'queer culture', 'queer theory', and even a 'queer nation' in some western post-industrial societies. These developments in social practice and theory have been experienced by some as liberating, and have been described by others as deeply problematic. I already have considered some of the challenges raised by queerness in earlier chapters – surrounding issues of identity, categorical thinking, and the coherence of gender as an identity concept. Throughout this analysis, it has become increasingly apparent that a tension exists between, on the one hand, the queer 'desire' to deconstruct the categories of identity and render them problematic; and, on the other, the necessity of asserting coherent categories as a strategy of political reform and transformation. I bring this dilemma to the forefront in this chapter and I argue that the tension between the assertion and deconstruction of identity categories is irresolvable and should be understood as a continuing contestation. I will also consider the relation of queer social theory and practices to law, in order to begin to develop what I term a 'queer legal theory'. I will argue, as I have done throughout this book, that while law may be repressive in its relationship to lesbians and gay men (or, indeed, to 'queers'), law as a locus of struggle can be dynamic, unstable, and unpredictable. I will suggest that law and legal reasoning can inadvertently contribute to the development of a 'queer' political stance and identity. In this regard, legal discourse often inscribes sexuality in a queer fashion and, in the process, legal reasoning itself becomes a queer phenomenon. That is, opportunities for resistance within the legal realm may be opened up through the spaces in the reasoning left by the law and it is through these gaps that the weakness in the system might be subverted and even queered.

QUEER PRACTICES, QUEER THEORIES: A PRIMER

Defining the parameters of 'queer' is no easy task. Queerness undoubtedly means different things to different people, at different moments, in different contexts.

This ambiguity in meaning underscores the fluidity of the term; the fact that its boundaries, rather than being fixed, possess a high degree of flexibility. Sometimes 'queer' is deployed as a synonym for lesbian, gay, and bisexual sexualities. Given how troublesome it is to continually say (and write) that triumvirate of sexual identities, the employment of a single word that can signify a range of sexualities which have been socially constructed as deviant, often proves useful.

However, for my purposes, the term 'queer' can be used in a somewhat different sense. I want to consider the implications of the term as signifying a provisional category of identity in its own right. The meaning of a queer identity again is not easily definable; that of course contributes to its current popularity. Central to a queer identity, though, is the problematisation of categories of sexual identity and boundaries of sexual propriety, as they have been historically constituted. Queerness in part suggests an unwillingness to fix difference in any ultimate literality. Rather, queers favour a strategically articulated commonality forged from differently located subject positions. A unity is sought without imposing closure on any identity category through fixed conditions of membership:

> Queer Nation affirms an abstract unity of differences without wishing to name and fix these. This positioning resembles the poststructuralist refusal to name the subject, as if any anchoring of the flux and abundant richness of experience marks the beginning of conflict, domination and hierarchy.[1]

Queerness thus suggests the 'subversion of identity' at the same time that a category of identity is tenuously constituted.[2] In a sense, then, queerness might provide a challenging response to my discussion of the emergence of the gay subject in Chapter 1. While the gay subject may have emerged at a particular historical moment as a coherent subjectivity, queerness now aims to deconstruct the identity and contest its stability. Queer signifies a more fluid conception of subjectivity, a 'new elasticity in the meanings of lesbian and gay' in which the fixity of sexual identity is loosened.[3] It also thereby challenges the coherence of the subject and, in so doing, it simultaneously underscores the exclusions that the closure of identity categories inevitably bring.

Consequently, queerness has been characterised as a stance generated from a position of dissent and resistance to the attempt at categorisation within both dominant culture and sexual subcultures. Queerness thus inhabits an interesting position, as both an identity category and an explicit challenge to the attempt at categorisation (and all at the same time!). In particular, it challenges the fixity of the categories of gender and sexual identity and the binary opposition of hetero- and homosexuality. It thus is a 'stance constituted through its dissent from the hegemonic, structured relations and meanings of sexuality and gender, but its actual historical forms and positions are open, constantly subject to negotiation and renegotiation'.[4] To the extent that the coherent gay subject depends upon the construction of sexuality as a binary opposition dependent upon the gender of object choice, the articulation of a gay subjectivity can reinforce and reify the hetero–homo dichotomy which forms the basis of categorical thinking around sexuality. Of course, it is this construction of rigid sexual categories that provides the framework within which a system of compulsory heterosexuality so often flourishes.[5] The alternative, according to queers, is to undermine and destabilise sexual (and other) identities as the basis of both activism and theory, rather than reinforcing them through the assertion of categories that historically have been deployed in an oppressive manner.

A less fixed conception of identity also is a means to respond to issues of exclusion that have surfaced within the lesbian and gay movements, along lines of race, sexual practices, (dis)ability, age, gender, and so on. While identity categories may demand boundaries in order to be constituted in a coherent fashion, lesbian and gay politics has often seemed in practice less inclusive of difference than in stated theory. Membership in a sexual category defined in terms of its 'otherness' to the heterosexual norm implicitly (and sometimes explicitly) has been constructed in a totalising fashion. That is, sexual identity provides the singular difference which is similarly inscribed upon all who claim membership in the group. The focus on sexual categories thus slides easily into a one-dimensional view of 'otherness', which frequently has obliterated the complexity of the matrices of oppression in which subjects operate.

For example, Arlene Stein has argued that the lesbian feminist movement was plagued by a double bind in which, on the one hand, membership in the movement was universally available; indeed, the movement 'positioned itself as the expression of the aspirations of *all* women'.[6] On the other hand, in so doing, the identity became totalised, such that 'at its worst, it hardened the boundaries around lesbian communities, subsumed differences of race, class, and even sexual orientation, and set up rather rigid standards for living one's life'.[7] The lesbian feminist movement thus to some extent was faced with an irresolvable conflict between a stabilised minority status with a set of (contested) criteria of membership; and the constitution of itself as unbounded in the sense of being able to tap into the woman-centredness of *all* women (leaving aside, of course, the problematic of defining an essential woman).

Queerness in part is a reaction to the double bind faced by lesbian feminism and it also highlights a certain generational division within the lesbian movement. Some lesbians, for example, have questioned the coherence of the category 'lesbian', and the nexus between gender and sexuality that lesbian feminism posited:

> An emergent lesbian politics acknowledged the relative autonomy of gender and sexuality, sexism and heterosexism. It suggested that lesbians shared with gay men a sense of "queerness", a non-normative sexuality which transcends the binary distinction between homosexual/heterosexual to include all who feel disenfranchised by dominant sexual norms – lesbians and gay men, as well as bisexuals and transsexuals.[8]

The stance of queerness thus potentially provides a point of unity across differences of gender, sexual practices, and sexual orientation. It represents simply a positioning in relation to a dominant, background norm, and it demands only a refusal to conform to normalcy. Queerness thereby might challenge the rigid binary thinking through which categories have been constructed. It also provides a means to dissolve the fixity of sexual and gender categories as they have been employed to inscribe subjects and through which subjects also have constituted themselves.

At the same time, the transcending of categories cannot, in itself, dissolve the structural inequalities that emerge out of the process of categorisation within dominant culture. While queer sexuality may be perceived as a means to break down barriers between lesbians and gay men, bisexuals, transsexuals, and others, social categories still have a material reality that impacts upon people's lives. As Stein has suggested, within queer political movements, 'lesbians and gay men were often divided along much the same lines as heterosexual women and men'.[9]

However, despite the intransigence of these power differentials, which continue to demand political mobilisation in their own right, lesbian and gay sexualities perhaps uniquely lend themselves to being queered. In large measure, queerness signifies a self-reflexive questioning of the naturalness and coherence of any identity category and a recognition of the contingency of categorisation. Furthermore, if lesbian and gay individual and collective identities can be defined by any single phrase, it is surely that of 'coming out'. This is, of course, the rallying cry of the last twenty years of the lesbian and gay movements. Indeed, the closet is a metaphor carrying sufficient rhetorical power for it to seem increasingly capable of appropriation in a plethora of different contexts. But coming out evokes the idea of bounded space and it implies that the self is engaged in a simple 'one off' movement from a constrained sphere into a broader public realm. The process of coming out, however, is fundamentally performative. It is also highly ambiguous in that, while it suggests a clear boundary through which one can 'pass', the process of coming out is ongoing. The subject is always *engaged* in coming out – how far, to whom, and in what contexts. Moreover, the lesbian or gay subject not only comes out in the first person, but also must remember who's in and who's out (or 'outish') and in what circumstances. This process is an ongoing negotiation of borders. Thus, lesbians and gay men have long been aware through experience that borders are not always as stable as they seem, and that the spaces of 'in' and 'out' can be inhabited simultaneously.

In another respect lesbians and gay men are well aware of the contingency and provisionality of identity categories. While a sexual identity can be claimed by oneself through the performative of coming out, identities also are frequently inscribed by others onto the gay subject (and often before one has asserted the identity, even to oneself). People are queered involuntarily all the time, in that categorisation is undertaken both within dominant culture and also subculturally. The boundaries of a lesbian and gay sexuality thus are contested and continually crossed.[10] Lesbian and gay sexualities thereby become particularly conducive to self-reflexivity. That is, for lesbians and gay men, it is perhaps *relatively* easy to recognise that categories have no natural or essential character, and that identities are assumed and inscribed in multiple and conflicted ways. Identity then becomes politically indeterminate and a product of an ongoing contestation over social meanings and definitions.

The stance of queerness also is a form of resistance to the binaries and boundaries of identity as they have been imposed within the lesbian and gay communities. To reiterate, queerness is partly a reaction to the perceived exclusivity and exclusions that are the result of sexual identity categories. As I already have discussed, queerness may be a product of exclusions that have been experienced through the multiplicity of intersecting identities around race, sexual practices, and gender identification. But queerness also is a form of resistance to the agenda of the lesbian and gay movement, as it has been formulated and implemented in the past. The *perception* in some quarters is that the movements around sexual orientation largely have been tied to a politics of liberal assimilation – a politics derived from the belief in the essential 'sameness' of minority sexual preferences (the 'we are just like you' position). Queerness is a response to this political stance; it is 'a form of resistance, a refusal of labels, pathologies and moralities. It is defined more by what it is against than what it is for'.[11]

In the context of the 1980s, a sexual politics of liberal assimilation appeared increasingly lacking in viability in the context of many of the issues that I have analysed in this book: official (and unofficial) government (non)reaction to the Aids pandemic; the success of Senator Helms and others in implementing a conservative political agenda in America; the enactment of section 28 of the *Local Government Act* in Britain; the relative inability to secure anti-discrimination legislation based upon sexual orientation in many jurisdictions and, finally, the decision of the United States Supreme Court in *Bowers v. Hardwick*, which held that private consensual sexual relations between same sex partners are not constitutionally protected as a right of privacy (an issue I will discuss in more depth shortly).[12] In the face of these sometimes startling (and frightening) developments, an assimilationist approach appeared spent as a political strategy. Furthermore, the urgency and anger felt by many around HIV and Aids also fuelled the rise of a more radical, uncompromising politics:

> Queer finds its firmest tap-root here, in the cultural experience of a devastation unique outside wartime, where whole populations were seen to be surplus, disposable: Other. Queer claims this otherness as its own, donning the mantle of pariah, acknowledging the failure of assimilation, a strategy demonstrably broken-backed in the light of straight America's response to Aids . . . rage rather than mere acceptance, rejection of a flawed tolerance rather than demands for integration, such were the tenor and tone of the times.[13]

Queerness also serves as a form of resistance to a lesbian and gay politics that in large measure has assumed the centrality of sexual identity to individual subjectivity and, furthermore, that has often assumed a unitary and essential sexual identity. Within such a model, identity as lesbian, gay or straight has been inscribed unproblematically upon the subject. For that matter, the same rigid categories of sexual identity have been utilised within dominant culture, by a gay and lesbian movement espousing a liberal assimilationist agenda, and by more 'radical' elements of the movement in the practice of 'outing'. Outers, for example, assume that sexual identity can be ascribed and articulated, and that a 'true' sexual identity can be revealed for the greater good:

> Outers generally not only believe in the existence of a gay nation, but are confident of their ability to identify its members and of their authority to do so. They have no doubts about definitions or boundaries, and do not hesitate to override the welfare and autonomy of individuals "in the national interest".[14]

The problem, of course, is that in assuming a primary and coherent sexual identity, the complexity of identity which many subjects experience is overlooked. It is not surprising therefore that, to the extent that a political stance depends upon the primacy and centrality of a coherent sexual identity, it so often 'ultimately represents the view from the subject position "20th-century Western white gay male"'.[15]

To repeat, a queer stance challenges the unitary 'givens' of sexual identity as they have been developed in the past across the political spectrum. Thus, queerness might challenge binary and categorical thinking which has inscribed the 'normal' and the 'other'. Central to the project is the contestation of boundaries and categories, not only of sexual identity, but more widely to include all the boundaries of normalcy. Queerness is a rejection of minority group categorisation in general, and it underscores the complexity of the logic of identity:

> along dimensions that can't be subsumed under gender and sexuality at all: the ways that race, ethnicity, postcolonial rationality criss-cross within these and other identity-constituting, identity-fracturing discourses.[16]

Rather than constituting a totalised identity category itself, queerness highlights the contingency of all boundaries of social practice and identity, including its own. It represents a subversion of categorical thinking so that 'queer' is capable of constant reworking to serve new political purposes. Queer theory, then, is closely related to the critical approaches of deconstruction and poststructuralism. In fact, the latter has been described as 'a sort of theoretical wing of Queer Nation'.[17]

At its highest, queerness also seeks to challenge the binary opposition between theory and practice in the realm of sexuality. So too, it could be employed to develop the relationship between sexual practices and political activism, and might explain how a theoretical position spins off of both. The recent work of Eve Sedgwick represents a self-conscious attempt to cross these categories. For Sedgwick, queerness suggests:

the open mesh of possibilities, gaps, overlaps, dissonances and resonances, lapses and excesses of meaning when the constituent elements of anyone's gender, of anyone's sexuality aren't made (or can't be made) to signify monolithically.[18]

She thus links queerness explicitly to the performativity of gender (and all other) categories.[19] Sedgwick has coined the term 'queer performativity', drawing upon Judith Butler's analysis of gender performativity, which might provide insights into the significance of queer social practices.[20] Performativity as a concept facilitates an anti-essentialist view of identities by suggesting that it is through the repetition of actions alone that all identities come to be naturalised. Queerness, though, in its disruptive capacity, might undermine the dominant performatives of gender and sexuality. Through acts that challenge the category of the sexually 'normal', a queer identification can be understood, not as an essential sexual category, but rather as an identity that emerges from a 'self' awareness of its own contingency: '"queer" seems to hinge much more radically and explicitly on a person's undertaking particular, performative acts of experimental self-perception and filiation'.[21]

Queerness thus becomes principally based upon how the subject sees herself in relation to dominant background norms of sexuality, rather than how the subject slots into any particular sexual identity category as it has been historically constituted. Queer no longer then is coterminous with a lesbian or gay sexual identity. Nor is it synonymous with any particular sexual act, nor reducible to the genders of the participants. Rather, queer has an ambiguous quality both in terms of act and identity:

> I'd venture that queerness in this sense has, at this historical moment, *some* definitionally very significant overlap – though a vibrantly elastic and temporally convoluted one – with the complex of attributes today condensed as adult or adolescent "gayness". Everyone knows that there are lesbians and gay men who could never count as queer, and other people who vibrate to the chord of queer without having much same-sex eroticism, or without routing their same-sex eroticism through the identity labels lesbian or gay.[22]

In the way that Sedgwick understands it, queerness depends largely (or exclusively) upon the individual identifying as such. The category thereby is devoid of essential content, so that it can be invoked by queers everywhere. The identity thus is always open to resignification, it is self-consciously provisional and tenuous, and it knows no bounds. Rather, it transgresses and problematises the boundaries of other identities, underscoring the contingency of categories and contesting any attempt to naturalise them. The inside/out binary thereby is transcended through a mode of resistance to a history of categorisation and the essentialising of categories.

However, queerness as a stance and an identity cannot possibly live up to this idealistic billing in practice. For instance, it is rather presumptuous of Sedgwick to suggest that 'everyone' knows that there are lesbians and gay men who are not 'queer'. This comment implies that there are some boundaries to queerness (at least set by Sedgwick herself) and, for the cynic, this may give rise to some scepticism as to the all-inclusiveness and anti-essentialism of the identity. Consequently, queer may (and perhaps must) effect its own set of exclusions which reproduce the inside/out binary. This may make some of us rather reluctant to take on a sexual identity that definitionally excludes, for reasons that remain unarticulated, some lesbians and gay men. So too, I suspect that many lesbians and gay men would be reluctant to identify, in terms of a shared sexual identity, with people who primarily have cross-gender sexual relations. While the problematising of categorical thought may be a positive development, categories continue to be invested with social meaning and, as a result of categorisation, different subjects experience a different material reality. In terms of the categories of sexual identity, the position of men and women who primarily or exclusively have sexual relations with each other is *different* because it has been socially constructed as such (no matter what the sexual practice, if any, in which they are engaged).[23] After all, categories cannot be divested of social significance simply through wishing it were so.

This analysis also raises the fundamental question of whether, in constituting itself, an identity can avoid creating a series of exclusions through a set of boundaries by which the identity is coherently constituted. If this in fact is the case, then it is debateable whether queer is simply a broader category of identity – seemingly more inclusive in some respects – but effecting new sets of exclusions along different axes. For example, 'queer culture' (which presently has attained a particular prominence in the mainstream media) in many respects is founded upon consumer consumption. Culture, in this context, appears to be the ability to purchase and consume goods and services aimed at a 'queer' market, which then fortifies the identity. While I argued in Chapter 3 that consumption historically has been conducive to the formation of a gay male identity, the heightened focus on consumerism also exacerbates distinctions based upon social class in the delineation of the identity category. Furthermore, queer identity, being in many ways a reaction to a previous generation of lesbians and gay men, is itself a rather youth-oriented (and urban) community. Finally, while queerness idealistically may be defined in cross-gender terms, queer activism in the 1990s has not easily transcended the political and economic inequalities as between gay men and lesbians.

QUEER/LAWS

Despite its drawbacks, I still want to argue that the creation of queerness as a theoretical and political stance is an important occurrence that can provide insights worth employing.[24] At this point, I also want to bring the analysis back to its relevance for legal theory. In providing a critique of categorical thinking in general, and by denaturalising the meaning which has been discursively invested in categories, queer theory has obvious applications to law. Categorical thought is the foundation of the common law method of analysis. Through the process of drawing analogies and distinctions, students of the common law are taught how to categorise legal problems. While we also are taught to recognise that the contours of the categories sometimes must be redrawn, common law method ultimately demands some degree of essentialism in its use of categories. However, queer theory underscores the contingency and contestability of categories – that there is nothing natural about them. While the employment of categories and their investment with meaning may be necessary in order for us to process information both in law and in life, it is useful to be reminded that when we invoke those categories we should do so prepared to see them deconstructed.

In this regard, common law legal scholars in the last twenty years also have been witnesses to and participants in the critique posed by the school of Critical Legal Studies (CLS). In particular, many Critical Legal Scholars challenged the naturalness of the public/private distinction, arguing that it was a social construction which was employed in order to justify the intervention of law in some (but not other) areas. The divide between the public and the private justified a *laissez faire* judicial philosophy in the spheres of property law and economic regulation.[25] Like queer theorists, proponents of CLS have sought to denaturalise categories of thought which had been inscribed with a meaning that was made to appear historically and culturally invariant. In the case of CLS, the categories are those of legal analysis. With respect to queer theory, the categories are primarily sexual.

However, in response to the CLS critique of the public/private divide, the importance of a zone of privacy has been defended as important both as a symbolic and practical matter. For example, privacy as a constitutional value has been justified on the basis of its connections to personal (sexual) autonomy.[26] As well, for lesbians and gay men, the private has been a crucial realm of safety from a metaphoric and literal violence that lurks within the public sphere. Although that private sphere has been tenuously protected at the best of times, it has remained an important area of *relative* security.

Of course, the private sphere also serves as the basis of the metaphor of the closet. While privacy has a protective function for lesbians and gay men in allowing some freedom in determining where to position oneself in terms of outness (although this varies from person to person), the public/private distinction has also acted as a regulatory boundary by which sexual minorities are removed from a public dialogic sphere into a realm of 'discretion'. Furthermore, the public/private distinction has a particularly queer function in how it must be utilised by lesbians and gay men seeking a *legally* protected sphere of sexual privacy. In order to achieve a legal guarantee of privacy, it first becomes necessary to come 'out' into the public sphere. The closet can only be protected to the extent that someone has crossed the public/private divide.[27]

This paradox of the public and private spheres relates to legal attempts to secure rights of privacy to consensual sexual activity in the United States (as well as in a number of other countries). There are, however, other connections between legal discourse and queer identities in this regard. In my view, queerness as a political and theoretical stance in some measure might be traced to the now notorious decision of the United States Supreme Court in *Bowers v. Hardwick*. In that case, the factual background of which is now well known, the Supreme Court considered whether, in its words, 'the Federal Constitution confers a fundamental right upon homosexuals to engage in sodomy and hence invalidates the laws of the many States that still make such conduct illegal and have done so for a very long time'.[28] As many commentators have pointed out, the issue was whether the right of privacy, which has been judicially recognised in the American Constitution, encompassed the right of private, consensual sexual conduct *in general*. The statute in question criminalised the *act* of sodomy (defined as 'any sexual act involving the sex organs of one person and the mouth or anus of another') and created a penalty of imprisonment 'for not less than one nor more than 20 years'.[29] However, on the face of the statute, it was not the act of same-sex sodomy that was made illegal; rather the statute was neutral regarding the genders of the participants. The majority of the Supreme Court, though, construed the statute as a criminal prohibition on homosexual sodomy. In a very brief judgment, Justice White, for the majority, held that there is no general, constitutionally imposed zone of privacy for private, consensual sexual activity. Furthermore, to claim a right of privacy for homosexual sodomy was, 'at best, facetious'.[30] For the majority of the Supreme Court, the moral basis of the law was beyond review:

> respondent asserts that there must be a rational basis for the law and that there is none in this case other than the presumed belief of a majority of the electorate in Georgia that homosexual sodomy is immoral and unacceptable. This is said to be an inadequate rationale to support the law. The law, however, is constantly based on notions of morality, and if all laws representing essentially moral choices are to be invalidated under the Due Process Clause, the courts will be very busy indeed.[31]

For my purposes, the decision of the Supreme Court in *Bowers v. Hardwick* provides an interesting point of departure for considering the rise of queer politics. To reiterate, the decision to challenge Georgia's sodomy law in court required a crossing of the public/private divide by Michael Hardwick as a means of securing a constitutionally protected zone of privacy. Of course, the boundary between public and private already had been crossed in the events leading up to his arrest.[32]

Furthermore, the queerness of the decision is evident in how the 'homosexual' is publicly inscribed as a class of persons, through a particular deployment of categories. Once again, the Georgia law was apparently neutral *vis-à-vis* sexual orientation. It prohibited heterosexual acts of sodomy as well as same-sex sexual acts. Thus, the focus was a set of sexual activities, rather than a prohibition on the expression of any particular sexual identity (other than 'sodomite'). It simply 'happened' that the individual charged in this case was engaged in a *same*-sex act. However, the majority of the court 'queers' the statute so that the boundary between acts and identities is muddied, leaving acts of sodomy coextensive with the sexual identity of the 'homosexual'. Sodomy becomes defined as an act engaged in by the class of homosexuals and, presumably, only that class is capable of committing such an act. A category of identity thus is invested with meaning through judicial discourse. However, as I have argued throughout this book, categories are never created without an 'other' against which they are constituted. In *Hardwick*, the court succeeds in inscribing an identity through the constitution of the class of heterosexuals, a category of persons who presumably also can be defined in terms of sexual acts. Heterosexuals thus must be the non-sodomites. An interesting judicial manoeuvre is made as the separation of sexual acts from identities is obliterated. At the same time, sexual identities are essentialised in terms of particular sexual acts. A 'constellation of prohibitive practices'[33] provides the essential meaning of a sexual identity and the hetero–homo binary thereby is further strengthened.

The incoherence of this judicial consolidation of acts and identities has been demonstrated by others, who have sought to deconstruct the Court's reasons.[34] To create a binary division of sexual identity categories through the mutually exclusive categorisation of sexual acts can only be realised through the use of a legal fiction. Acts and identities do not cleave 'naturally' (or unnaturally) in such a neat division and by drafting the law in a facially neutral manner, presumably the Georgia legislature appreciated that point. However, *Hardwick* exemplifies the discursive construction of incoherent, essentialised and opposing identity categories that are used to constitute the hetero–homo binary. This movement is reinforced through the repressive and discriminatory employment of the law. As Janet Halley has argued, in the context of the enforcement of sodomy laws (and the judicial imprimateur they have received), 'definitional incoherence is the very mechanism of material dominance'.[35] Through the use of force, an act provides the basis for the definition of an identity, and that identity is inscribed upon the gay body as its total and essential meaning.

One of the more incredible aspects of a case that is, on many levels, quite astonishing is that constitutional precedents could easily have been applied to reach the opposite result. A general right of privacy, understood as grounded in the value of individual autonomy, in the area of consensual, private sexual relations seems implicit in earlier Supreme Court judgments.[36] *Hardwick* might be read then as exemplifying the failure of liberal assimilationist arguments around lesbian and gay male sexuality in American constitutional discourse in the 1980s. The message sent by the Supreme Court was that gays were sodomites and sodomy was not constitutionally protected because it is viewed as immoral by the general public. Therefore, in a logical leap, lesbians and gay men are not constitutionally protected categories of citizens. In the aftermath of *Bowers v. Hardwick*, numerous lower courts have been prepared to perform precisely such a move, holding that lesbians and gay men do not constitute a category subject to heightened judicial scrutiny under the Equal Protection clause of the Bill of Rights (a point which I considered in the context of the 'gays in the military' example in Chapter 5). For many in America, *Bowers v. Hardwick* provided a rude awakening to the realities of American political and judicial thinking in this period. In my view, it was an event which contributed, at least symbolically, to the crystallisation of a new radicalism and rejection of liberal assimilationist rhetoric in the lesbian and gay rights movement.

The predominant factor, however, which may have fuelled an anti-assimilationist politics was the urgency, panic, frustration, and anger that was experienced around the American government's gross inaction over the Aids pandemic in the 1980s. The message here was completely compatible with the Supreme Court's reasoning in *Hardwick*, namely that gay men were sodomites and that sodomy led inexorably to death from Aids. Gay men thus were *the* cause of Aids, which was the logical result of engaging in sodomy. Within these rhetorical tropes, gay men were constitutionally unprotected and, furthermore, their lives were beyond protection from the relentless pursuit of the virus (no matter what 'protection' was adopted). As I suggested in Chapter 2, the conclusion drawn by conservatives was that the only safe gay male sex was abstinence or conversion to a heterosexual (and, therefore, non-sodomotical) sexuality. It is thus not surprising that the thrust of activism shifted in light of the articulation of such reasoning.

The emergence of queerness as a political stance, then, in part is a response to these developments and the perceived failure of the language of liberal rights as a means to realise social change. Arguments based upon the 'sameness' of lesbians and gay men have withered in the face of their continuing construction within dominant culture as 'other', as perverse, as pornographic. In some respects, queerness may be a self-conscious attempt to reclaim this 'otherness'. If, as the American Supreme Court accepted, gays are defined in terms of a set of sexual practices, then queerness appropriates that discourse and throws those sexual practices back 'in their faces'. In an earlier generation, some lesbians and gay men argued that sexual orientation was *more* than 'just sex'. Now, in the 1990s, we are witnessing a radically different strategy. Queers are reclaiming the identity of sodomite which has been inscribed upon them by dominant culture. This phenomenon exemplifies what Judith Butler has described as occurring in the discursive employment of the term queer:

> The contemporary redeployment enacts a prohibition and a degradation against itself, spawning a different order of values, a political affirmation from and through the very term from which in a prior usage had as its final aim the eradication of precisely such an affirmation.[37]

QUEER/FUTURES

In queer times, the status of sexual outlaw has become something of a badge of honour – a celebration of one's position outside the culturally constituted boundaries of normalcy. So too, to the extent that the private has now been officially deemed a constitutionally unprotected zone for lesbians and gay men in America, there may be less incentive to exercise 'discretion' by remaining silenced within that sphere.[38] Queerness challenges the boundaries through which constraints have been imposed upon sexual expression, for 'crucial to a sexually radical movement for social change is the transgression of categorical distinctions, between sexuality and politics, with their typically embedded divisions between public, private, and personal concerns'.[39] For example, Queer Nation's appropriation of public space as a realm of openly sexual expression transgresses the boundaries of public and private. Queers are attempting to redeploy the sexual self in a confrontational manner within public cultural arenas. In this sense, queer activism is a direct challenge to a liberal assimilationist agenda: 'the confrontational queer identity is a critique and a displacement of the homosexuality which wants to occupy a legitimate space within an unchanged social order'.[40]

The challenge to sexual boundaries offered by many queers in the 1990s also includes sexual practices themselves. Once again, if a liberal assimilationist approach as enunciated by lesbians and gay men downplayed sex and sought to normalise minority sexual preferences, queers have focused upon sexual practices so as to problematise normalcy itself. This strategy also is a product of the alteration of sexual behaviour in the age of Aids – the need to reimagine sexual practices and to redefine the erotic. For example, the current interest in sadomasochistic practices and fetishism amongst some segments of the queer community (and the development of a sadomasochistic identity itself) serves to flout sexual rules. It also reappropriates perversion and the identity of the sexual 'pervert'.

In that sense, a queer identity has come to be associated with 'transgressiveness'. Just as queerness might be defined as a challenge to the boundaries of identity, queer social practices (and theory) are self-consciously transgressive of attempts to normalise them: 'what is implied is a flouting of the rules, or a rule, behaviour antagonistic to what is established, the opposite, a radical challenge to what is prescribed'.[41] Thus, queers rejoice in deviance as a strategy of defiance.

For example, the current re-emergence of a gay male culture of sexual adventurism and experimentation exemplifies this development. After a period of retrenchment in the first decade of the Aids pandemic, there now appears to be a renaissance of a gay male *sexual* culture, emphasising safe sex practices, eroticism, and experimentation. This is largely (but not exclusively) centred in major urban areas. Sex clubs, sadomasochism, saunas, phone sex, and 'jerk off' parties all exemplify a carnivalesque reassertion of a gay male eroticism that transgresses the cultural equation of homosexuality with disease and death. Thus, we may be witnessing the reappropriation of a sexual liberationist ethic within the cultural conditions of the Aids pandemic:

It is as though the very discursive openness that followed on the epidemic here has loosened many of the old certainties that underpinned the strategies of containment and public order. Ten years into the epidemic here and Britain has a slowly growing culture of sexual tolerance and experimentation, albeit subject to abrupt and unpredictable reversals, that have led to a sexual golden age for gay men of a certain style.[42]

Indeed, this resurgence comes after a period in which, in some American cities, gay male sexual spaces were closed by local authorities ostensibly on the basis of a public health risk. Of course, such spaces have always functioned in the shadow of the law, with continuing threats of police intervention in the name of public morals. We are witnessing then a new queering of space; a contesting of the privatisation of gay sexuality and its erasure from the public sphere. At the same time, the issue of what is public and what is private space itself is interrogated. Since the Supreme Court determined that the private sphere is not a legally safe space for sexual activity, then one response is to take safe sex into public spaces – to resignify and subvert the public as sexual and as queer. If we are defined exclusively by our sexual practices, then our sexual practices will be everywhere.

A related aspect of the challenge posed by queerness focuses on the binary of hetero- and homosexuality and the immutability of sexuality. A queer sexuality seeks to destabilise the entrenched categories of identity and the essentialising of those categories through a discourse of immutability. Instead, sexual identities might be conceived as multiplicitous, shifting, fluid, and fragmented. Queerness thus is closely related to the postmodern conception of identity which I described in Chapter 1. Also connected to a queer identity stance is the emergence of an activist bisexual rights movement. Bisexuality as identity is sometimes constructed as the 'ultimate' postmodern and queer identity, because of the ways in which it might challenge the fixity of object choice as the foundation of sexual identity.[43] Bisexuality has been characterised as transgressive because it disrupts the fixity of sexual identity categories. Ironically, within the lesbian and gay movements, bisexuals at some moments seem to have appropriated opposite-gender sexual acts as the paradigm of a transgressive sexuality.[44]

However, I am sceptical whether bisexuality as an identity or, for that matter, 'queer' sexual practices engaged in by those who would not (or could not) define themselves as lesbian or gay, *necessarily* are of particular political importance. That is, I question whether such practices and identities are likely to interrupt the constitution of sexual and gender categories by revealing their contingency and social constructedness. As Elizabeth Wilson has queried, how can a male–female couple act in a sexually transgressive manner if, 'so far as the world is concerned they are still a heterosexual couple – it's just that they are a kinky heterosexual couple'.[45] Moreover, with respect to a bisexual identity, it has been argued that, rather than undermining an essentialist, immutable conception of sexual identity, bisexuality has appropriated the discourse of fixed sexual identities and simply created a new category. The use of the politically correct language of 'lesbian, gay, and bisexual' highlights that, rather than engaging in a deconstruction of lesbian, gay and heterosexual identities, bisexuality appears increasingly to provide an-other container in which to pour one's sexuality:

> Activists have used the term "bisexual" to disrupt the natural status of the dualism heterosexual/homosexual. But they have then paradoxically re-instated sexual polarity through the addition of a third naturalized term, as rigidly gendered as the original two, only doubled. The tendency of bisexual writers and organizations to appropriate wholesale the rhetoric of the lesbian and gay rights movement reinforces the latter effect.[46]

At the same time, there has been a noticeable tendency on the part of some bisexual activists to overlook the degree to which this appropriation is prob-lematic from the perspective of lesbian and gay politics. To the extent that a bisexual identity challenges the assumption that gender is a relatively fixed and central consideration in the choice of sexual partners, it creates what might well be an irresolvable political division. For bisexual activists who seek a space within the lesbian and gay movements, this tension has been brought 'out', often causing quite significant ruptures.

But such disagreements and stresses provide a useful example in practice of the tension between, on the one hand, the deconstruction of the categories of identity, and, on the other, the political necessity of invoking (often in a fairly totalising way) those same categories. This, of course, is the problematic of both asserting and interrogating the fixity and meaning of identity and it is sympto-matic of the cultural conditions of postmodernity.[47] Identities will always effect exclusions, but a provisional unity and coherence is required to engage in col-lective political struggles. The utility of queerness in part lies in the fact that it has provided a focal point around which coalitions have been developed that cross barriers which previously had proven largely impenetrable, achieving some contingent unity across recognised difference.[48] However, as I have suggested, queer as identity also effects its own exclusions, but the self-reflexiveness and indeterminacy of its boundaries may make them more easily negotiable (although this remains to be seen).

While the categories of identity may be constraining and exclusionary, they must also be recognised as politically necessary and personally liberating. As Elizabeth Wilson has argued, the transgression of the boundaries of identity alone will not *transform* the meaning inscribed on social categories.[49] The goal of any social theory and practice today thus must be the self-conscious attempt to negotiate this paradox between the construction and deconstruction of identity categories, and to connect identities back to the social structures within which they operate in relation to dominant background norms. In the end, we must remember that 'identity constructions are not disciplining and regulatory only in a self-limiting and oppressive way; they are also personally, socially, and politically enabling'.[50]

The assertion of coherent identity categories can also be *legally* enabling. For example, in the context of American Equal Protection jurisprudence, the failure of arguments calling for heightened judicial scrutiny of governmental classifications based upon sexual orientation in large measure is a result of the inability to persuade judges that a lesbian or gay sexual *identity* is a meaningful category which can be analogised to those categories which are strictly scrutinised. For a conservative judiciary, lesbians and gay men do not constitute such an identity category. Instead, homosexuality is constructed, first, as 'behavioural' – a set of sexual practices centred upon sodomy. However, sexual *identity* (at least for men) also is read by those same judges as contingent, capable of alteration, mutable, fluid, acquired – queer. Such an analysis has forced some 'liberals' to argue in favour of a very theoretically conservative model of sexuality, sometimes including the claim that sexual identity categories are fixed and immutable. For a gay legal strategy, then, this issue highlights the difficulty of asserting the logic of identity while not essentialising identity through rigid (and exclusionary) categories.

Thus, sexual orientation as a category underscores the problems of categorical thinking more generally. Claims that the category warrants legal protection from invidious discrimination demand that it be understood as coherent, possessing some degree of stability, and also that sexual orientation is a relatively central aspect of individual identity. In other words, it must be argued that the primary gender direction of sexual object choice creates a category that *matters* and that warrants legal protection. The category is important because it has been historically invested with a meaning which must be acknowledged and remedied. At the same time, the category must maintain a certain provisionality in its deployment, so that:

> as much as identity terms must be used, as much as "outness" is to be affirmed, these same notions must become subject to a critique of the exclusionary operations of their own production.[51]

The strategy is to both assert categories as meaningful and strategically important, while avoiding a closure in their definition. Indeed, queerness itself is a reappropriation and reinscription of a category that previously had been imposed within dominant culture in a harsh and hateful fashion. This point underscores how identity categories are never fully owned, never essentially defined, but are always subject to 'democratizing contestations that have and will redraw the contours of the movement in ways that can never be fully anticipated in advance'.[52] While the exclusionary forces of political movements should always be recognised, political life continues and our efforts must be aimed, not simply at the exclusions performed around identities, but principally at the exclusions caused by the constitution of the dominant background norm itself.

CONCLUSION

In this final chapter, I have examined queerness as a provisional identity category which has come to be articulated in the 1990s. I also have attempted to apply queer theory and queer social practices to the arena of law and legal discourse in order to expose the tension between the assertion of sexual identities and their transgression. I also have suggested that legal discourse is sometimes queer in its own right. Law desires the homosexual body – it constructs it within discourse – and it desires the category of the 'homosexual'. Shifts between sexual acts and identities underscore the permeability of sexual boundaries, which are continually manipulated and exploited by the law. The response, I have argued, must be a stance that recognises the importance of deploying categories of identity while, at the same time, maintaining an awareness of the provisional character of their use. Moreover, it is important to retain a preparedness to interrogate legal, social, and political categories and to recognise that there is nothing essentially fixed about them. Rather, both law and legal identities are social constructions, but that does not negate the fact that both are invested with meaning which gives rise to material consequences. Finally, I have argued throughout this book that the law remains a powerful (but not 'all powerful') tool in the constitution and regulation of identities, as well as in their repression. In the end, the law is an arena which demands and warrants social struggle, for despite the frequent failures of the past, it can prove to be (sometimes unintentionally) one mechanism for social/sexual change.

NOTES

INTRODUCTION

1 478 U.S. 186 (1986).
2 [1993] 2 All E.R. 75 (H.L.).

1 IDENTITIES, SEXUALITIES, AND THE POSTMODERN SUBJECT

1 The National Foundation on the Arts and the Humanities Act, Pub.L.No. 89-209, 79 Stat. 845 (1965).
2 135 Congressional Record, 7 October 1989, S12969.
3 135 Congressional Record, 26 July 1989, S8806.
4 On Helms' and others' tactical appropriation of the language of group harm and minority rights, see generally J.H. Garvey, 'Black and White Images', *Law and Contemporary Problems*, 1993, vol. 56.4, p. 189.
5 135 Congressional Record, 13 Sept. 1989, H5633, per Rep. Rohrabacher.
6 Ibid. at H5638, per Rep. Green.
7 Ibid. at H5633, per Rep. Crane.
8 Ibid. at H5637, per Rep. Dornan.
9 Ibid. at H5635, per Rep. Dannemeyer.
10 C.S. Vance, 'Misunderstanding Obscenity', *Art in America*, May 1990, p. 49.
11 The test devised by the Supreme Court of the United States in *Miller v. California*, 413 U.S. 15 (1973) emphasises three aspects: '(a) whether "the average person, applying contemporary community standards" would find that the work, taken as a whole, appeals to the prurient interest, (b) whether the work depicts or describes, in a patently offensive way, sexual conduct specifically defined by the applicable state law, and (c) whether the work, taken as a whole, lacks serious literary, artistic, political, or scientific value' (ibid. at 24).
12 20 U.S.C.A. 959(c) (Supp. 1992).
13 L. Hart,'Karen Finley's Dirty Work: Censorship, Homophobia, and the NEA', *Genders*, 1992, vol. 14, p. 1.
14 20 U.S.C. 954 (Supp. 1993).
15 W.H. Honan, 'Arts Chief Vetoes 2 Approved Grants', *New York Times*, 13 May 1992, p. C13.
16 In fact, the NEA is now threatened with closure by the Republican-controlled Congress, which by law must reauthorise the Endowment's budget in 1995. See

L. Hodges, 'Republicans Gun for Arts Cash', *The Times Higher Education Supplement*, 10 February 1995, p. 8.

17 N. Hunter, 'Identity, Speech, and Equality', *Virginia Law Review*, 1993, vol. 79, p. 1695 at 1696.

18 *Perry v. Sindermann*, 408 U.S. 593, 597 (1972).

19 754 F.Supp. 774 (C.D. Cal. 1991).

20 Ibid. at 783.

21 795 F.Supp. 1457 (C.D. Cal. 1992).

22 Ibid. at 1471.

23 Ibid. at 1473.

24 Ibid. at 1475.

25 See K. Baynes, *et al.* (eds), *After Philosophy: End or Transformation?*, Cambridge, MA, MIT Press, 1987, p. 68.

26 J. Lyotard, *The Postmodern Condition: A Report on Knowledge*, Minneapolis, University of Minnesota Press, 1984, p. 15.

27 N. Hartsock,'Foucault on Power: A Theory for Women?', in L.J. Nicholson (ed.), *Feminism/Postmodernism*, New York, Routledge, 1990, p. 157 at 160.

28 See S. Bordo, 'Feminism, Postmodernism, and Gender-Scepticism', in Nicholson, *Feminism/ Postmodernism*, p. 133 at 145. But, for a critique of the metaphor of the body as container, see J. Nedelsky, 'Law, Boundaries, and the Bounded Self', *Representations*, 1990, no. 30, p. 162.

29 This point has been cogently developed by psychoanalyst Jane Flax; see J. Flax, *Thinking Fragments: Psychoanalysis, Feminism, and Postmodernism in the Contemporary West*, Berkeley, University of California Press, 1990, pp. 218–219.

30 See J. Wicke, 'Postmodern Identity and the Legal Subject', *University of Colorado Law Review*, 1991, vol. 62, p. 455 at 462: 'to efface or erase the legal subject, however much predicated on an illusory unity, singularity, intentionality, would be an enormous political loss'.

31 Seyla Benhabib takes this point to its logical conclusion. See S. Benhabib, 'Critical Theory and Postmodernism: On the Interplay of Ethics, Aesthetics and Utopia in Critical Theory', *Cardozo Law Review*, 1990, vol. 11, p. 1435 at 1439:

> We must begin to probe the implications of the postmodernist project not just in aesthetics but in ethics as well. Postmodernism gestures its solidarity with the other, with the "différend," with "women, children, fools, and primitives," whose discourse has never matched the grand narrative of the modern masters. Yet can there be an ethic of solidarity without a self that can feel compassion and act out of principle? Can there be a struggle for justice without the possibility of justifying power by reason? What is justice if not the rational exercise of power?

32 This point draws upon a wealth of scholarship which has been succinctly summarised by Richard Thomas; see R.M. Thomas, 'Milton and Mass Culture: Toward a Postmodernist Theory of Tolerance', *University of Colorado Law Review*, 1991, vol. 62, p. 525.

33 Flax, *Thinking Fragments*, p. 41.

34 See A. Ross, 'Introduction', in A. Ross (ed.), *Universal Abandon: The Politics of Postmodernism*, Minneapolis, University of Minnesota Press, 1988, p. vii at xi.

35 Ibid. at xii.

36 S. Phelan, 'Specificity: Beyond Equality and Difference', *Differences*, 1991, vol. 3.1, p. 128 at 137.

37 See S. Connor, *Postmodernist Culture*, Oxford, Blackwell, 1989, p. 228.

38 M. Foucault, *The History of Sexuality Volume One: An Introduction* (R. Hurley, trans.), London, Penguin, 1980, p. 96.

39 R.J. Coombe, 'Publicity Rights and Political Aspiration: Mass Culture, Gender Identity,

and Democracy', *New England Law Review*, 1992, vol. 26, p. 1221 at 1247. See also M. Featherstone, *Consumer Culture and Postmodernism*, London, Sage Publications, 1991, pp. 62–63.

40 Connor, *Postmodernist Culture*, p. 232.

41 Ibid. at 233.

42 J. Baudrillard, *In the Shadow of the Silent Majorities or, the End of the Social and Other Essays*, New York, Semiotext(e), 1983, pp. 42–43.

43 P. Willis, *Common Culture*, Milton Keynes, Open University Press, 1990, p. 20.

44 Ibid. at 136.

45 Ibid. at 137.

46 Ibid. at 139.

47 See generally E. Laclau and C. Mouffe, *Hegemony and Socialist Strategy*, London, Verso, 1990.

48 C. Mouffe, 'Radical Democracy: Modern or Postmodern?', in Ross, *Universal Abandon*, p. 31 at 43.

49 E. Laclau, 'Politics and the Limits of Modernity', in Ross, *Universal Abandon*, p. 63 at 78.

50 Laclau and Mouffe, *Hegemony and Socialist Strategy*, p. 36.

51 Ibid. at 87.

52 Ibid. at 96.

53 Ibid. at 104.

54 See ibid. at 113.

55 Ibid. at 138.

56 R.J. Coombe, 'Objects of Property and Subjects of Politics: Intellectual Property Laws and Democratic Dialogue', *Texas Law Review*, 1991, vol. 69, p. 1853 at 1860.

57 See e.g., P. Chevigny, *More Speech: Dialogue Rights and Modern Liberty*, Philadelphia, Temple University Press, 1988, p. 4.

58 D.Cornell, 'Toward a Modern/Postmodern Reconstruction of Ethics', *University of Pennsylvania Law Review*, 1985, vol. 133, p. 291 at 298. For an extended explanation of the meaning and implications of dialogic equality, see D.Cornell, *The Philosophy of the Limit*, New York, Routledge, 1992.

59 See Cornell, 'Toward a Modern/Postmodern Reconstruction of Ethics', p. 368.

60 Ibid. at 378.

61 See D. Fuss, 'Inside/Out', in D. Fuss (ed.), *Inside/Out*, New York, Routledge, 1991, p. 1.

62 Ibid. at 6. Fuss points out, however, that the capacity for an oppositional subject to redeploy the language of inside/out depends upon a relatively privileged positioning as both within and outside the binary (ibid. at 5).

63 S. Watney, 'School's Out', in Fuss, *Inside/Out*, p. 387 at 388.

64 See R. Dyer, 'Believing in Fairies: The Author and the Homosexual', in Fuss, *Inside/Out*, p. 185 at 188.

65 See E. Jackson, Jr., 'Scandalous Subjects: Robert Gluck's Embodied Narratives', *Differences*, 1991, vol 3.2, p. 112 at 121.

66 E. Kosofsky Sedgwick, 'Across Gender, Across Sexuality: Willa Cather and Others', *South Atlantic Quarterly*, 1989, vol 88.1, p. 53 at 56.

67 Watney, 'School's Out', p. 400.

68 J. Butler, 'Imitation and Gender Insubordination', in Fuss, *Inside/Out*, p. 13 at 15.

69 See ibid. at 17.

70 See generally J. Butler, *Gender Trouble*, New York, Routledge, 1990.

71 Ibid. at 24–25.

72 Ibid. at 121.

73 Here I am relying upon the analysis of Andrew Ross; see A. Ross, *No Respect: Intellectuals and Popular Culture*, New York, Routledge, 1989. Ross summarises theories of cultural consumption as follows:

More radical theories of "creative consumption" would later come to be posed as a way of explaining how people actually express their resistance, symbolically or otherwise, to everyday domination, by redefining the meanings of mass-produced objects and discourses in ways that go against the "dominant" messages in the text.

(ibid. at 53)

74 J. Leo, 'The Familialism of "Man" in American Television Meledrama', *South Atlantic Quarterly*, 1989, vol 88.1, p. 31 at 46.
75 Coombe, 'Objects of Property', pp. 1876–1877.
76 Ross, *No Respect*, p. 146.
77 Ibid. at 157.
78 See A. Sinfield, 'Private Lives/Public Theater: Nöel Coward and the Politics of Homosexual Representation', *Representations*, 1991, no. 36, p. 43 at 44.
79 See ibid.: '[U]ntil 1958 all mention of homosexuality was specifically forbidden.'
80 A. Sinfield, 'Closet Dramas: Homosexual Representation and Class in Postwar British Theater', *Genders*, 1990, vol. 9, p. 112 at 115.
81 Ibid. at 116.
82 Sinfield, 'Private Lives/Public Theater', p. 49.
83 Butler, 'The Force of Fantasy: Feminism, Mapplethorpe and Discursive Excess', *Differences*, 1990, vol. 2.2, p. 118.
84 Ibid. at 111.
85 Sinfield, 'Private Lives/Public Theater', p. 49.
86 Ibid.
87 Ross, *No Respect*, p. 177.
88 Ibid. at 189.

2 OF PROHIBITIONS AND PROMOTIONS

1 Department of Education, 'Sex Education at School', Circular No. 11, 1987, s.19.
2 Ibid., s.22.
3 Lords, *Hansard*, 18 December 1986, 336.
4 On the 'Positive Images' campaign, see generally D. Cooper, *Sexing the City: Lesbian and Gay Politics within the Activist State*, London, Rivers Oram Press, 1994.
5 Lords, *Hansard*, 18 December 1986, 310.
6 Ibid. at 311.
7 Ibid. at 313.
8 Ibid. at 318.
9 Ibid. at 324.
10 Ibid. at 326.
11 Ibid. at 329, per Baroness Faithfull.
12 Ibid. at 330.
13 Ibid. at 337.
14 Commons, *Hansard*, 8 May 1987, 1002–1003 [emphasis added].
15 Commons, *Hansard*, 15 December 1987, 992.
16 Ibid. at 1007 [emphasis added].
17 Ibid. at 1014.
18 D.T. Evans, 'Section 28: Law, Myth and Paradox', *Critical Social Policy*, 1989/90, vol. 27, p. 73 at 90.
19 Ibid. at 91.
20 See generally D. Cooper and D. Herman, 'Getting "The Family Right": Legislating

Heterosexuality in Britain, 1986–1991', *Canadian Journal of Family Law*, 1991, vol. 10, p. 41.

21 This manoeuvre exemplifies Eve Sedgwick's description of the system of 'double binds' that underpins the dominant understanding of homosexuality; see E. Sedgwick, *Epistemology of the Closet*, Berkeley, University of California Press, 1990, p. 85:

> it is organized around a radical and irreducible incoherence. It holds the minoritizing view that there is a distinct population of persons who "really are" gay, at the same time, it holds the universalizing view that sexual desire is an unpredictably powerful solvent of stable identities.

22 S. Watney, 'School's Out', in D. Fuss (ed.), *Inside/Out*, New York, Routledge, 1991, p. 387 at 392.

23 Ibid.

24 Evans, 'Section 28', p. 80.

25 M. McIntosh, 'The Homosexual Role', *Social Problems*, 1968, vol. 16, p. 182.

26 M. Colvin, *Section 28: A Practical Guide to the Law and its Implications*, London, National Council for Civil Liberties, 1989, p. 13.

27 Ibid.

28 Commons, *Hansard*, 9 March 1988, 424.

29 Lords, *Hansard*, 16 February 1988, 611–612.

30 Colvin, *Section 28*, p. 45.

31 Ibid.

32 Evans, 'Section 28', p. 79, citing K. Norrie, 'How to Promote Homosexuality', *Gay Scotland*, 1989, no. 44, p. 9.

33 Evans, 'Section 28', pp. 81–82. The list is more extensive and is also documented in Cooper and Herman, 'Getting the Family Right', p. 74.

34 Cooper and Herman, 'Getting the Family Right', p. 73.

35 Ibid. at 74.

36 Ibid.

37 Lords, *Hansard*, 18 December 1986, 324. Interestingly, Lord Kilbracken, in his defence of 'heterosexual life', made mention of his five year old son, about to enter public school (as well as his teenage grandson). Note, again, that he himself was at public school in the 1930s!

38 Lords, *Hansard*, 18 December 1986, 337.

40 See Cooper and Herman, 'Getting the Family Right', p. 74.

40 R. Wintemute, 'Sexual Orientation Discrimination', in C. McCrudden and G. Chambers (eds.), *Individual Rights and the Law in Britain*, Oxford, Clarendon Press, 1994, p. 491 at 510.

41 J. Weeks, *Against Nature*, London, Rivers Oram Press, 1991, p. 137.

42 Lords, *Hansard*, 16 February 1988, 627.

43 Department of Education, Circular No. 12, 1988.

44 See Evans, 'Section 28' at p. 85: this attitude was 'typified by Mrs. Thatcher's reputed response to the initial draft of the first advertising campaign in 1986 which she vetoed for being "like writings on a lavatory wall"'. The government's attitude towards official explicit safe sex education has continued in the same vein; see 'Tory Right Halt Sex Education Campaigns', *The Independent on Sunday* (UK), 17 April 1994, p. 3, which describes the halting of the government's Aids and sexual health education programmes as a result of their 'offensiveness'.

45 Commons, *Hansard*, 8 May 1987, 998.

46 Cooper and Herman, 'Getting the Family Right', p. 75.

47 S. Jeffery-Poulter, *Peers, Queers, and Commons*, London, Routledge, 1991, p. 234.

48 Weeks, *Against Nature*, p. 137.

49 Watney, 'School's Out', p. 394.

50 N. Hunter, 'Identity, Speech, and Equality', *Virginia Law Review*, 1993, vol. 79, p. 1695 at 1709.

51 Ibid. at 1710.

52 See S.C. Dubin, *Arresting Images*, New York, Routledge, 1992, p. 242; Senator Helms:

> tried to block emergency disaster relief to major US cities in 1990 to help them cope with the Aids crisis. Helms argued that this legislation was an hysterical response. Stronger morals, not more money, was what was needed . . . Helms also fought to prevent anti-Aids workers from giving bleach to addicts to clean their needles, wrote the 1987 law which denied entry of people with Aids into the country, and in 1991 proposed that health care workers who were HIV-infected and did not inform their patients before performing invasive procedures be subject to penalties of up to ten thousand dollars and ten years in jail.

53 133 Congressional Record, 14 October 1987, S14216.

54 133 Congressional Record, October 20, 1987, H8800, per Rep. Dannemeyer.

55 Ibid.

56 133 Congressional Record, 14 October 1987, S14204. This description of the spread of the virus has been described by Cindy Patton; see C. Patton, 'Tremble, Hetero Swine!', in M. Warner (ed.), *Fear of A Queer Planet*, Minneapolis, University of Minnesota Press, 1993, p. 143 at 154:

> AIDS discourse has a curious retrograde motion that I have called "the queer paradigm": you can begin as a queer, and therefore as uniquely susceptible to AIDS, but whatever your cultural status, once you test positive for the HIV antibody, regardless of how you contracted the virus, you become nominally queer.

57 133 Congressional Record, 14 October 1987, S14204.

58 See ibid. at S14207, per Senator Helms:

> this Senator sees no way that the situation is going to be improved as long as groups which advocate homosexuality, which . . . is the original source of the Aids virus, and in every known case insofar as the information available to me.

59 See ibid. at S14204, per Senator Helms:

> Until we are ready and willing to discourage and do our level best to eliminate these types of activities which have caused the spread of the Aids epidemic, I do not believe we are ever going to solve it.

60 Ibid. at S14208.

61 See 133 Congressional Record, 20 October 1987, H8801, per Rep. Dornan: 'What is offensive, outrageous, about any Federal money being spent on this, is that, like all pornography – the writing of whores, in this case male prostitutes – it is to stimulate sexual desire. It is written lustfully.' As Mark Barnes suggests, within this discourse all representations of a gay male sexuality that are other than negative are constructed as pornographic; see M. Barnes, 'Toward Ghastly Death: The Censorship of AIDS Education', *Columbia Law Review*, 1989, vol. 89, p. 698 at 714:

> Confused information about how HIV is transmitted (that every AIDS case can be traced to homosexuality) is united with disgust toward homosexual sex and drug use – a disgust that is assumed to be evident to all and that is explicitly based on certain religious tenets. Any portrayal of homosexual sex is deemed to fall within the category of pornography, without definition of that category.

62 C. Patton, 'Safe Sex and the Pornographic Vernacular', in Bad Object-Choices (ed.), *How Do I Look?*, Seattle, Bay Press, 1991, p. 31 at 43.

63 E. King, *Safety in Numbers*, London, Cassell, 1993, p. 121.

64 See Barnes, 'Toward Ghastly Death', p. 715: 'legal prohibitions on the explicitness of Aids education in fact will discriminate between low and high-income populations, between the less and the better-educated, and between the less than literate and the fully literate'.

65 *Gay Men's Health Crisis v. Sullivan*, 792 F.Supp. 278 (S.D.N.Y. 1992).

66 Ibid. at 296.

67 Ibid. at 303–304.

68 The closest analogy would be a challenge to section 28 as in breach of the European Convention of Human Rights; for a discussion of this issue see generally Colvin, *Section 28*, p. 60.

69 Barnes, 'Toward Ghastly Death', pp. 720–721.

70 Ibid. Barnes goes further and asks 'how do strong arguments for colloquial and erotic Aids education force us to imagine not simply legal problems with government-imposed content restriction, but further, to posit a constitutional duty of government to allow accurate and relevant AIDS education?' (ibid. at 720).

71 J. Butler, *Bodies That Matter*, New York, Routledge, 1993, pp. 15–16.

72 Ibid. at 109–110.

73 In the American context, the protest organisations ACT UP and Queer Nation exemplify this process of social movement activism.

74 Of course, while those categories may be consolidated by virtue of discursive prohibitions enacted in law, excluded categories of sexual identity themselves must be interrogated for their own exclusions which are necessary for their consolidation. Butler refers to this as the 'double movement'; see ibid. at 222: she describes the task as 'to invoke the category and, hence, provisionally to institute an identity and at the same time to open the category as a site of permanent political contest'.

75 Ibid. at 232.

3 THE PORN WARS

1 The veneer of unity was cracked, however, by the issue of lesbian pornography. The issue is a complex one which is beyond the scope of this book, for it deserves discussion in its own right. In this chapter, I do not in any way want to suggest that everyone who identifies themselves as a feminist subscribes to the same theory of pornography or that feminist views on this issue are in any way monolithic. See e.g., C.S. Vance (ed.), *Pleasure and Danger: Exploring Female Sexuality*, New York, Routledge, 1984; V. Burstyn (ed.), *Women Against Censorship*, Vancouver, Douglas & McIntyre, 1985; A. Carol, *Nudes, Prudes and Attitudes: Pornography and Censorship*, Cheltenham, New Clarion Press, 1994; S. Jeffreys, *The Lesbian Heresy*, London, Women's Press, 1994.

2 C. MacKinnon, *Towards a Feminist Theory of the State*, Cambridge, MA, Harvard University Press, 1989, p. 137.

3 C. MacKinnon, *Feminism Unmodified*, Cambridge, MA, Harvard University Press, 1987, pp. 54–55.

4 MacKinnon, *Towards a Feminist Theory of the State*, p. 145.

5 See J. Stoltenberg, *Refusing to be a Man*, New York, Meridian, 1990, p. 127.

6 MacKinnon, *Feminism Unmodified*, p. 148.

7 MacKinnon, *Towards a Feminist Theory of the State*, pp. 210–211.

8 For a description of the model and a discussion of its implementation by city ordinance in Minneapolis and Indianapolis see A. Dworkin and C. MacKinnon,

Pornography and Civil Rights: A New Day for Women's Equality, Minneapolis, Organizing Against Pornography, 1988. The story of the Indianapolis ordinance, culminating in its invalidation by Easterbrook, J. in the Seventh Circuit Court of Appeals is an interesting one, but beyond the scope of this book. See *American Booksellers Ass'n v. Hudnut*, 771 F.2d 323 (7th Cir. 1985) [ordinance prohibiting distribution of materials depicting coercion in performance unconstitutional because of invalid definition of pornography]. The Supreme Court refused to hear oral argument in the case: 106 S.Ct. 1172 (1986).

9 MacKinnon, *Feminism Unmodified*, p. 210.

10 The ordinances are reproduced in Dworkin and MacKinnon, *Pornography and Civil Rights*, pp. 99–132. For a discussion of the civil cause of action, see ibid. at 41–52.

11 See ibid. at 101:

> Pornography is the sexually explicit subordination of women, graphically depicted, whether in pictures or in words, that also includes one or more of the following: (i) women are presented dehumanized as sexual objects, things or commodities; or (ii) women are presented as sexual objects who enjoy pain or humiliation; or (iii) women are presented as sexual objects who experience sexual pleasure in being raped; or (iv) women are presented as sexual objects tied up or cut up or mutilated or bruised or physically hurt; or (v) women are presented in postures of sexual submission or (vi) women's body parts – including but not limited to vaginas, breasts, and buttocks – are exhibited, such that women are reduced to those parts; or (vii) women are presented as whores by nature; or (viii) women are presented being penetrated by objects or animals; or (ix) women are presented in scenarios of degradation, injury, abasement, torture, shown as filthy or inferior, bleeding, bruised, or hurt in a context that makes these conditions sexual.

12 Ibid.

13 MacKinnon, *Towards a Feminist Theory of the State*, p. 141.

14 Ibid. at 142. Andrea Dworkin suggests that while male homosexuality is intolerable in a patriarchal society, male homosexuals engage in a similar willingness to exploit and objectify as do heterosexual men; see A. Dworkin, *Pornography: Men Possessing Women*, New York, Dutton, 1989, p. 62.

15 Dworkin, *Pornography: Men Possessing Women*, p. 43.

16 Ibid. at 44–45.

17 MacKinnon, *Feminism Unmodified*, p. 172 [emphasis added].

18 Stoltenberg, *Refusing to be a Man*, p. 109.

19 Ibid.

20 Ibid. at 53.

21 Ibid. at 132.

22 The signifier can be understood as operating on two levels; see E.A. Kaplan, 'Pornography and/as Representation', *Enclitic*, 1987, vol. 9.1 and 2, p. 8:

> [pornography] consists of signifiers, whether we think of it on the level of fantasy/dream/hallucination inside the subject's mind; or on the level of more materialist signifiers, i.e. words/images/sounds produced for, and to a degree constructing, the subject-spectator.

23 S. Watney, *Policing Desire: Pornography, Aids and the Media*, (second edn), Minneapolis, University of Minnesota Press, 1987, p. 71.

24 T. Yingling, 'How the Eye is Caste: Robert Mapplethorpe and the Limits of Controversy', *Discourse*, 1990, vol. 12.2, p. 3 at 9–10.

25 M. Foucault, *The History of Sexuality Volume One: An Introduction* (R. Hurley, trans.), London, Penguin, 1990, p. 48. I am not suggesting that gay male pornography

operates as a completely excluded discourse undermining a dominant discourse of
sexual relations. Rather, it may operate within the dominant discourse as an oppositional strategy; see ibid. at 101:

> we must make allowance for the complex and unstable process whereby dis-
> course can be both an instrument and an effect of power, but also a hindrance, a
> stumbling-block, a point of resistance and a starting point for an opposing
> strategy. Discourse transmits and produces power; it reinforces it, but also
> undermines and exposes it, renders it fragile, and makes it possible to thwart it.

26 Yingling, *How the Eye is Caste*, p. 3. See also S. Tucker, 'Gender, Fucking and
    Utopia', *Social Text*, 1990, no. 27, p. 3 at 21, for his description of gay sex as an act
    of resistance.
27 Yingling, *How the Eye is Caste*, p. 8.
28 C.S. Vance, 'Pleasure and Danger: Toward a Politics of Sexuality', in Vance,
    Pleasure and Danger, p. 1 at 15.
29 Yingling, *How the Eye is Caste*, p. 7.
30 A. Echols, 'The New Feminism of Yin and Yang', in A. Snitow, C. Stansell and S.
    Thompson (eds), *Powers of Desire: The Politics of Sexuality*, New York, Monthly
    Review Press, 1983, p. 448.
31 A. Ross, *No Respect: Intellectuals and Popular Culture*, New York, Routledge, 1989,
    p. 196.
32 Watney, *Policing Desire*, p. 73. See also M. Bronski, *Culture Clash: The Making of
    Gay Sensibility*, Boston, South End Press, 1984, p. 165:

> While it is true that the viewer, sexually aroused, lusts after the object, it is
> equally true that he may also want to *be* that object. This element of identifi-
> cation *with* as well as desire *for* the sexual object distinguishes gay and straight
> porn.

33 G. Rubin, 'Thinking Sex: Notes for a Radical Theory of the Politics of Sexuality', in
    Vance, *Pleasure and Danger*, p. 293. This is not to suggest that feminist theory is
    incapable of grappling with issues of sexuality. Rather, as Vance argues, it is to
    suggest that questions of sexuality must be recognized as posing a unique method-
    ological challenge; see Vance, *Pleasure and Danger*, p. 16.
34 J. Butler, *Gender Trouble: Feminism and the Subversion of Identity*, New York,
    Routledge, 1990, p. 7.
35 Ibid. at 13.
36 Ibid. at 24–25.
37 Ibid. at 121.
38 Ibid. at 139.
39 See also D. Altman, *The Homosexualization of America*, Boston, Beacon, 1982, p. 13:

> If the man dressed as a woman was, in effect, mocking the assumptions society
> makes about men and women, then the man dressed as a stereotypical man is
> also mocking the assumption that to be gay is to want to be a woman.

40 C. Sunstein, 'Pornography and the First Amendment', *Duke Law Journal*, 1986, p.
    589 at 595.
41 Butler, *Gender Trouble*, p. 6.
42 J. Butler, 'The Force of Fantasy', *Differences*, 1990, vol 2.2, p. 105 at 114.
43 L. Bersani, 'Is the Rectum a Grave?', in *AIDS :Cultural Analysis, Cultural Activism*,
    Cambridge, MA, MIT Press, 1988, p. 197.
44 Ibid. at 207.
45 Ibid. at 208.
46 Ibid. at 213.

47 See ibid. at 215.
48 Ibid. at 218.
49 Ibid. at 222.
50 Tucker, 'Gender, Fucking and Utopia, p. 3.
51 See J. Benjamin, 'Master and Slave: The Fantasy of Erotic Domination', in Snitnow *et al.*, *Powers of Desire*, p. 280; and see generally, J. Benjamin, *The Bonds of Love*, London, Virago, 1988.
52 Benjamin, 'Master and Slave', p. 281.
53 Ibid. at 286.
54 Ibid. at 285.
55 Ibid. at 282.
56 Bersani, 'Is the Rectum a Grave?', p. 222.
57 Ibid. at 218.
58 Ross, *No Respect*, p. 177.
59 See also Bronski, *Culture Clash*, p. 173:

> [gay porn magazines] have made images of gay male sexuality available to a large number of people, an especially important thing for gay men who may be insecure in their identities. They have also promoted a notion of a gay sensibility, and a gay community – albeit one based on consumerism – both to the straight and the gay worlds.

60 Butler, *Gender Trouble*, p. 93.

4 OF REPRESENTATION AND REALITY

1 s.163(8), R.S.C. 1985, c. C-46.
2 (1992), 89 DLR (4th) 449.
3 Ibid. at 467 [emphasis mine].
4 Ibid. at 470.
5 Ibid. at 471.
6 Cited in K. Busby, 'LEAF and Pornography: Litigating on Equality and Sexual Representations', *Canadian Journal of Law and Society*, Spring 1994, vol. 9.1, p. 165 at 180.
7 M. Landsberg, 'Canada: Antipornography Breakthrough in the Law', *Ms.*, May/June 1992, p. 14.
8 However, Busby states categorically that the relevant videos were not shown to the judiciary in open court; see Busby, 'LEAF and Pornography', p. 179.
9 Ibid. at 183.
10 Ibid. at 185.
11 Toronto 619/90 (Ontario Court, General Division), 14 July 1992 [unreported].
12 Ibid.
13 Ibid.
14 See Busby, 'LEAF and Pornography', pp. 185–187.
15 S. Scott, 'A Secretive Band of Bureaucrats Decide What we Read and Watch', *Toronto Star*, 18 April 1993, p. B7.
16 On this point, see A.M. Smith, '"What is Pornography?" An Analysis of the Policy Statement of the Campaign Against Pornography and Censorship', *Feminist Review*, 1993, no. 43, p. 71 at 76.
17 See Revenue Canada Customs and Excise, Memorandum D9-1-1, 1 January 1988.
18 Scott, 'A Secretive Band', p. B7.
19 My thanks to José Arroyo for bringing this incident to my attention.
20 See e.g., Busby, 'LEAF and Pornography', pp. 184–187.

21 An indication that such a reversal might be forthcoming can be found in the language of the Ontario Court of Appeal in *R. v. Hawkins et al.* (1993), 15 OR (3d) 549 (C.A.) at 567:

> I cannot accept that *Butler* compels the conclusion that once the portrayal of sexually explicit acts is found to be degrading or dehumanizing, it necessarily follows that the films are harmful and therefore obscene. In my opinion, it remains open to the court to find that the harm component of the offence has not been established. Just as there is a range of opinion as to what is degrading or dehumanizing, there is a range of opinion as to whether such material causes social harm or the risk of such harm.

22 In New Zealand, the Indecent Publications Tribunal explicitly accepted this position in its application of the *Indecent Publications Act, 1963* to gay male pornography, and in so doing, the Tribunal included extensive references to my earlier work; see Decision No. IND 100/92, 2 March 1993.

23 See generally D. Pendleton, 'Obscene Allegories: Narrative, Representation, Pornography', *Discourse*, 1992, vol. 15.1, p. 154 at 160–164; L. Williams, 'Pornographies on/scene, or Diff'rent Strokes for Diff'rent Folks', in L. Segal and M. McIntosh (eds), *Sex Exposed: Sexuality and the Pornography Debate*, New Brunswick, N.J., Rutgers University Press, 1993, p. 233 at 257.

24 For an equally sceptical view of judicial attitudes, see P. Wollaston, 'When Will They Ever Get it Right? A Gay Analysis of *R. v. Butler*', *Dalhousie Journal of Legal Studies*, 1993, vol. 2, p. 251.

25 See C.N. Kendall, '"Real Dominant, Real Fun!": Gay Male Pornography and the Pursuit of Masculinity', *Saskatchewan Law Review*, 1993, vol. 57, p. 21.

26 Ibid. at 32.

27 See ibid. at 29–32.

28 Ibid. at 36.

29 C.S. Vance, 'The Meese Commission on the Road', in G. Chester and J. Dickey (eds), *Feminism and Censorship*, Bridport, Prism, 1988, p. 87 at 93.

30 See e.g., R. Gorna, 'Delightful Visions: From Anti-porn to Eroticizing Safer Sex', in Segal and McIntosh, *Sex Exposed*, p. 169; C. Patton, 'Safe Sex and the Pornographic Vernacular', in Bad Object-Choices (ed.), *How Do I Look?*, Seattle, Bay Press, 1991, p. 31; R. McGrath, 'Health, Education and Authority: Difference and Deviance', in V. Harwood *et al.* (eds), *Pleasure Principles*, London, Lawrence & Wishart, 1993, p. 157.

31 See Patton, 'Safe Sex', p. 32: 'The concern to produce "responsible" sexual fantasy material was clear in most video porn by 1989'. Oddly, Kendall cites Patton from the same article for the opposite proposition; see Kendall, '"Real Dominant"', p. 34, n.34.

32 The work of the Gay Men's Health Crisis in New York City and the Terrence Higgins Trust in London are well-known examples.

33 McGrath, 'Health, Education', p. 178. McGrath illustrates this point using safe sex 'photographic narratives' produced by the Terrence Higgins Trust, which eroticise bondage as a safe sex practice; see ibid. at 175–178.

34 Kendall, '"Real Dominant"', p. 34.

35 Ibid. at 31.

36 R. Fung, 'Looking for my Penis: The Eroticized Asian in Gay Video Porn', in Bad Object-Choices, *How Do I Look?*, p. 145.

37 Ibid. at 158.

38 The complexities of the intersection of race and a gay male sexuality in the arena of sexual representations have been the subject of fascinating work. In addition to Fung, 'Looking', see K. Mercer, 'Skin Head Sex Thing: Racial Difference and the Homoerotic Imaginary', in Bad Object-Choices, *How Do I Look?*, p. 169; I. Julian, 'Performing

Sexualities: An Interview', in Harwood, *Pleasure Principles*, p. 124; I. Julian, 'Confessions of a Snow Queen: Notes on the Making of *The Attendant*', *Critical Quarterly*, Spring 1994, vol. 36.1, p. 120; T.D. Smith, 'Gay Male Pornography and the East: Re-Orienting the Orient', *History of Photography*, Spring 1994, vol. 18.1, p. 13. On the complex meanings of Nazi symbolism in gay male sadomaso- chism from the perspective of a Jewish, gay male sadomasochist, see A. Kantrowitz, 'Swastika Toys', in M. Thompson (ed.), *Leatherfolk: Radical Sex, People, Politics and Practice*, Boston, Alyson Publications, 1991, p. 193.

39 See e.g., S. Jeffreys, *The Lesbian Heresy*, London, Women's Press, 1994; R.R. Linden *et al.*, *Against Sadomasochism: A Radical Feminist Analysis*, Palo Alto, Ca., Frog in the Wall Press, 1982.

40 See S.E. Keller, 'Viewing and Doing: Complicating Pornography's Meaning', *Georgetown Law Journal*, July 1993, vol. 81.6, p. 2195 at 2221:

> If part of the appeal of fantasy is that it is fantasy, then part of the appeal of viewing may be that it is *not* doing. When laboratory subjects report that they are more prone to consider violence after viewing pornography, it is possible that a layer of distance is still in effect. For example, one can be said to be more prone to consider "sadomasochism" than one who merely fantasizes, but there are still layers between that consideration and actually brutalizing someone.

41 Ibid. at 2218. Keller emphasises the importance of differentiating between physically abusive relationships (which she refers to as 'lived s&m') and 'a relationship in which a couple engages in a specific, ritualized sexual practice of inflicting and receiving pain for mutual pleasure' (ibid.). Keller also discerns two other 'levels' of s&m: 'pretend s&m' (a ritual in which pain occurs in the imagination) and 'fantasy s&m' (fantasising about the other levels of s&m) (ibid. at 2219). Keller's framework is not gender- or sexuality-specific and is an important tool for avoiding the conflating of what are profoundly different social practices.

42 For a general introduction to sadomasochistic sexualities and related 'leather' sexualities (which cross lines of gender and sexuality) see Thompson, *Leatherfolk*. For a specifically gay male focus, see G. Mains, *Urban Aboriginals*, San Francisco, Gay Sunshine Press, 1984.

43 See P. Califia, 'The Limits of the S/M Relationship, or Mr Benson Doesn't Live Here Anymore', in Thompson, *Leatherfolk*, p. 221 at 223–224. I recognise that I have presented an idealised vision of sadomasochistic relationships, which may not be realised in practice due to the power imbalances within relationships. However, it none the less may provide a model to which sadomasochists may be particularly well suited to aspire. It is also a curious, but frequent observation that there is inevitably a shortage of 'tops' in the gay male sadomasochistic community.

44 Kendall, '"Real Dominant"', p. 39.

45 Ibid. at 45. This proposition has been disputed; see e.g., Pendleton, 'Obscene Allegories'. Kendall relies upon the work of Richard Dyer in support. However, Dyer recently has suggested that some gay male pornography 'has consistently been marked by self-reflexivity, by texts that have wanted to draw attention to themselves as porn, that is, as constructed presentations of sex' (R. Dyer, 'Idol thoughts: Orgasm and Self-reflexivity in Gay Pornography', *Critical Quarterly*, 1994, vol. 36.1, p. 49 at 54). This self-reflexive quality makes a literal reading of gay male pornography problematic, for self-reflexivity within a representation suggests that there is nothing 'essential' about sexual positioning or indeed about the fact that the participants are sexually positioned.

46 Kendall, '"Real Dominant"', p. 44.

47 Ibid.

48 Ibid., p. 51.

49 On this point I can add nothing in addition to the following report of a conversation, which brilliantly captures the response to the 'passing' issue:

> Late in the 1970s there was discussion in the gay liberation movement as to what this new aura of masculinity and the emergence of an S/M style and politic might mean. I remember being at a *Gay Community News* meeting when a very politically correct man opined that the new leatherman was trying to "pass as straight". Several of us fumbled for a response when one of the more conservative dykes said, "Give me a *break*. You think that someone wearing chaps, a black leather jacket, a motorcycle cap, handcuffs on his belt, two different color hankies, and 36-inch-high black boots looks *straight!*"
>
> (M. Bronski, 'A Dream is a Wish your Heart Makes:
> Notes on the Materialization of Sexual Fantasy',
> in Thompson, *Leatherfolk*, p. 56 at 61)

50 On 'drag' as a form of gender subversion, see J. Butler, *Gender Trouble*, New York, Routledge, 1990, pp. 121–141; and, for a clarification of her position on the politics of drag, see J. Butler, *Bodies That Matter*, New York, Routledge, 1993, pp. 124–140.
51 See Vance, 'The Meese Commission', pp. 93–94.
52 C. Smart, 'Law, Feminism, and Sexuality: From Essence to Ethics?', *Canadian Journal of Law and Society*, 1994, vol. 9.1, p. 15 at 36.
53 I am not suggesting that gay men have a non-misogynist or non-racist essence. Obviously, there are gay men who are sexist or racist or both, and who converse and behave in ways that demonstrate their bigotry. The ethical duty on other gay men is to speak up and respond when we witness such bigotry within our community.
54 In this regard, I am thinking of 'out' gay men who, nonetheless, act in what I would describe as an assimilationist fashion in their everyday public lives. The position of closeted gay men is quite different again and beyond the scope of this argument.

5 INSIDE AND OUT OF THE MILITARY

1 C. Isherwood, *The World in the Evening*, New York, Ballantine, 1967, pp. 265–266.
2 For a fascinating account of the history of gay men and lesbians as soldiers during the Second World War, see generally A. Bérubé, *Coming Out Under Fire*, New York, Penguin, 1990.
3 See ibid. at 8:

> Before the war, the military had had no official procedure for preventing gay men from entering its ranks. But when the war heated up in Europe, psychiatric consultants to the Selective Service system in Washington began to piece together a rationale and initial procedure for excluding homosexuals.

4 Of course, this change in emphasis was documented historically by M. Foucault (*The History of Sexuality Volume One: An Introduction* (R. Hurley trans.), London, Penguin, 1990), who described 'homosexuality' as

> characterized . . . less by a type of sexual relations than by a certain quality of sexual sensibility, a certain way of inverting the masculine and the feminine in oneself. Homosexuality appeared as one of the forms of sexuality when it was transposed from the practice of sodomy onto a kind of interior androgyny, a hermaphrodism of the soul. The sodomite had been a temporary aberration; the homosexual was now a known species.

> (ibid. at 43)

5 Bérubé, *Coming Out Under Fire*, p. 33.

6 See Uniform Code of Military Justice, 10 U.S.C. 925 (1988):

> (a) Any person subject to this chapter who engages in unnatural carnal copulation with another person of the same or opposite sex or with an animal is guilty of sodomy. Penetration, however slight, is sufficient to complete the offense. (b) Any person found guilty of sodomy shall be punished as a court-martial may direct.

7 See J.C. Hayes, 'The Tradition of Prejudice Versus the Principle of Equality: Homosexuals and Heightened Equal Protection Scrutiny After *Bowers v. Hardwick*', *Boston College Law Review*, 1990, vol. 31, p. 375 at 388–389:

> The military has a long tradition of discrimination against homosexuals. Currently, the military administrative discharges anyone who, prior to or during a period of military service, engaged in or attempted to engage in a homosexual act, stated that they were homosexual or bisexual, or married or attempted to marry a person of the same sex. The military, however, can retain some who commit homosexual sodomy if it concludes that the act was an aberration and that the person was not actually a homosexual.

8 780 F.Supp. 1 (D.D.C. 1991).

9 Ibid. at 2.

10 Ibid. at 3.

11 Ibid. at 2.

12 Ibid. at 5–6.

13 C.W. Stedman, 'The Constitution, the Military, and Homosexuals: Should the Military's Policies Concerning Homosexuals be Modified?', *Dickinson Law Review*, 1991, vol. 95, p. 321.

14 *Steffan*, 780 F.Supp. at 3.

15 Ibid. at 4–5.

16 Ibid. at 5.

17 83 U.S. 587 (1987).

18 *Steffan v. Cheney*, 780 F.Supp. at 5.

19 Ibid. at 5–6.

20 Ibid. at 6.

21 Ibid.

22 On the 'double bind' of disclosure, see E. Sedgwick, *Epistemology of the Closet*, Berkeley, University of California Press, 1990, p. 70:

> The most obvious fact about this history of judicial formulations is that it codifies an excruciating system of double binds, systematically oppressing gay people, identities, and acts by undermining through contradictory constraints on discourse the grounds of their very being.

For a brilliant elaboration of the dynamics of the inside/out binary see D. Fuss, 'Inside/Out', in D. Fuss (ed.), *Inside/Out*, New York, Routledge, 1991, p. 1 at 4:

> "Out" cannot help but to carry a double valence for gay and lesbian subjects. On the one hand, it conjures up the exteriority of the negative – the devalued or outlawed term in the hetero/homo binary. On the other hand, it suggests the process of coming out – a movement into a metaphysics of presence, speech, and cultural visibility. The preposition "out" always supports this double sense of invisibility (to put out) and visibility (to bring out), often exceeding even this simple tension in the confused entanglement generated by a host of other active associations.

23 *Steffan*, 780 F.Supp. at 6.

24 Ibid. at 7.

25 Ibid.

26 The relevance of the 'political powerlessness' of the class in Equal Protection juris-prudence received its most famous articulation in *United States v. Carolene Products Co.* 304 U.S. 144 at 153 n.4 (1938):

> prejudice against discrete and insular minorities may be a special condition, which tends seriously to curtail the operation of those political processes ordinarily to be relied upon to protect minorities, and which may call for a correspondingly more searching judicial inquiry.

27 *Steffan*, 780 F.Supp. at 7–8. For evidence to support this conclusion, the Court noted that in New York City, Mayor Dinkins joined the 'homosexual groups and activists' in the St. Patrick's Day Parade (ibid. at 8–9).

28 Ibid. at 8, n.14.

29 Ibid. at 9.

30 Bérubé, *Coming Out Under Fire*, pp. 146–147. Bérubé does acknowledge, however, that punitive and regulatory use by the military of the 'homosexual' as an identity concept was a precursor to its redeployment in liberatory terms: 'The military, ironically, encouraged gay veterans to assume a stronger gay identity when it began to identify and manage so many people as homosexual persons rather than focus narrowly on the act of sodomy' (ibid. at 249).

31 *Steffan*, 780 F.Supp. at 10. The Court relied upon the Supreme Court decision in *Cleburne v. Cleburne Living Center Inc.*, 473 U.S. 432 (1985) [mental retardation held not to be a quasi-suspect classification]. The majority decision of White J. in *Cleburne* is relevant to this analysis particularly for the proposition that the mentally retarded are not 'politically powerless in the sense that they have no ability to attract the attention of lawmakers' (ibid. at 445). The implications of this argument have been described by E. Arriola, 'Sexual Identity and the Constitution: Homosexual Persons as a Discrete and Insular Minority', *Women's Rights Law Reporter*, 1988, vol. 10, p. 143 at 170:

> a more troubling aspect of *Cleburne*, however, is the majority's allusion to the idea that *any* degree of political power achieved by a socially harmed group (i.e. in the form of some protective legislation) negates the need for judicial pro-tection. By elevating the significance of "political powerlessness" the Court suggested that no socially harmed group could ever achieve suspect class status, if through organized help it gains the attention of a few lawmakers or of a court.

32 *Steffan*, 780 F.Supp. at 10.

33 On the separation of act and identity, see Sedgwick, *Epistemology of the Closet*, p. 54: 'To be gay, or to be potentially classifiable as gay . . . in this system is to come under the radically overlapping aegises of a universalizing discourse of acts or bonds and at the same time of a minoritizing discourse of kinds of persons'.

34 J. Halley, 'The Politics of the Closet: Towards Equal Protection for Gay, Lesbian and Bisexual Identity', *University of California at Los Angeles Law Review*, 1989, vol. 10, p. 915 at 923.

35 Ibid. at 956.

36 *Steffan*, 780 F. Supp. at 10, citing Department of Defense Directive 1332.14.

37 Ibid. at 13.

38 S. Harris, 'Permitting Prejudice to Govern: Equal Protection, Military Defence, and the Exclusion of Lesbians and Gay Men from the Military', *Review of Law and Social Change*, 1989–90, vol. 17, p. 171 at 173.

39 See e.g., *Cleburne*, 473 U.S. at 448 ['mere negative attitude or fear . . . are not permissible

bases']; *Palmore v. Sidoti*, 466 U.S. 429, 433 (1984) ['Private biases may be outside the reach of the law, but the law cannot, directly or indirectly, give them effect'].

40 Harris, 'Permitting Prejudice to Govern', p. 221.

41 *Steffan*, 780 F.Supp. at 13.

42 See Hayes, 'The Tradition of Prejudice Versus the Principle of Equality', pp. 388–389.

43 *Steffan*, 780 F.Supp. at 16.

44 S. Sontag, *AIDS and Its Metaphors*, New York, Farrar, Straus and Giroux, 1989, p. 11. Sontag also has traced the history of illness as metaphor and has demonstrated that 'the medieval experience of the plague was firmly tied to notions of moral pollution, and people invariably looked for a scapegoat external to the stricken community' (S.Sontag, *Illness as Metaphor*, Harmondsworth, Penguin, 1978, p. 74). See also S. Gilman, *Disease and Representation*, Ithaca, Cornell, 1988, p. 4. The connections between Aids and American nationalism were explored by Yingling; see T. Yingling, 'AIDS in America: Postmodern Governance, Identity, and Experience', in Fuss, *Inside/Out*, p. 291 at 297:

> In American political discourse, "America" and the nation-state are not synonymous, and while the slippage between the terms is ever conveniently manipulated, the mythic term virtually always takes precedence and value over the more material one; conservatives may thus not only ignore the need for the nation-state to respond to population groups not visible within "America" (predominantly gays and IV-drug users in the early years of the AIDS epidemic) but may even cast those needs as anti-American, as a danger *to* rather than *within* the state.

On the connections between political and social order and disease, see M. Douglas, *Purity and Danger: An Analysis of Concepts of Pollution and Taboo*, London, Routledge & Kegan Paul, 1966, p. 3.

45 Douglas, *Purity and Danger*, p. 139.

46 On a gay identity as a matrix of performances, see R. Dyer, 'Believing in Fairies: The Author and the Homosexual', in Fuss, *Inside/Out*, p. 185 at 187–188.

47 On the capacity of lesbians and gay men to denaturalise subjectivities, see J. Butler, *Gender Trouble: Feminism and the Subversion of Identity*, New York, Routledge, 1990, p. 31.

48 The new military directive provides that a 'statement by a Service member that he or she is a homosexual . . . creates a rebuttable presumption that the Service member engages in homosexual acts or has a propensity or intent to do so': Department of Defense Directive 1332.14.H.1.b (2) (22 December 1993).

49 See e.g., *Meinhold v. United States Department of Defense*, 1994 W.L. 467311 (9th Cir. 1994), in which the Court held that the military classification of the 'homosexual' was irrational because of its presumption that homosexual persons will violate military regulations concerning sexual conduct (while not making analogous presumptions concerning heterosexual military personnel).

50 *Steffan v. Aspin*, 8 F.3d 57 (D.C. Cir. 1993).

51 Ibid. at 67.

52 Ibid. at 68.

53 Ibid. at 69.

54 Ibid.

55 *Steffan v. Perry*, 41 F.3d 677 (D.C. Cir. 1994).

56 Ibid. at 685.

57 Ibid.

58 Ibid. at 686.

59 Ibid. at 688.

60 Ibid. at 701.

61 Ibid. at 709.

62 Ibid. at 715.

63 'Gay Ex-Midshipman Drops Bid to Appeal', *New York Times*, 4 January 1995, p. A12. Finally, it is worth noting that the ten judges of the Court of Appeal divided neatly according to which President of the United States had appointed him or her to the bench. The majority judges were all Reagan/Bush appointments, while the dissenters were either appointed by Carter or Clinton. See 'En Banc D.C. Circuit Rejects Steffan Challenge to Old Military Policy', *Lesbian/Gay Law Notes*, December 1994, p. 139.

6 EQUALITY RIGHTS IDENTITY POLITICS, AND THE CANADIAN NATIONAL IMAGINATION

1 For an introduction to this emerging literature on identity, see e.g., J. Rutherford (ed.), *Identity: Community, Culture, Difference*, London, Lawrence and Wishart, 1990; 'The Identity in Question: A Special Issue', *October*, 1992, no. 61; I.M. Young, *Justice and the Politics of Difference*, Princeton, Princeton University Press, 1990; S. Lash and J. Friedman (eds), *Modernity and Identity*, Cambridge, Blackwell, 1992. Of course, 'identity politics' emerged, not from a vacuum, but from a history of minority practices and theory which highlighted the political implications of oppressed identities.

2 M. Smiley, 'Gender Justice Without Foundations', *Michigan Law Review*, 1991, vol. 89, p. 1574 at 1579.

3 J.C. Williams, 'Dissolving the Sameness/Difference Debate: A Post-Modern Path Beyond Essentialism in Feminist and Critical Race Theory', *Duke Law Journal*, 1991, p. 296 at 307.

4 S. Best and D. Kellner, *Postmodern Theory: Critical Interrogations*, Basingstoke, Macmillan, 1991, p. 205.

5 On the relationship of equality rights in Canada and the new social movements, see generally D. Herman, *Rights of Passage: Struggles for Lesbian and Gay Legal Equality*, Toronto, University of Toronto Press, 1994.

6 See generally E. Laclau and C. Mouffe, *Hegemony and Socialist Strategy*, London, Verso, 1985.

7 Ibid. at 96.

8 A. Woodiwiss, *Social Theory After Postmodernism*, London, Pluto, 1990, p. 65.

9 J.W. Scott, 'Experience', in J. Butler and J.W. Scott (eds), *Feminists Theorize The Political*, New York, Routledge, 1992, p. 22 at 33.

10 J. Butler, 'Contingent Foundations: Feminism and the Question of Postmodernism', in Butler and Scott, *Feminists Theorize The Political*, p. 3 at 13.

11 See A. Parker *et al.*, 'Introduction', in A. Parker, M. Russo, D. Sommer and P. Yaeger (eds), *Nationalisms and Sexualities*, New York, Routledge, 1992, p. 1 at 5:

> nationality is a relational term whose identity derives from its inherence in a system of differences. In the same way that "man" and "woman" define themselves reciprocally (though never symmetrically), national identity is determined not on the basis of its own intrinsic properties but as a function of what it (presumably) is not. Implying "some element of alterity for its definition", a nation is ineluctably "shaped by what it opposes". But the very fact that such identities depend constitutively on difference means that nations are forever haunted by their various definitional others.

12 See E. Sedgwick, 'The Age of Wilde', in *Nationalisms and Sexualities*, p. 235 at 241:

> The "other" of the nation in a given political or historical setting may be the pre-national monarchy, the local ethnicity, the diaspora, the transnational cor-

porate, ideological, religious, or ethnic unity, the sub-national locale or the ex-colonial, often contiguous unit; the colony may become national *vis-à-vis* the homeland, or the homeland become national *vis-à-vis* the nationalism of the colonies; the nationalism of the homeland may be coextensive with or oppositional to its imperialism; and so forth. Far beyond the pressure of crisis or exception, it may be that there exists for nations, as for gender, simply no normal way to partake of the categorical definitiveness of the national, no single kind of "other" of what a nation is to which all can by the same structuration be definitively opposed.

13 See H. Bhabha, 'Dissemination', in H. Bhabha (ed.), *Nation and Narration*, New York, Routledge, 1992, p. 291 at 296: 'The demand for a holistic, representative vision of society could only be represented in a discourse that was *at the same time* obsessively fixed upon, and uncertain of, the boundaries of society, and the margins of the text'.

14 See D.E. Pease, 'National Identities, Postmodern Artifacts and Postnational Narratives', *Boundary 2*, 1992, vol. 19.1, p. 1 at 3.

15 Ibid. at 4.

16 H. Bhabha, 'Introduction: Narrating the Nation', in Bhabha, *Nation and Narration*, p. 1 at 4.

17 Pease, 'National Identities', p. 6.

18 Bhabha, 'Dissemination', p. 299.

19 Ibid. at 300.

20 Indeed, it has been argued that the 'New Europe' may provide a forum for the practice of many of these ideas from postmodernism; see A. Huyssen, 'The Inevit- ability of Nation', *October*, 1992, no. 61, p. 65 at 71:

> what may be desirable as a first modest step might be a broad public debate about an alternative notion of nation, one that emphasizes negotiated heterogeneity rather than homogeneity imposed from above, federalism rather than centralism, regionalism as indeed an important layer of national identity rather than its alleged opposite.

Surely, these words could be transposed to the context of modern Canadian federalism.

21 R.J. Coombe, 'Tactics of Appropriation and the Politics of Recognition in Late Modern Democracies', *Political Theory*, 1993, vol. 21.3, p. 411 at 412.

22 Ibid. at 419.

23 Ibid.

24 N. Duclos, 'Lessons of Difference: Feminist Theory on Cultural Diversity', *Buffalo Law Review*, 1990, vol. 38, p. 325 at 380–381.

25 I do not deny the utopianism of this approach, nor do I wish to underestimate the existence of historical and current practices of exclusion which deny to many Canadians the benefits of full citizenship. My aim simply is to develop a model of full citizenship to which Canada might be particularly well suited to aspire.

26 Section 15 of the Canadian *Charter of Rights and Freedoms* reads as follows:

> 15 (1). Every individual is equal before and under the law and has the right to the equal protection and equal benefit of the law without discrimination and, in particular, without discrimination based on race, national or ethnic origin, colour, religion, sex, age or mental or physical disability.
>
> 15 (2). Subsection (1) does not preclude any law, program or activity that has as its object the amelioration of conditions of disadvantaged individuals or groups including those that are disadvantaged because of race, national or ethnic origin, colour, religion, sex, age or mental or physical disability.

27 (1989) 56 D.L.R. (4th) 1.

28 Ibid. at 18.

29 Ibid. at 33.

30 Ibid. at 32.

31 9 O.R. (2d) 495.

32 Ibid. at 503.

33 Ibid. at 508.

34 (1989) 44 C.R.R. 364; appeal dismissed, 109 N.R. 300 (Fed.C.A.).

35 Ibid. at 370–371.

36 Ibid. at 371.

37 For an introduction to the debate, see E. Stein (ed.), *Forms of Desire: Sexual Orientation and the Social Constructionist Controversy*, New York, Routledge, 1992. The terms of the debate have been summarised by S. Epstein, 'Gay Politics, Ethnic Identity: The Limits of Social Constructionism', in Stein, *Forms of Desire*, p. 239 at 250–251:

> where essentialism took for granted that all societies consist of people who are either heterosexuals or homosexuals (with perhaps some bisexuals), constructionists demonstrated that the notion of "the homosexual" is a sociohistorical product, not universally applicable, and worthy of explanation in its own right. And where essentialism would treat the self-attribution of a "homosexual identity" as unproblematic – as simply the conscious recognition of a true, underlying "orientation" – constructionism focused attention on identity as a complex developmental outcome, the consequence of an interactive process of social labelling and self-identification.

38 D. Fuss, *Essentially Speaking*, New York, Routledge, 1989, p. 109.

39 S. Seidman, 'Postmodern Anxiety: The Politics of Epistemology', *Sociological Theory*, 1991, vol. 9.2, p. 180 at 183. See also C.S. Vance, 'Social Construction Theory: Problems in the History of Sexuality', in H. Crowley and S. Himmelweit (eds), *Knowing Women: Feminism and Knowledge*, Cambridge, Polity, 1992, p. 132 at 134.

40 Epstein, 'Gay Politics, Ethnic Identity', p. 269.

41 Ibid. at 289.

42 Vance, 'Social Construction Theory', p. 142.

43 Epstein, 'Gay Politics, Ethinic Identity', p. 291.

44 Ibid.

45 J. Rutherford, 'A Place Called Home: Identity and the Cultural Politics of Difference', in Rutherford, *Identity: Community, Culture, Difference*, p. 9 at 22.

46 Ibid. at 23.

47 As Spelman has argued, this capacity to rework existing identity structures can have positive effects on disadvantaged groups; see E. Spelman, *Inessential Woman: Problems of Exclusion in Feminist Thought*, Boston, Beacon Press, 1988, p. 152.

48 J. Scott, 'Multiculturalism and the Politics of Identity', *October*, 1992, no. 61, p. 12 at 19.

49 (1992) 9 O.R. (3d) 495 at 497.

50 See *Douglas v. The Queen*, 98 D.L.R. (4th) 129 (F.C.T.D.).

51 I choose not to define at this point what I mean here by the use of 'queer', as I utilise it as a term that has come to denote, in some sexual subcultures, the transgressive power of numerous minority sexualities. A queer identity also might redefine and subvert the articulated identities of lesbians and gay men. I elaborate upon the phenomenon of queer theory and political practices in Chapter 8.

52 In general, see L. Berlant and E. Freeman, 'Queer Nationality', in M. Warner (ed.), *Fear of a Queer Planet*, Minneapolis, University of Minnesota Press, 1993, p. 193. Berlant and Freeman argue that the phenomenon of 'queer nationality' has 'taken up the project of coordinating a new nationality. Its relation to nationhood is multiple and ambiguous, however, taking as much from the insurgent nationalisms of oppressed peoples as from

the revolutionary idealism of the United States' (ibid.). As a primarily American phenomenon, it is difficult to graft such a movement into a Canadian context. However, it is possible that the goals of Queer Nation which include the attempt to cross the boundaries between individual and national space and to radically reconstitute notions of citizenship, might be more readily incorporated within a national discourse that is substantially more open to new nationalist articulations of identity. On the other hand, that fact alone might rob Queer Nationals of their radicalism.

53 Ibid. at 205–206.

7 UNMANLY DIVERSIONS: THE CONSTRUCTION OF THE HOMOSEXUAL BODY (POLITIC) IN LAW

1 The two phenomena are closely related; see K. Thomas, 'Beyond the Privacy Principle', *Columbia Law Review*, 1992, vol. 92, p. 1431.
2 [1993] 2 All ER 75 (HL).
3 Ibid. at 78.
4 Ibid. at 83.
5 Ibid. at 79.
6 Ibid. at 82.
7 Ibid.
8 Ibid.
9 Ibid. at 83.
10 Ibid.
11 Ibid.
12 Ibid. at 84.
13 Ibid. at 85.
14 Ibid.
15 Ibid. at 91.
16 Ibid. at 92.
17 Ibid.
18 Ibid.
19 Ibid. at 100.
20 Ibid. at 101.
21 Ibid. at 113.
22 Ibid. at 116.
23 Ibid. at 117.
24 Ibid. Lord Slynn, in further dissenting reasons, found it reasonable to draw the line where consent is overriden based upon the seriousness of the injury: 'grievous bodily harm I accept to be different by analogy with and as an extension of the old cases on maiming' (ibid. at 122). On the facts, as these acts did not result in permanent or serious injury, the onus rested on the prosecution to prove the absence of consent of the assaulted person.
25 G. Rubin, 'Thinking Sex: Notes for a Radical Theory of the Politics of Sexuality', in C.S. Vance (ed.), *Pleasure and Danger: Exploring Female Sexuality*, Boston, Routledge & Kegan Paul, 1984, p. 267 at 279.
26 Ibid. at 282.
27 Ibid. at 291. For a similar treatment of the issue of gay male sadomasochism in terms of the law of assault, but within an American context, see *People v. Samuels*, 58 Cal. Rptr. 439 (Ct. App. 1967), *cert. denied* 390 U.S. 1024 (1968).
28 J. Gange and S. Johnstone, '"Believe Me, Everybody Has Something Pierced in California": An Interview With Nayland Blake', *New Formations*, 1993, no. 19, p. 51 at 61.

29 [1993] 2 All ER 75 at 82, per Lord Templeman.

30 Ibid.

31 Ibid. at 100, per Lord Lowry.

32 T.S. Weinberg, 'Sadomasochism in the United States: A Review of Recent Sociological Literature', *Journal of Sex Research*, 1987, vol. 23.1, p. 50 at 52. In this chapter, I am not attempting to discern the 'truth' of sadomasochism, but rather to highlight the difficulties involved in providing any single 'true' reading of a sexual encounter of this (or any) type. The fact that social science based arguments have been made that contradict the meaning ascribed by the House of Lords to the sexual relationships, calls into question the majority's characterisation of the meaning of sadomasochism.

33 Ibid. at 63.

34 Ibid. In a somewhat different vein, the relationship between control and spontaneity within the s&m relationship was analysed by Foucault in terms of 'regulation' and 'openness'; see M. Foucault, 'Sexual Choice, Sexual Acts: An Interview with Michel Foucault', *Salmagundi*, 1982–1983, vol. 58–59, p. 12:

> sexual relations are elaborated and developed by and through mythical relations. S and M is not a relationship between he (or she) who suffers and he (or she) who inflicts suffering, but between the master and the one on whom he exercises his mastery. What interests the practitioners of S and M is that the relationship is at the same time regulated and open. It resembles a chess game in the sense that one can win and the other lose. The master can lose in the S and M game if he finds he is unable to respond to the needs and trials of his victim. Conversely, the servant can lose if he fails to meet or can't stand meeting the challenge thrown at him by the master. This mixture of rules and openness has the effect of intensifying sexual relations by introducing a perpetual novelty, a perpetual tension and a perpetual uncertainty which the simple consummation of the act lacks.
>
> (ibid. at 20)

35 See Weinberg, 'Sadomasochism in the United States', p. 64. Trust therefore to some extent might distinguish the long term sadomasochistic relationship from the 'one off' encounter.

36 [1993] 2 All ER 75 at 100 [emphasis added].

37 [1992] 1 W.L.R. 1006 (C.A.).

38 Ibid. at 1010.

39 Ibid.

40 Ibid. at 1018.

41 Ibid. at 1019–1020.

42 Ibid. at 1020.

43 This closely resembles the role of consent in the law of sexual assault.

44 S. Tendler, 'Gay-killer Tells Police he will Murder One Victim a Week', *The Times* (UK), 17 June 1993, p. 1. The press also reported on the HIV status of some of the deceased. The ethics of such disclosure of course is a subject of serious concern, but is beyond the scope of this chapter.

45 Ibid.

46 A. Thomson and J. Llewellyn-Smith, 'Death goes cruising', *The Times* (UK), 17 June 1993, p. 14.

47 W. Bennett, 'Four of the Victims were Regular Visitors to Gay Pubs', *The Independent* (UK), 17 June 1993, p. 3.

48 See J. Dalrymple and B. Deer, 'Killed for kicks', *Sunday Times* (UK), 20 June 1993, p. 1 at 11; Thomson and Smith, 'Death goes Cruising'; Bennett, 'Four of the Victims were Regular Visitors to Gay Pubs'.

49 E. Kosofsky Sedgwick, 'Epidemics of the Will', in J. Crary and S. Kwinter (eds), *Incorporations Zone 6*, Cambridge MA, MIT Press, 1992, p. 582 at 582–583.
50 Ibid. at 584.
51 Ibid.
52 M. Seltzer, 'Serial Killers (1)', *Differences*, 1993, vol. 5.1, p. 92 at 111.
53 Sedgwick, 'Epidemics of the Will', p. 587.
54 Seltzer, 'Serial Killers (1)', p. 112.
55 Sedgwick, 'Epidemics of the Will', p. 589.
56 Ibid.
57 S. Seidman, *Embattled Eros*, New York, Routledge, 1992, p. 159.
58 J.W. Jones, 'Discourses on and of AIDS in West Germany, 1986–90', in J.C. Fout (ed.), *Forbidden History*, Chicago, University of Chicago Press, 1992, p. 361 at 364.
59 Dalrymple and Deer, 'Killed for kicks', p. 11.
60 Ibid. [emphasis added].
61 [1993] 2 All ER 75 at 82.
62 Ibid. at 91.
63 Ibid. at 100 [emphasis added].
64 J. Derrida, 'The Rhetoric of Drugs: An Interview', *Differences*, 1993, vol. 5.1, p. 1 at 7.
65 Ibid. at 12.
66 Ibid. at 14.
67 Ibid. at 19.
68 [1993] 2 ALL ER 75 at 84.
69 The creation of a film of the sadomasochistic sexual encounters heightens the effect of simulacrum and representation, one step removed from the 'reality' of sex.
70 Derrida, 'The Rhetoric of Drugs: An Interview', p. 19.
71 I recognise, of course, that members of the judiciary may be members of this community in their 'private' lives.
72 See B. Brown, 'Troubled Vision: Legal Understandings of Obscenity', *New Formations*, 1993, no. 19, p. 29 at 39:

> public spaces were not to be places of diversity and debate in which tolerance would be a civil necessity and, ideally, consensus might be born out of the experience of everyday exposure to variety. On the contrary, difference and diversity were to bloom unseen, cordoned off in the private domain.

The Wolfenden Report of 1957 was the product of an independent committee, established by the British government, to make recommendations on the laws dealing with prostitution and with male homosexuality. In regard to the latter, the committee recommended the decriminalisation of consensual homosexual sex between two adult men over the age of twenty-one years *in private*. On the Wolfenden Report and the struggle for gay law reform in the United Kingdom, see generally S. Jeffery-Poulter, *Peers, Queers and Commons*, London, Routledge, 1991.

73 Brown, 'Troubled Vision', p. 40. Within these cultural conditions, the use of codes which cannot be read outside the subculture become an important means of self-defence; see C. Patton, 'Safe Sex and the Pornographic Vernacular' in Bad Object-Choices (ed.), *How Do I Look?*, Seattle, Bay Press, 1991, p. 31 at 47. The interrogation of a subculture in light of the decision in *Brown* was exemplified by a police raid of a house in a South Yorkshire village. Acting on information suggesting that stolen goods were being received, the police instead found a group of thirty eight 'partying homosexuals in various states of undress' (M. Macdonald, 'Stolen Goods Raid Surprises Gay Party', *The Independent* (UK), 11 May, 1993, p. 3). Although no sex acts were taking place, some of the men were found 'bound in leather' and a 'large quantity of clothes and sexual apparatus were seized' (ibid.). Charges of conspiracy to commit gross indecency were later dropped due to lack of evidence.

74 L. Edelman, 'The Plague of Discourse: Politics, Literary Theory, and AIDS', *South Atlantic Quarterly*, 1989, vol. 88.1, p. 301 at 309--310.

75 S. Watney, 'The Spectacle of AIDS', in D. Crimp (ed.), *AIDS: Cultural Analysis Cultural Activism*, Cambridge, MA., MIT Press, 1988, p. 71 at 77.

76 S. Watney, *Policing Desire*, (second edn), Minneapolis, University of Minnesota Press, 1989, p. 42.

77 [1993] 2 All ER 75 at 82.

78 Ibid. at 83, citing to 94 Cr App R 302 at 310.

79 Ibid. at 92. The strictly legal response to these arguments was provided by Lord Mustill in dissent, who recognised the circularity of the argument:

> The element of the corruption of youth is already catered for by the existing legislation; and if there is a gap in it which needs to be filled the remedy surely lies in the hands of Parliament, not in the application of a statute which is aimed at other forms of wrongdoing.
>
> (ibid. at 117)

80 M. Douglas, *Purity and Danger: An Analysis of Concepts of Pollution and Taboo*, London, Routledge & Kegan Paul, 1966, p. 3.

81 Ibid. at 87.

82 Ibid. at 97.

83 Ibid. at 113.

84 Ibid. at 133.

85 S. Gilman, *Disease and Representation: Images of Illness from Madness to AIDS*, Ithaca, Cornell University Press, 1988, p. 4.

86 Seidman, *Embattled Eros*, p. 160.

87 Watney, *Policing Desire*, p. 49.

88 Ibid. at 85.

89 Ibid. at 73.

90 C. Patton, *Inventing Aids*, New York, Routledge, 1990, pp. 127–128.

91 S. Watney, 'Aids, "Moral Panic" Theory and Homophobia', in P. Aggleton and H. Thomas (eds), *Social Aspects of Aids*, London, Falmer Press, 1988, p. 52 at 58–59.

92 J. Gamson, 'Silence, Death, and the Invisible Enemy: AIDS Activism and Social Movement "Newness"', *Social Problems*, 1989, vol. 36.4, p. 351 at 358.

93 L. Singer, *Erotic Welfare*, New York, Routledge, 1993, p. 117.

94 Ibid. at 118.

95 S. Sontag, *AIDS and its Metaphors*, New York, Farrar, Straus and Giroux, 1989, p. 25.

96 [1993] 2 All ER 75 at 100 [emphasis added].

97 Ibid. at 91.

98 Ibid. at 83 [emphasis added].

99 Ibid.

100 M. Foucault, *The History of Sexuality Volume One*: An Introduction (R. Hurley trans.), London, Penguin, 1976, p. 147.

101 Ibid. at 149.

102 Ibid. at 156.

103 M. Foucault, *The Birth of the Clinic* (A.M. Sheridan trans.), New York, Vintage, 1973, p. 120.

104 Ibid. at 153.

105 Ibid. at 172.

106 Dalrymple and Deer, 'Killed for Kicks', p. 1 at 11.

107 Tendler, 'Gay Killer tells police he will Murder One Victim a Week', p. 1. The HIV revenge theory proved unfounded. The convicted killer, apparently heterosexual, had expressed a desire 'of doing the perfect murder'; see P. McGowan, 'This Man Must Never Go Free', *Evening Standard*, 20 December 1993, p. 1 at 2.

108 J. Dalrymple and B. Deer, 'Police on Alert at Gay Rally', *Sunday Times* (UK), 20 June 1993, p. 1.
109 See Foucault, *The Birth of the Clinic*, p. 162.
110 See ibid. at 107.
111 J. Butler, 'The Force of Fantasy: Feminism, Mapplethorpe, and Discursive Excess', *Differences*, 1990, vol. 2.2, p. 105 at 111.
112 Ibid. at 117.
113 Ibid.

8 TOWARDS A QUEER LEGAL THEORY

1 S. Seidman, 'Identity and Politics in a "Postmodern" Gay Culture: Some Historical and Conceptual Notes', in M. Warner (ed.), *Fear of a Queer Planet*, Minneapolis, University of Minnesota Press, 1993, p. 105 at 133. For an introduction to the politics of queer sexuality, see also A. Stein (ed.), *Sisters, Sexperts, Queers: Beyond the Lesbian Nation*, New York, Penguin, 1993.
2 Seidman, 'Identity and Politics', p. 133.
3 L. Duggan, 'Making It Perfectly Queer', *Socialist Review*, 1992, vol. 22, p. 11 at 21.
4 Ibid. at 23.
5 See Seidman, 'Identity and Politics', p. 130.
6 A. Stein, 'Sisters and Queers: The Decentering of Lesbian Feminism', *Socialist Review*, 1992, vol. 22, p. 33 at 45.
7 Ibid.
8 Ibid. at 50.
9 Ibid.
10 See M. Warner, 'Introduction', in Warner, *Fear of a Queer Planet*, p. vii at xxv.
11 M. McIntosh, 'Queer Theory and the War of the Sexes', in J. Bristow and A.R. Wilson (eds), *Activating Theory: Lesbian, Gay, Bisexual Politics*, London, Lawrence & Wishart, 1993, p. 30 at 31.
12 478 U.S. 186 (1986).
13 P. Derbyshire, 'A Measure of Queer', *Critical Quarterly*, 1994, vol. 36.1, p. 39 at 41.
14 Duggan, 'Making It Perfectly Queer', p. 16.
15 Ibid. at 18.
16 E.Kosofsky Sedgwick, 'Queer and Now', in *Tendencies*, Durham, Duke University Press, 1993, p. 1 at 9.
17 Seidman, 'Identity and Politics', p. 131.
18 Sedgwick, 'Queer and Now', p. 8.
19 See my discussion of performativity in the context of gender in Chapter 1.
20 See E. Kosofsky Sedgwick, 'Queer Performativity: Henry James's *The Art of the Novel*', *GLQ: A Journal of Lesbian and Gay Studies*, 1993, vol. 1.1, p. 1; and, for a reply, see J. Butler, 'Critically Queer', *GLQ: A Journal of Lesbian and Gay Studies*, 1993, vol. 1.1, p. 17.
21 Sedgwick, 'Queer and Now', p. 9.
22 Sedgwick, 'Queer Performativity', p. 13. In fact, I once read a personal advertisement in which the advertiser sought a gay male, non-queer companion.
23 Of course, the social positioning of lesbians and gay men is 'different' *vis à vis* each other.
24 Despite its claims to 'newness', it has been noted that many of the ideas surrounding queer theory and practice received their original hearing in the Gay Liberation movement in the late 1960s and early 1970s; see F. Mort, 'Essentialism Revisited?: Identity Politics and Late Twentieth-Century Discourses of Homosexuality', in

J. Weeks (ed.), *The Lesser Evil and the Greater Good*, London, Rivers Oram Press, 1994, p. 201 at 210.

25 See e.g., D. Kennedy, 'The Structure of Blackstone's Commentaries', *Buffalo Law Review*, 1979, vol. 28, p. 205; M. Horwitz, 'The History of the Public/Private Distinction', *University of Pennsylvania Law Review*, 1982, vol. 130, p. 1423; K. Vandevelde, 'The New Property of the Nineteenth Century: The Development of the Modern Concept of Property', *Buffalo Law Review*, 1980, vol. 29, p. 325; K. Klare, 'The Public/Private Distinction in Labor Law', *University of Pennsylvania Law Review*, 1982, vol. 130, p. 1358.

26 D. Richards, 'Sexual Autonomy and the Constitutional Right to Privacy', *Hastings Law Journal*, 1979, vol. 30, p. 957.

27 See C. Patton, 'Tremble Hetero Swine!', in Warner, *Fear of a Queer Planet*, p. 143 at 170.

28 478 U.S. 186 at 190.

29 Ibid. at 188.

30 Ibid. at 194.

31 Ibid. at 196.

32 For a description of the factual background to the case, see K. Thomas, 'Beyond the Privacy Principle', *Columbia Law Review*, 1992, vol. 92, p. 1431 at 1436–1443.

33 Ibid. at 1441.

34 See ibid.; J. Halley, 'The Politics of the Closet: Towards Equal Protection for Gay, Lesbian, and Bisexual Identity', *University of California at Los Angeles Law Review*, 1989, vol. 36, p. 915; K. Thomas, 'Corpus Juris (Hetero)Sexualis: Doctrine, Discourse, and Desire in *Bowers v. Hardwick*', *GLQ: A Journal of Lesbian and Gay Studies*, 1993, vol. 1.1, p. 33.

35 J.E. Halley, 'The Construction of Heterosexuality', in Warner, *Fear of a Queer Planet*, p. 82 at 98.

36 See *Griswold v. Connecticut*, 381 US 479 (1965); *Eisenstadt v. Baird*, 405 US 438 (1972); *Roe v. Wade*, 410 US 113 (1973).

37 J. Butler, *Bodies That Matter*, New York, Routledge, 1993, p. 231.

38 In fact, there has been some success in eradicating sodomy laws via state constitutional law and also through the political process. However, I am here referring both to the practical and particularly the overwhelming symbolic effect of the decision in *Bowers v. Hardwick*.

39 L. Berlant and E. Freeman, 'Queer Nationality', in Warner, *Fear of a Queer Planet*, p. 193 at 196–197.

40 A.M. Smith, 'Resisting the Erasure of Lesbian Sexuality: A Challenge for Queer Activism', in K. Plummer (ed.), *Modern Homosexualities: Fragments of Lesbian and Gay Experience*, London, Routledge, 1992, p. 200 at 206.

41 E. Wilson, 'Is Transgression Transgressive?' in Bristow and Wilson, *Activating Theory*, p. 107 at 109.

42 Derbyshire, 'A Measure of Queerness', p. 43.

43 See Wilson, 'Is Transgression Transgressive?', p. 112.

44 Ibid. at 113.

45 Ibid.

46 Duggan, 'Making It Perfectly Queer', p. 20.

47 See A.M.Smith, 'Hegemony Trouble: The Political Theories of Judith Butler, Ernesto Laclau and Chantal Mouffe', in Weeks, *The Lesser Evil and the Greater Good*, p. 222 at 228.

48 See Duggan, 'Making It Perfectly Queer', p. 26.

49 See Wilson, 'Is Transgression Transgressive?', pp. 114–116.

50 Seidman, 'Identity and Politics', p. 134.

51 Butler, *Bodies That Matter*, p. 227.

52 Ibid. at 228.

INDEX